Touched by Angels

Sallon caricature. *Daily Mirror*
Executive, 1977 – by the brilliant
caricaturist Sallon.

TOUCHED BY ANGELS

Derek Jameson

EBURY PRESS • LONDON

Published by Ebury Press
Division of The National Magazine Company Ltd
Colquhoun House 27–37 Broadwick Street
London W1V 1FR

First impression 1988

ISBN 0 85223 741 3

Jacket photography by Richard Brook

Computerset by Chapterhouse, The Cloisters,
Formby, L37 3PX
Printed and bound in Great Britain by
Butler & Tanner Limited, Frome and London

Contents

FOR MY CHILDREN

Barbara, Peter, Ben and Dan

Preface

————

My story is simple enough. I grew up poor and hungry on the streets of London's East End and decided at an early age it was better to be rich and successful. This chronicle of fifty turbulent years tells how it came to pass.

Fame and glory never came into it, though the great British public gave me both in large measure. It is really the story of a fight for survival. What makes Jameson run is not a desire to lie on a beach in Bermuda nor drive a Rolls. Rather, to make people aware of my existence, to be considered as good as the next. Most of all, to fill my belly.

Surprisingly enough, I seem to have pulled it off. Just about everyone knows me. Quite a few even love me. Not many realise that old gravel guts, making them laugh on radio and telly, is a bastard out of a home for waifs and strays, still as hungry as ever. Not that I had much to do with my success. My life has been determined by fate, not calculation. The only thing I had going for me from the start turned out to be the greatest gift of all. A way with words. I remember broadcaster Eamonn Andrews telling me not long before his death that I seemed to be heading for stardom.

'That's because I'm like you, Eamonn,' I said. 'I've got the gift of the gab.'

'It's not the gift of the gab,' he said, 'it's the gift of God.'

He was right there. It has to be divine inspiration. Nothing else could explain why fortune should favour me so abundantly. I come from the bottom of the heap, the product of a slum with little education. Many of my contemporaries could neither read nor write, yet I knew beyond any doubt that I would make it. As Ma Wren, who brought me up, said: *You are touched by the angels*.

Who would have bet twopence on my chances in life when I was begging

1

money on the streets? By all the rules, I should have become a criminal. Instead I took myself off to Fleet Street at the age of fourteen, became a messenger boy and clawed my way up the ladder to become managing editor of the *Daily Mirror* and editor of the *Daily Express, Daily Star* and *News of the World.*

That world crashed in 1984. First I was fired by Rupert Murdoch, then my life savings went down the pan in a disastrous libel action against the BBC. I was broke, unemployed and fifty five. I had blown Fleet Street. It seemed there was no hope for me beyond an obscure job in advertising or public relations.

The telephone rang. It was publishing magnate Robert Maxwell. He put me to work crusading to save the NSPCC. 'It will get you back in the land of the living,' he said. And so it did. Within days I was talking to top industrialists, editors and programme makers. 'Don't write me off,' I told them in passing.

Author Jeffrey Archer invited me to tea. 'What do you do best?' he wanted to know. 'Communicate,' I said. 'Well, don't sit there feeling sorry for yourself, go out and communicate!' Two powerful men holding no particular brief for me, came to my rescue. *The angels again.*

I appeared on just about every chat show, panel game, news and current affairs programme known to radio and television. My big break came within months with a modest BBC2 series called *Do They Mean Us?* on how foreign television views Britain. It made my name – and gave me the catchphrase that still pursues me everywhere.

David Frost was another who took a hand in my comeback. He gave me a regular slot on his Sunday morning TV programme, dubbing me "Lord Jameson of Fleet Street." I was invited to stand in for Jimmy Young on Radio 2. We received 800 letters in a week and critics urged the Beeb to sign me up immediately. They did just that.

The Jameson Show hit the airwaves on Radio 2 in April, 1986, with six million listeners. Within two years it had grown to ten million. Television offers soon followed. My Thames TV series *Headliners* and *People* on BBC1 run at peak time on television most weeks of the year. On top of that, I write a weekly column in *Woman's Own.* Sixty million people a week tuning in to Jameson! I am surrounded by warmth and affection. That should satisfy my desire for my fellows to hold me in some regard. An old hack from Fleet Street, reborn as the man of the people. *Do they mean me?*

Oddly enough, it probably would not have happened without that libel action. Looking back, it proved to be the watershed in my life. The British public always champion the underdog and they realised I had been fighting for my honour and dignity. So did the BBC. Instead of leaving me to rot, as most would have done, they made me a star. Not that I ever wanted to go into court. At the beginning, I feared the case that ultimately made me would destroy everything I stood for. It nearly did. The memory of it was so painful that for years I couldn't even bear to look at the mountain of legal documents, legacy of those twelve days in the High Court.

Now, for the first time, I have put together my own account of that courtroom drama. The perfect place, of course, to begin the story of my life. . . .

To the best of my knowledge, this is a fair and accurate account of my life. However, it does span more than half a century and the old brainbox sometimes plays tricks when called upon to harvest memories of the past. My apologies to anyone relevant to my story who feels he or she has been treated badly or, even worse, left out altogether. It was never my intention to hurt anyone. By the same token, a few names have been altered so not to cause pain or embarrassment.

Derek Jameson

CHAPTER ONE

East End boy made bad

David Bealing's spiky red beard shook in a mirthless grin. His eyes glinted behind steel-framed spectacles. He seemed to be highly pleased with himself – and making a lousy job of not showing it. Someone must be in trouble. It turned out to be me.

'Did you hear? Did you hear?' he wanted to know. 'Boy, they really tore you apart on Radio 4 on Friday. Reckoned you're an illiterate yob! You were DESTROYED . . .' He made it sound like the knell of doom.

Picture editors tend to look on the bright side of other people's misfortunes. *I mean, there's got to be a story and pictures there somewhere* . . . Bealing's nose is permanently tuned in to the follies of mankind. In later years it was to earn him a lot of pennies. His agency, People in Pictures, specialises in the kiss-'n-tell revelations of Page 3 girls. I don't think Sir Ralph Halpern has met Dave. The tycoon would find him most interesting.

This bearer of bad tidings was at that time London picture editor of the *Daily Star*, fledgling sister paper of the *Daily Express*. It was this strange alliance that gave special significance to our encounter in the lift taking us up to the *Star*'s offices in the Black Lubyianka, as everyone called *Express* headquarters in Fleet Street, Lord Beaverbrook, the founding father, had a thing about black marble.

Bealing's ill-concealed delight that I had been carved up was quite understandable. This was March, 1980, and he pounced as I was playing the heavy in a drama without parallel even in the crazy world of newspapers. As editor of the *Daily Express*, I had just fired his boss, Peter Grimsditch, editor of its rival stablemate, the *Daily Star*. No wonder he was laughing under his beard. The man with the axe had been given a mighty kick in the balls.

Inside my office I quickly buzzed the news desk on the editor's hotline. 'Get

RTNS,' I told the voice at the other end. 'Some bastard had a go at me on Radio 4 last Friday and I want to know what he said.' RTNS is Radio and Televison News Service, an enterprising agency which monitors the airwaves and delivers reports to newspapers for an appropriate fee. Most useful. It keeps us in touch with what those jokers in radio and television are up to. In this case it proved unnecessary to order a special delivery. Bad news travels fast in newspapers.

'We've already got it, boss,' said the news desk assistant. 'Phew! They marked your card alright!'

A boy brought in the report. For the first time I read the words that were to change my life. They came in a late-night programme called *Week Ending*, which I had heard of vaguely as some kind of satire show. RTNS helpfully said in a preamble that *Radio Times* described it as 'an irreverently critical look back at the week's news.'

By now millions of people in Britain know how I became enmeshed in a nasty libel action over the programme's suggestion that I was some kind of illiterate yob. Many are aware that I was born illegitimate and grew up in poverty in the East End, starting work in Fleet Street as a messenger boy at the age of fourteen and finishing up an editor. To be exact, I climbed the ranks to become managing editor of the *Daily Mirror*, editor and editor-in-chief of the *Daily Express* and *Daily Star* and finally (after the broadcast) editor of the *News of the World*. What is not generally known is how *Week Ending* viewed my life's work. Only their satirical betters at *Private Eye* published the words in full. I think they deserve a wider audience. This version is exactly as it appeared on the original script produced in court:

MALE ACTOR: This week we burrow into the no-bars-barred world of Fleet Street, to pay tribute to an Editor who sees reality with half an eye, humour with half a wit and circulation figures with half an aspirin. Yes, the Daily Star's editor of the month and our MAN OF THE WEEK is Derek Jameson.

Rousing martial music at this point. Elgar's *King of the Barbarians*, to be precise.

In Derek Jameson we have the archetypal East-End boy made bad, narrowly surviving a term of active service on the Mirror *he retired from newspaper work to become editor of the* Daily Express. *He arrived uncluttered with taste or talent and took to his new role like a duck to orange sauce, displaying an editorial policy characteristically simple – all the nudes fit to print and all the news printed to fit. But it's as a craftsman we remember him best: the writer who thinks from the wrist, the author who is to journalism what lockjaw is to conversation and the creative force who's made the* Express *what it is today – the thinking man's bin-liner. Never lost for clichés, Derek Jameson is always ready to speak his mind, however small. But tonight we honour him for his promotion to the lofty obscurity of the* Daily Star. *We salute him as an editor with the common touch, who regards nudity as only skin deep, and who still believes that 'erudite' is a glue.*

More music.

So join with us now as we congratulate this man of a few syllables as he approaches his new labour of lust and starts the bull rolling in the paper that put the media in mediocrity. Derek Jameson, the nitty-gritty titivation tout from Trafalgar House, is our MAN OF THE WEEK.

Music reaches a crescendo.

So much for the self-appointed guardians of good taste and proper use of language. Their grammar, spelling and punctuation are up the creek, of course, and clearly *titivation* should read *titillation*. As a piece of satire, it has about as much literary merit as a Christmas cracker joke. All the same, I could envisage the mirth it must have caused around the Manchester and London offices of the *Star* in the wake of the sudden demise of their champion Grimsditch at my hands. I felt like Judas myself.

Editors come and go in Fleet Street faster than football managers in the first division. Nevertheless, it still makes the troops uneasy. Quite apart from anything else, new brooms have a nasty habit of sweeping out old rubbish. The pain was greater in the case of 'Grimbles,' as Peter was known to one and all. He had put the *Star* together from scratch, grafting up to 16 hours a day to make the paper succeed and their jobs secure.

It was launched on November 2nd, 1978, with the smallest staff of any national daily, little money to spend and massive production problems. On

top of all that its headquarters were in Manchester, from where it was supposed to take on and smite *The Sun* and the *Daily Mirror*. Grimbles' only
crime in the eyes of his loyal followers was to upset the management by asking
for more of everything on their behalf.

Peter had been my choice to run the *Star*. We worked together at the
Sunday Mirror and to me he was a roaring genius. He looked like manic Steve
MacQueen and had immense drive and a great capacity for work. Emotional,
noisy, reckless – but still superb at his job. Just the man to edit a new, down-
market tabloid. Builder-turned-publisher Victor Matthews, who had taken
over Lord Beaverbrook's dwindling *Express* empire for the Trafalgar Group,
was not too sure.

'What's he done, this *Grimm-er-um*?' Matthews wanted to know. Like
many another, he never could quite get the hang of the name Grimsditch. My
man's claim to the editor's chair was none too promising. His top job to date
had been deputy editor of the defunct weekly *Reveille*.

Matthews and his chief lieutenant, the aristocratic Jocelyn Stevens,
brightened considerably when I told them Grimbles was a Greek classical
scholar with an honours degree at Oxford. They agreed to give him the job.
There were strings. I was to take the title of editor-in-chief and supervise the
birth of Matthews' brainchild. He dreamed up the idea in the bath, an
immaculate conception that did not prevent him telling the world two weeks
before the *Star*'s launch that it was not the kind of paper he would have
around the house.

Editors do not take kindly to other editors being put on top of them, even
when they come clucking sympathetically and dressed up in fancy titles like
Editor-in-Chief or Editorial Director. It is the editor, not the proprietor's
visiting poodle, who does the work, labouring long and hard in a world
bordering on insanity. The editor, if he is doing his job, is in charge in fact and
in law. He carries the can for the millions of words that pour off his presses.

Grimbles was no exception. Although I was supposed to be in charge, he
kept me at arm's length and ploughed his own furrow to disaster. I could not
blame him. As I say, it is a difficult relationship at the best of times. What
made it worse in this case was that I was also editor of the rival *Express*.
Nobody with the faintest idea of how newspapers work could have expected
him to take me into his confidence. All the same, when relations between

Grimbles and management reached the point of no return, turning into a series of slanging matches, the bosses exercised the editor-in-chief option. Grimsditch was fired in March, 1980, for failing to maintain proper relations with Derek Jameson. And the aforementioned editor-in-chief was instructed to go to Manchester to deliver the chop personally. I was also told to take over full control of the paper.

'One of us had to go,' I told Radio Manchester, 'and you can guess who that was.' They kindly put my tough words on the national grid, Radio 4's early morning *Today* programme. Messrs. Matthews and Stevens were outraged. I got a fearful wigging for speaking out so harshly. It was a tragedy totally in character with Fleet Street. Grimbles, my friend and protégé, has not spoken to me from that day to this. A couple of years back I happened to hire a Polish lady mini-cab driver of his acquaintance – he collects the most extraordinary people – and hoped she would bring about a reconciliation. I suggested she arrange a meeting, but heard nothing. He must have turned down the idea.

In our day we made a devastating combination. My first 15 months at the *Express* saw the circulation climb ever upward, on occasion reaching 2,500,000 copies daily, an increase of 25 per cent. It was an achievement unequalled in modern times. Grimbles and I then went on to take the *Star* from nil to 1,250,000 in less than two years. Before very long, under new management, the *Express* would be struggling to hold 1,700,000 and we would see the *Star* going through a brief marriage with soft porn merchants in a bid to stop sales dipping below a million.

To me *Week Ending*'s crude attack was the portent of disaster to come. You do not spend forty years in the Street without being able to sniff which way the wind is blowing. Here was total madness. Having been forced to fire one of my own, I was left holding the baby – running not one, but two national dailies. Simultaneously. 'Two editors for the price of one,' Victor Matthews told Jocelyn Stevens, 'what are you complaining about!' Total madness. It could not be long before I joined Grimbles on the cobbles – and now friend Bealing had brought the glad tidings that someone had already struck the first blow.

'Character assassination', I screamed in protest on reading the words. *Defamatory, offensive, unfair and untrue.*

Nothing of the kind, the BBC replied to our first salvo. The said words are fair comment upon a matter of public interest.

The argument sounds simple enough up to this point. Now the lawyers enter the arena. Four years of mumbo-jumbo were to follow. The legal eagles soared to ever greater heights of verbosity. More and more letters, briefs, affidavits, statements, opinions. Most of all, more postponements and more expenditure. I should have listened to my old Mum. *Find out who wrote it and go and punch him in the nose,* she said. *The worst that can happen is you'll be fined fifty quid.*

But then that would have made me a yob, wouldn't it?

The name of Peter Carter-Ruck brings a grimace to the face of every editor in Fleet Street. He is the nation's top libel lawyer, his reproving letters instantly recognisable as they drop into *IN*-trays across the media. They are printed on pale yellow paper. The contents are usually short and to the point:

> *The statements made in your publication dated so-and-so are highly defamatory of our client; it is difficult to comprehend how you could be party to such vicious and scurrilous denigration; kindly make amends immediately by publishing a full apology in terms to be agreed; and we await your proposals for compensating our client and paying his costs.*

Peter's fearsome reputation as the man who never loses is such that legal advisers usually recommend editors to settle on the best possible terms they can extract. Carter-Ruck doesn't give much away, though he can be merciful when detractors come to heel immediately rather than take their chances in the High Court of Justice.

So there was a touch of black comedy about my request to Carter-Ruck to represent my interests in seeking redress from the BBC. All my previous dealings with him had been as defending editor, not plaintiff. I surrendered every time.

'Much as I enjoy a good laugh at my own expense, I find this goes beyond the bounds of either humour or satire,' I wrote to him in a letter enclosing the *Week Ending* transcript on March 27, 1980. My secretary put a terse message on my desk a few days later: *Peter Carter-Ruck phoned from a callbox in Glencoe*

and will try to ring after lunch. He does consider it highly deflamatory (sic).
Considers it so serious that a statement should be issued as well as damages. He is
proceeding with the case...'

First shot in the battle of words that was to go on unremittingly for years.
The BBC did not cop out, as their newspaper cousins tend to do when
confronted by that pale yellow paper. Aunty's policymakers obviously took
the view that it would spell the end of satire and much of comedy itself if
artists were not able to clobber people like myself who occupied seats of
power. They saw it as a fight for free speech. Jameson's hurt feelings were of
secondary importance.

Our statement of claim followed conventional lines. The remarks broadcast
on March 21 and repeated the following day were defamatory and damaging,
causing my reputation to be brought into public scandal, odium and
contempt. Specifically, we said the offending words bore the meaning that I
was illiterate and stupid, narrowly avoided being dismissed for incompetence
by the *Daily Mirror*, presented news in a distorted or misleading way, and was
not fit to hold the posts of editor of the *Daily Express* and editor-in-chief of the
Daily Star. We sought an injunction restraining the defendants from a repeat
performance and asked for damages.

The BBC responded promptly. It agreed the programme had been
broadcast, but contested everything else. It did not accept that the words used
were capable of the meanings we alleged or were defamatory. Furthermore, it
was fair comment on a matter of public interest.

From the start it was obvious that this case would revolve around the
meaning of words. Difficult at the best of times. We all have differing views on
the rich treasures of the English language and no two people stick to the same
vocabulary. Here we were not dealing merely with statements of fact, but
rather the airy-fairy world of something passing under the holy name of *satire*.
Just to complicate matters more, the lawyers have a language of their own
totally at odds with the rest of mankind. They call it legalese. Jargon would be
a better description.

One thing was certain. The BBC was going to go to incredible lengths to
prove that I was a disreputable product of the gutter press, a tit-and-bum
merchant. They had to make those words uttered in the name of satire ring
true. Needless to say, they did not delve into my fifteen years at Reuters, the

world news agency famous for honest, decent journalism. Nor did they go into the fact that I had made my reputation in newspapers as the *Mirror* executive responsible for sales in Ireland, where sex stories and Page 3 girls were light on the ground, thanks to the presence of the Irish Censorship Board.

Admittedly, I have often handled pictures of girls wearing not very much and run stories to match. For much of my life in journalism I was editor of popular tabloid newspapers. One rumbustious period in the seventies found me editing the Northern editions of the *Daily Mirror*. My brief then was to stop the onward march of Rupert Murdoch's *Sun*. We were a million readers down nationally and that meant I had to go like the clappers to keep ahead.

For starters I would have to snitch Page 3 girls, trade mark of *The Sun* and a key factor behind its soaring circulation. I soon seized my chance. Having been a picture editor in the past, I was on first name terms with just about every glamour photographer in the business. In those days they were selling Page 3 pictures to our rival at £120 a throw. They offered a selection of ten or twelve prints, *The Sun* would pick its favourite and return the rest to the photographer. My ploy was to buy second rights for £60 and promptly acquire these 'overs' from the snappers. We would publish them in the Northern editions of the *Mirror* after a decent interval had elapsed. Usually three or four days.

It was a factor in our success, though by no means the whole story. Page 3 girls might turn on a high percentage of young men, but what really kept Rupert's troops at bay was our ability to produce two or three pages of picture reports on late football matches plus powerful treatment of late news stories. *The Sun* was printed in London hours earlier and could not compete with our Manchester advantage. This is the bread-and-butter of pop tabloids – hard news tailored to the working class audience, lashings of sport, bingo and other gimmicks, provocative features and big pictures. Sex most certainly comes into it. It is not the main ingredient. Quite apart from anything else, the women readers who form the bulk of the audience would not wear it – as the *Star* was to discover to its cost in later years.

It was my success over *The Sun* publishing the *Mirror* out of Manchester that led to my promotion to London. Incidentally, the Southern editions did not publish or approve of topless girls. There was no way the *Mirror* bosses were going to appoint a sexpot as managing editor.

It was the same story again when I joined Grimbles in launching the *Daily Star* back in Manchester in 1978. A tit-and-bum paper, the cry went up. *The Sun* even had the cheek to blow up a headline with some spurious quotes pinned on me in the Sunday *Observer*: 'The *Daily Star* will be all tits, bums, QPR and roll your own fags – DEREK JAMESON, EDITOR-IN-CHIEF.'

I told *The Sun* angrily that it was a phoney quote, pointing out that the editor-in-chief of a Manchester newspaper initially circulating only in the North was hardly likely to take Queen's Park Rangers as his text. The next day's *Sun* published a most peculiar correction:

NOT ME, SAYS MR JAMESON

Derek Jameson, editor-in-chief of the Daily Star, *says he never used the quote, attributed to him in Thursday's* Sun, *that the new paper would be 'all bum and tit, QPR and roll your own fags.' Sorry, Derek, but it did sound like you.*

By then the rot had set in. Even Victor Matthews got cold feet and came out with his remarkable statement that he would not have the *Star* inside the house. Yet I had published a job memo spelling out in detail just what the first new daily paper for seventy five years was all about:

★ Forget all the talk about the *Daily Star* being a tit-and-bum paper grovelling in the dust with *The Sun*. Not likely. Quite apart from anything else, it isn't that easy. Imitations rarely succeed.

★ What kind of paper will it be? In basic terms, a popular working class tabloid, strong on pictures and bright words, hitting the market midway between *The Sun* and the *Daily Mirror*.

★ Some key words to memorise: lively, vigorous, optimistic, youthful, caring, crusading, irreverent, provocative, protective, curious. Never talk down to the reader. Nor lose touch with the way he lives, thinks, feels, hopes and dreams.

That just about sums up my philosophy as a newspaperman. It doesn't seem to come out quite like that in Fleet Street, however worthy our intentions. It certainly works a treat on Radio 2 every morning.

The mountain of legal dross on my desk grew ever higher. It soon became evident that this was to be a battle involving the sex dragon. BBC strategy was all there in the vast quantity of paper before me. The lawyers had gone back twelve years in their efforts to dredge up material designed to destroy my case. Out came muzzy photostat copies of dozens of lurid headlines and sexy pictures presumably aimed at proving I was nothing more than a titillation tout. One of their 'bundles', as they call files, featured a stunning beach picture of Anthea Redfern, who was to become Mrs Bruce Forsyth; photographs illustrating the streaking craze were there; and so, too, was a topless dancer smuggled aboard a nuclear submarine; plus dozens of model girls with and without strategically placed wisps of chiffon.

I would not recommend accepting a lawyer's definition of titillation as the last word on the subject. They certainly had no doubts as to what they considered any reasonable person, as they call Mr Average Citizen, should not be reading in the columns of a newspaper.

Elaborate graphs were produced of papers between 1972–77 showing column inches devoted to sex compared with news, sport and other contents. The highest count came in the *Daily Mirror* of 1st March, 1976. 'Sexually titillating' material claimed $17\frac{1}{2}$ columns against $42\frac{1}{2}$ columns for news and features, $38\frac{1}{2}$ columns sport, 9 columns TV and radio and $73\frac{1}{2}$ columns advertising. Fourteen of those $17\frac{1}{2}$ 'titillating' columns were occupied by a feature on the meaning of physical love written by Marje Proops, the most respected agony aunt in Britain.

Ah, well, any stick to beat a dog.

CHAPTER TWO

Sexual titillation, Mr Jameson?

S tep beyond Fleet Street into the Strand and there stands the Victorian
Gothic palace where virtue finally is rewarded and vice receives its just
desserts. Or so they say. The Royal Courts of Justice, otherwise known
as the Law Courts, possess all the ambience of a Corporation crematorium.
Those unfortunate enough to be drawn inside the most famous courts in the
land look far from happy. They appear to be walking on thin ice. Fear gets
you in the legs and stomach. Only the barristers seem at home in the gloom.
Juniors in tow, they scurry through the cold stone corridors like worker ants,
their urgent whispers sending a sibilant hiss upwards to the legal battlements.
In their black robes and wigs, it is difficult to tell one from the other, friend
from foe.

Not that anyone could miss the stern features of Mr John Wilmers, Queen's
Counsel, eminent advocate, part-time judge, outdoor man (skiing, walking,
gardening) and front runner for the BBC. Leading for the defence, they call it.
He strode into Court 14, Queen's Bench Division, on the opening day of the
trial, February 13, 1984, at the head of a formidable support team of lawyers,
clerks, BBC executives, scriptwriters and radio and television technicians.
The engineers had been in court beforehand to install a battery of radio and
TV transmitters. It was going to be a high tech trial. This army occupied most
of the pews to the right of the court while my own counsel cut a somewhat
lonely figure, sitting to the left at the front of the court. A music lover like
myself, Mr David Eady was then in his early 40s, some twenty years younger
than his learned friend opposite. He was a rising star at the Bar and a top man
in the complex field of libel and contempt. He had just been made QC. I
believed in him totally. It was only later I learned that his confidence in the
outcome did not match my faith in him, though that was not his fault.

Presiding over the celebrated libel action was a man of very few words indeed. The Hon. Sir James Comyn, then sixty three. This Dubliner, wit and raconteur and breeder of prize cattle was said to have a special fondness for newspapermen. It did not show in my case, which is only fair and proper. Mr Justice Comyn ruled over the court with total authority, though I cannot recall him speaking more than a dozen times throughout the proceedings.

The most significant person in court, or so it seemed to me, did not speak at all. My solicitor, Mr Peter Carter-Ruck, wartime artillery officer, ocean racer (Royal Yacht Squadron) and a leading member of the Law Society that governs the conduct of the nation's solicitors. Although approaching his seventies, this veteran of a thousand libel battles seemed to have lost none of his will to win as he fussed and fretted amid the flood of paper that threatened to engulf us all.

I had already been through the *interrogatories* stage. These are written questions set by the plaintiffs before the trial commences.

Yes, I dutifully replied in August, 1983, I was brought up from childhood in the East End of London. It was true I described the said upbringing as 'tough . . . tougher than any editor before.' I did follow a policy of publishing photographs of nude or bare-breasted women in the Northern editions of the *Daily Mirror*. Ditto the *Daily Star*.

It all seemed dreadfully unfair to me, having to tick "Yes" or "No" to a series of questions taken out of context. What are they doing, I wondered? Studying anthropology or setting me up as a sex maniac from Stepney Green? I didn't realise how near the truth the latter was.

On Day One of the hearing, the jury of six men and six women looked suitably neutral, betraying nothing of their feelings as they weighed up the supposed East End boy made bad who thought erudite was a glue. It did not seem to have stopped his progress to the top in Fleet Street. *All the nudes fit to print, and all the news printed to fit*. Could that be the explanation? David Eady opened vigorously, taking the court through the *Week Ending* broadcast and pointing out why I felt so affronted by what the BBC called satire. In his view it was schoolboy humour.

'Whether it is funny or not, it was of the gravest concern for him. It really knocked him for six. He found it personally offensive, rather spiteful and damaging to his professional reputation as a journalist.

15

'The implications of the piece are that he is unfit to edit a national newspaper and that he is illiterate or stupid.'

The BBC denied libel, contending that the words complained of did not have the meaning alleged and that they were fair comment on a matter of public importance. Mr Eady said the other side would be relying on copies of the newspapers involved and television interviews given by Mr Jameson to support their defence of fair comment. However, he told the jury, the newspapers were really only examples of tabloid journalism generally. 'They are no proof of the competence, skill or intelligence of Mr Jameson.'

It was time for me to climb the steps into the witness box, taking me eye level with judge and jury and looking down into the courtroom, which was to remain crowded with friend and foe alike throughout the trial. First the easy bit. In a matter of minutes Mr Eady took me through my life. Started at Reuters as a messenger, worked up the ladder to become Northern editor of the *Sunday Mirror* and then *Daily Mirror*, went on to become managing editor of the paper in London, and then editor of the *Daily Express* as well as the *Daily Star*. More recently editor of the *News of the World*.

'I see myself as an all-round journalist. I am totally involved in the whole spectrum of newspapers and my professional reputation is the dearest thing to me.' As Northern editor of the *Mirror*, I agreed, I had introduced nudes in a bid to beat off *The Sun*. At the *Express*, I insisted on a no nudes policy. I was simply a professional doing his job.

I agreed that being called 'an archetypal East End boy made bad' had caused me the greatest pain. 'I consider it offensive, an insult to all those people who helped me along the way,' I said.

It was John Wilmers' turn. He stood there in his half-moon spectacles, looking for all the world like a history master at a public school. Though icily polite – he even referred to my speech as 'splendid Cockney' – he still managed to convey the impression I was something nasty he had found on the sole of his shoe.

Well, I thought, it will only last three or four hours, a day at most. I had been told a dozen times that the trial would be over in five days. Wilmers was to keep me in that box for six days – more than twenty hours of intense, painful, hectoring interrogation. The trial itself lasted twelve days.

I have never felt so isolated in my life. Nobody came to my assistance.

Presumably there was no reason why they should. So this is what they call the majesty of the law. I stood there trying to appear calm, answering politely, wisecracking, hitting back where I could. 'You like your little digs, don't you, Mr Jameson,' he admonished me once in those stentorian tones.

Inside I was raging. That's me up here, I thought. They're out to destroy me – my name, my reputation, everything I've done in my life, I'm going to be wiped out – and I'm supposed to be the injured party. God help me, I've fallen among lawyers.

The purpose of Mr Wilmers' onslaught was to prove that I was nothing more than a tit-and-bum merchant, a muckraker, someone who deserved everything thrown at him by the literary set at Radio 4. 'You make it sound as though every paragraph I have ever handled in my life was concerned with sex,' I told him at one point.

Wilmers began his marathon by asking whether it was not true that I was known as Sid Yobbo, the nickname given to me years earlier by another satirist, Richard Ingrams of *Private Eye*.

'Nobody in Fleet Street ever called me Sid Yobbo,' I snapped back, 'I'm a newspaperman, not a professional Cockney.'

Solemnly, pausing here and there for effect, Mr Wilmers went through the mass of papers before him page by page as if reading *Mein Kampf* at a Nazi war crimes trial. His favourite bundle appeared to be a huge blue file. I weighed it afterwards: six pounds.

The paper mountain included what are called *disclosures* – documents exchanged in advance by either side relevant to the case. This material included entries from my own cuttings book, a collection of various bits and pieces about myself published over the years. The fact I had stuck an item from *Private Eye* or elsewhere in the book did not imply it was a fair and accurate report. Quite the opposite, in many instances. So I was shaken in mid-trial when Wilmers battered me about the head with material taken from this cuttings book – with the name of the newspaper and date in my own handwriting!

One of these stories that particularly caused damage was a tongue-in-cheek gossip piece in the London *Standard* saying I had been given only hours to clear my desk at the *Mirror* and vacate the building. It was used in court to back up the programme's suggestion that I had 'narrowly survived' at the

Mirror. In truth, *Mirror* editorial boss Tony Miles ordered me to vacate the premises pronto because I had been made editor of the rival *Express*. He had only recently brought me to London from Manchester and made me the *Mirror*'s managing editor.

Wilmers also used my cuttings to hit me with the spurious 'tit-and-bums, QPR and roll your own fags' quote described earlier – despite the fact the *Observer*'s diary man, Tom Davies, retracted the following week and admitted 'I got it wrong.' The cutting with that disclaimer was ignored.

Every now and then the technicians lolling about at the rear of the court were roused to relay various television programmes in which I expounded my professional views. In one programme, *The Editors*, I told George Scott that as new editor of the *Express* I had to fight *The Sun* and *Mirror* with one arm tied behind my back because I had no intention of printing nudes. Elsewhere I admitted that topless *Starbirds* were part of that paper's diet because there was a market for them among its younger readers. I personally had little taste for them and they could not be defended journalistically – 'they don't win Pulitzer prizes, but they do sell newspapers.'

So it went on day after day. The mud had to be made to stick. He ponderously picked his way through carefully selected evidence from papers going back over the years. More and more pictures of girls in various states of undress – and yet still not adding up to more than a fraction of those papers' overall content. I would have been on my feet fifty times to demand what all this had to do with Derek Jameson. Why were not *all* the newspapers being exhibited in their entirety? My counsel stayed firmly seated. Perhaps they only interrupt in Hollywood films. Altogether the lawyers dredged up more than sixty pages. I had not been the editor responsible for more than two or three of them. They were someone else's baby.

The pages primarily were from Manchester editions of the *Daily Mirror* going back ten years. The lawyers in selecting material had failed to appreciate that they were devised and drawn up for all editions by head-quarters in London and were not my responsibility as Northern editor. Similarly, pages from the *Star* had been approved by Grimsditch in Manchester and I knew nothing of them sitting in my *Express* office in London.

It had become obvious that it was not Jameson on trial, but Fleet Street.

Not all of it. Just the part that produces two out of every three newspapers read in this country. And I *could* quite easily have edited them, not that more than a handful would have brought a blush to a maiden aunt's cheek.

As if to prove what a farce the trial had become, the BBC had problems finding salacious material in the *Daily Express*, still my paper at the time of the broadcast. Although I was supposed to publish 'all the nudes fit to print,' they were able to produce only two tame samples to air before the jury: a girl who appeared to be naked under a shawl, and a picture of comedian Leslie Crowther alongside a model girl. It measured less than three inches square.

'Sexual titillation, Mr Jameson?' Wilmers boomed for the umpteenth time.

'She's wearing a top hat,' I answered helpfully.

On another occasion he wanted to know why a holiday feature about Spain was illustrated by a girl wearing a bikini.

'Sexual titillation, Mr Jameson?'

'What should I have put in there?' I asked him 'A picture of General Franco?'

This interminable nonsense – a juror had to be woken up at one stage – was enlivened by the showing of a BBC documentary on runaway Joyce McKinney, the girl in the case of the Manacled Mormon. She caused a sensation in April, 1978, by skipping bail while awaiting trial at the Old Bailey accused of kidnapping Mormon missionary Kirk Anderson. Millions had followed sensational reports of the preliminary hearing in which the peachy blonde was accused of abducting Kirk, chaining him to a bed in a rented cottage in Devon and forcing him to have sex. It was all part of an elaborate love ritual, Joyce told the magistrates. 'I loved Kirk so much I would have skied down Mount Everest in the nude with a carnation up my nose.'

To the surprise of many, the magistrates at Epsom, where Kirk had been living, granted bail to Joyce and her close friend Keith May. Pending trail, the irrepressible Joyce promptly began courting Fleet Street. She disappeared shortly after attending a film première with the editor of the now defunct William Hickey column, *Express* writer Peter Tory. Naturally he made it his business to scour the world for her – along with every other tabloid – if only to restore his scalded pride. As editor of the *Express*, I gave him *carte blanche* to seek her out. And that he did. The phone rang on my desk one sleepy afternoon in mid-May. It was Tory. The conversation went something like this.

'I've found her!'

'Where are you?'

'Atlanta, Georgia.'

'ATLANTA! How the hell did she get there?'

'Dressed as a nun!'

'A nun! Incredible. Have you got it all wrapped up – nobody else sniffing around?'

'No, we've got the whole story to ourselves – and Bill Lovelace (the chief photographer) has marvellous pictures. Dressed as a nun, an Indian princess, God knows what.'

'Does she want money?'

'No, not much. Just a nominal sum for expenses.'

'Tory, you're a ****ing genius!'

On May 18 we came out with a Page 1 splash proclaiming WE FIND JOYCE, with a picture of the errant blonde in a nun's habit. Scoop of the year, we boasted – just to rub the opposition's nose in it.

Alas, our joy lasted but two days. We had projected her as a dizzy blonde. A good girl at heart, God-fearing and true, who had erred only because of her deep love for missionary Kirk. Inspired by our success in finding Joyce, the rival *Daily Mirror* dusted off a dossier it had tucked away on her secret life in Los Angeles earlier in the Seventies. Our Southern belle turned out to be a model who had made about £25,000 in 18 months posing for kinky pictures and offering sex services. And they had pictures to prove it. They knocked the stuffing out of us. I was most impressed and went to the Mirror pub, known affectionately as The Stab (for Stab-in-the-back), to buy my former colleagues a drink by way of congratulation.

Like the *Mirror*, though for different reasons, Wilmers also took a poor view of our scoop. I was delighted when the court sat back to view a two-night special by the BBC *Tonight* programme telling this tale of our times complete with lengthy interviews with the protesting Miss ('I'm a good girl') McKinney. At last an opportunity for me to get the sanctimonious stench of all the dirt thrown at me out of my nostrils.

'There you are,' I told the court, 'two nights running on BBC television, Joyce McKinney talking about bondage, handcuffs, sex, massage, pictures reproduced of her in kinky gear. To take me to task over the *Daily Express* story is pure hypocrisy.'

There was as much sexual titillation – if you want to call it that – in that broadcast as there was in the *Daily Express*.

I admitted we had been 'out-McKinneyed' by our rivals, but my sweetest moment was yet to come.

'The BBC got those interviews with McKinney thanks to me,' I told the court. 'The *Tonight* programme came to me for help and I used my good offices to get her to talk to them'.

Wilmers was having none of it, of course. He said the BBC treatment of the subject 'differs totally and utterly' from the way my paper had treated it. He was right there. Unlike the BBC, we didn't have any of those kinky pictures. The Beeb got theirs from the same source as the *Mirror*.

Roger Bolton, former editor of *Tonight* and *Nationwide*, was summoned later to confirm that I had helped the BBC team to interview Miss McKinney and agreed I had been 'helpful and friendly'.

Incidentally, I told the court several times that I had always enjoyed the best relations with the Beeb. 'I have always been the BBC's greatest champion in Fleet Street,' I said. Alongside Lord Whitelaw, I had been guest speaker at the 25th anniversary dinner of BBC TV and was on first-name terms with many of the Corporation's top executives. They must have been wondering what I was doing there. So was I.

Learned counsel also took me to task over the *Star*'s sensational series telling the story of Mrs Soraya Khashoggi, the Leicester Girl and former wife of Adnan Khashoggi, the Arab tycoon who once excited much Press attention as one of the world's richest men. Among her revelations were alleged cavortings with Winston Churchill MP. She claimed to have driven with him along an American freeway, taking off her clothes as the car gathered more and more speed. The headline on February 5, 1980, said: *THE FASTER YOU GO, THE MORE I'LL TAKE OFF... In no time at all Winston was doing 100 mph.* When the inevitable speed cop caught up with them and demanded to know the driver's name, he was bowled over by the answer: Winston Churchill. America's favourite Englishman.

Reading from "Soraya's Own Story", Mr Wilmers demanded: 'Isn't that sexually explicit?'

I didn't think so. Well, how would I define it?

'Rabelaisian,' I said thoughtfully. 'Rabelaisian.'

So what did I consider was sex then?

'By sexually explicit, I mean the graphic details of sexual intercourse. The report was couched in the language of a romantic novel – rather mawkishly, I thought.'

Wilmers let me out of the box after six days. By that time I was ready to confess all rather than spend another minute under the interrogation of this master advocate. I remember thinking to myself: *If that's how they treat the innocent party, God help the defendants.*

I greatly admired John Wilmers. Nobody had treated me so appallingly in my entire professional life, or so it seemed. Presumably he was just doing his job. What fascinated me most of all was that I never saw him smile once. A man of iron. He died shortly after the case. I felt very sad about it.

We called only two character witnesses in my support. Both venerable and highly-respected figures in Fleet Street. Sir Edward Pickering, in his day the top editorial executive of *Express*, *Mirror* and *Times* newspapers, testified that I was 'a man of high talent.' Morris Benett, my managing editor at the *Express* and formerly a famous chief sub-editor, said I was 'a very able editor.'

I nearly fell of my pew in the front row of Court Fourteen when Wilmers opened the defence case saying the BBC regretted the 'personal hurt' the sketch had caused me.

'Having said that, let me add the exercise of free speech sometimes does just that.'

The defence witnesses went through their evidence in a matter of hours. Guy Jenkin, a freelance scriptwriter employed on *Week Ending,* described it as a satire combining comment on the week's news with comedy. Asked if he felt any ill will towards myself, he replied: 'No, not at all.'

Alan Nixon, producer of that particular edition, thought the sketch about Jameson was 'funny, pertinent – a tough piece – but fair.'

Had he any ill will or did he intend to be spiteful towards Mr Jameson as a man or a journalist?

'Not personally, no.'

Cross-examined by my counsel, Nixon denied the sketch was meant to portray me as 'ignorant, illiterate or stupid.' He agreed it was 'tough, hard-edged and intended to wound, but it was intended as comment.'

John Langdon, scriptwriter on several radio comedy programmes, said he wrote the entire sketch in question except for the line 'East End boy made bad.' That was contributed by journalist Peter Hickey. He got the idea from an interview ('One of us has to go') I had given the Radio 4 *Today* programme earlier in the week. 'I believed that he was interested in selling newspapers rather than giving them any literary or cultural merit and he often used the lowest common denominator,' he said. The *Star* pandered to the lowest denominator in content and price, but he bore Jameson no ill feeling. The line about the East End boy was a joke based on the cliché 'East End boy made good.' He added: 'There is nothing at all wrong with being an East End boy – my father is one.'

Bad or good, he did not specify.

Cross-examined by Mr Eady, the scriptwriter thought the *Daily Express* was right wing rubbish which, under my editorship, displayed 'a sort of nasty, seditious titillation involving low-cut dresses with the model bending forward.' He agreed that nudes in newspapers were commonplace, though he did not approve of them. Although he thought the *Express* was politically biased in its editorials and choice of columnists, he said he did not accuse me of printing lies or untrue facts.

On the tenth day of the trial Mr Wilmers began his summing up.

Editors of papers like the *Express, Mirror* and *Star* 'might expect the people they comment on to have fairly thick skins and be able to take criticism,' he said.

'One is entitled to say that what is good for the goose is good for the gander.'

The BBC did not deny, he said, that some of the words in the sketch were defamatory in the sense that they were derogatory of Mr Jameson in his capacity as an editor. However, the scriptwriter had read the *Daily Star* under my editorship carefully. An honest man might say it was not a tasteful paper and plainly not very literary or intellectual.

'Why shouldn't the scriptwriter be allowed to express a strong opinion? We are all entitled, in a free country, to express our views.'

As for Mr Jameson's complaint that the broadcast made him out to be illiterate or stupid, there was no suggestion that he could not read or was personally illiterate. The sketch was comment on an editor, not an individual, and a reasonable listener would have realised that. It was of the greatest importance to the freedom of speech that the jury should reject Mr Jameson's careful and deliberate attack on programmes of the *Week Ending* type and vindicate the BBC's right to broadcast what the scriptwriter honestly believed. Should, however, the jury find in my favour 'the smallest coin in the realm' would be adequate damages, he concluded. After all, the jury had heard me described as a 'tit and bum' man. I was not the editor of *The Times*.

David Eady, summing up on my behalf, said the BBC had mounted a huge operation to get Jameson and demolish him by fair means or foul.

'The BBC's time and vast resources have been turned on Derek Jameson in a vast military operation to leave no stone unturned to find anything they could to discredit him.

'This libel action has nothing to do with topless girls or nudes. If all the programme had said was that Mr Jameson printed nudes in his papers, he would not have brought the action.

'The reason why Derek Jameson is here is because this piece went well beyond any legitimate comment about newspapers. It was a personal attack. It is absolutely clear to any listener to that broadcast that this was a hatchet job on Derek Jameson – a demolition job on his personal reputation, his character and his integrity as a journalist.'

He questioned whether it was likely I would risk everything simply to mount a one-man crusade against the BBC's right to fair comment. As for freedom of speech, it was interesting to see how it had been taken down from the shelf and wheeled out 'like a frail and elderly relative being attacked by a bullying plaintiff.'

'The BBC's freedom of speech is hale and hearty, alive and kicking everyone in sight, loud and robust and constantly in evidence.'

Mr Eady added that the BBC had scraped every barrel in dredging up cuttings from newspapers I had edited to back up their insulting and intemperate sketch. Its author and producer did not honestly believe what they were saying, but it was broadcast nonetheless. 'The implication of that sketch is that Mr Jameson is a moron – the dregs.'

He asked the jury to award damages big enough 'to signify to all concerned that he is the straight and responsible journalist, the thoroughly respectable individual, that he had shown himself to be in this trial.'

Mr Justice Comyn advised the jury: 'You have been asked to look at Mr Jameson as an editor – but is he not also a man?'

Had the sketch gone 'too far in poking fun?' Should not Mr Jameson, as the BBC had suggested, 'be the last man to complain?' These were matters for the jury to decide.

The twelve men and women good and true certainly took the longest anyone could remember in any libel action of our time, a total of seven hours, on the 29th day of February, 1984, a bad omen if I ever heard one.

I was not surprised. Counsel between them had come up with five questions for the jury to answer that might have baffled Solomon himself. M'Lord Justice Comyn said he would have preferred a straight 'Yes' or 'No' to the question of defamation, but if counsel had decided otherwise, then so be it. Here are the questions and guidelines to the jury in full:

1. *Are any of the imputations defamatory?*
2. *If so, are any of the imputations factual rather than comment?*
3. *If comment, are the imputations 'fair' comment?*
4. *If 'fair' comment, has the plaintiff proved that either Mr Nixon or Mr Langdon was actuated by malice?*
5. *If any of the imputations are:*
    (a) defamatory AND
    (b) either
        (i) not comment, or
        (ii) 'unfair' comment, or
        (iii) actuated by malice,
then what sum do you award by way of damages?

GUIDELINES FOR THE JURY

1. *Did the broadcast convey to reasonable listeners any of the imputations pleaded in paragraph 4 of the Statement of Claim* (that I was illiterate and stupid, narrowly avoided being dismissed by the *Mirror*, presented news in a distorted or misleading way, and was not fit to hold the post of editor)? *If so, are any such imputations defamatory?*

2. *In so far as you find that the broadcast did convey to reasonable listeners any of the imputations pleaded in paragraph 4 of the Statement of Claim are those imputations fact or comment?*

3. *If the imputations are comment:*
   (i) *are the imputations such as could have been made by an* honest *person on facts proved or admitted and known to the BBC at the time of the broadcast?*
   (ii) *has the Plaintiff proved that anyone in the BBC responsible for broadcasting the item about the Plaintiff was actuated by malice?*

4. *If any of the imputations:*
   (i) *are both factual and defamatory; or*
   (ii) *are comment but could not be made by an honest person on the facts; or*
   (iii) *are comment which an honest person* could *make but malice has been proved against the BBC.*

what damages do you award to the Plaintiff?

Confused? So was the jury. After five hours the six men and six women returned to court with a request to borrow a dictionary.

Request refused, said the judge. Not possible in law.

The foreman then asked the judge to define the word 'imputation.' Mr Justice Comyn consulted the eminent Queen's Counsel of both sides. The judge then ruled that 'imputation' meant 'meaning.'

Rather simplified, that, I thought. In my book, imputation means to suggest that somebody has been up to something undesirable. It goes a great deal further than 'meaning.' But then I'm just a simple soul who thinks erudite is a glue. I kept my mouth shut. At least my thoughts belonged to me: *God help us, if they don't know the meaning of imputation, how the hell are they going to make any sense of the rest of it?*

The jury filed back, having been encouraged by His Lordship to look for an unanimous verdict – 'most desirable in this case above all others,' he said.

They came back one and a half hours later, a retirement of seven hours in all.

26

The foreman intoned the verdict of us all:

Yes, defamatory.

My fists unclenched. *I've won*, Oh, no, you haven't.

The imputations, though defamatory, were fair comment and not actuated by malice.

Mr Wilmers was on his feet in a second, cutting the foreman short. Anything after that was purely academic. The BBC had won. Defamatory, certainly. He had admitted as much in his closing speech. What mattered here was not the technicalities of the verdict, but who was going to pick up the bill for this little lot. And fair comment meant that I paid. Mr Justice Comyn accordingly made the orders for costs against me, overruling objections by David Eady that the BBC had introduced large amounts of paper into the proceedings.

The judge told Wilmers: 'I feel that certain things in your case have been overdone, but in view of the unanimous verdict of the jury I feel there is no option but to award you the full costs of the action.'

Outside the court, the reporters and photographers who had spent the day awaiting a dramatic finale were rewarded with an ashen-faced Jameson, clearly shaken, and the lady in my life, Ellen Petrie, in tears. I gave her a kiss.

I told them the costs would add up to some £75,000. It would take all my savings, the result of 40 years' hard work, but I hoped to come out on the right side of bankruptcy. Then came the words, which were to be quoted over and again, that were to change my fortunes in the years ahead:

'I brought this case to show that honesty, integrity, decency and fair play do exist in Fleet Street. I hoped that I had demonstrated those virtues. Clearly the jury has decided otherwise and I can only accept their verdict.'

That was the moment people took me to their hearts. One lone individual against a mighty Corporation, I had fought the good fight and lost. Now it was all over I was not going to moan about it.

The British always champion the underdog. And my greatest champion of all turned out to be – the BBC. When I emerged from the case, badly shaken and fearful of the future, it was Aunty Beeb who picked me up, dusted me down and handed me over to the care of the great British public.

Within two years the editor without a paper became the star of the airwaves. It could only happen in Britain.

CHAPTER THREE

Case of the missing lady

There was an extraordinary sequel to the case. Within days, I learned vital information which would have had a major bearing on my attitude had been deliberately withheld from me. Had I known, there was no way I would have gone ahead. It explained much about the farce in the High Court and my feeling we could not win.

From the beginning, I had been sustained by the compassion and solicitude of Mrs May Richards, Peter Carter-Ruck's senior legal executive. In the old days of quill pens she would have been called managing clerk. A diminutive, black-haired lady in her early forties, May had been through troubles of her own. She was divorced and bringing up a young daughter she somehow managed to keep at private school out of her own pocket.

May did all the donkey work, putting together the endless sheaves of documents, checking names, dates and facts, liaising with the other side in producing evidence, and most of all, dealing with the client. There were times when Jameson was a very difficult client indeed, breathing fire down the telephone in his efforts to understand what the hell was going on.

Never one to hide her feelings, May was totally sympathetic. She knew I had no taste for the High Court, wanted to get out on honourable terms and, most important of all, was terrified of the horrendous costs eating away at my savings. In the months up to the trial, I was out of work. Rupert Murdoch had fired me as editor of the *News of the World*. One of our differences had been over the case. He advised me to drop it without any further shilly-shallying.

On that first day of trial a procession of us walked from Peter's offices in Essex Street, across the wide zebra crossing in the Strand where London's traffic halts in double-quick time for Her Majesty's judges, into the Law

Courts seen a thousand times in television news reports. I suddenly realised someone was missing. May Richards. My all-knowing lady of litigation. She was off the case, as they say in Hollywood. Peter muttered something about the strain of it getting to her. It was considered to be in the best interests of all that she should drop out. Sad, I thought, but did not pursue the subject. There were more desperate matters ahead.

Subsequently, I learned that May resigned three days after the case ended. As she wrote at the time, she had worked for Peter Carter-Ruck for twenty eight years. Apparently she pulled out of the trial because of her concern about the consequences. May's sympathy for me was such that she could not bear to see the last act. She did not express her doubts and fears to me, despite the fact she had been the person closest to the case for four years. Presumably she felt it would be indiscreet to raise the matter with me direct. But surely the client had a right to know? It would most certainly have influenced my thinking.

There was to be an even more extraordinary development. I had been deliberately kept in the dark about the views of my counsel, David Eady QC. The most important document in the entire case, so far as I was concerned, was not shown to me.

It happened this way. Top barristers-at-law are the consultant surgeons of the legal profession. They are frequently asked to deliver Opinions on the way they consider a case is likely to go. Based on knowledge of law and courtroom experience, they advise a client whether they consider he or she is on a winner, might force it to a draw – or have no chance. These Opinions from on high are intended to spare the client a great deal of money and mental turmoil. They do not come cheap.

It is a brave man who goes into court in a costly civil action against the Opinion of his learned counsel. I didn't even see mine and it certainly would have tipped the balance in favour of an immediate settlement, whatever the cost. Indeed, I could have got out lightly at that stage because the BBC had paid £10 into court, a technical device that meant they were willing to accept a degree of liability and pay the lion's share of the costs. I learned about this disturbing omission purely by chance. One of the questions repeatedly fired at me by the army of waiting reporters as I stumbled out of court on the final day was why had I taken legal action in the first place?

'Right from the beginning all my lawyers said I had a strong case for exemplary damages,' I told them.

When I went to see Carter-Ruck in the week following the trial, he obviously was disturbed about something. It soon came out. 'Look here, Derek', he said gravely, 'you mustn't go around saying all your lawyers said you had a strong case. David Eady is most upset. He never thought so.'

It was my turn to look confounded. 'How d'you mean?' I wanted to know. 'Are you saying David wasn't for me?' It was rather late in the day for me to be hearing that my own top man had not been all that confident that the case would go my way.

Peter tried to calm the waters. He explained that David had sent an Opinion a few months earlier saying he regarded it as a high risk case, which would leave me very much out of pocket. My solicitor hastened to add that we were not committed in any way by Counsel's opinion. In any case, he asserted, David Eady had later changed his mind.

In my one brief meeting in four years with Mr Eady – just hours before the trial – there was no discussion of risk, though he did make clear that the evidence involved matters of opinion rather than fact. Complex questions of free speech and fair comment were involved. Clearly he was not a happy man. There was no reference to any Opinion.

'So why wasn't I shown this Opinion?' I asked Carter Ruck.

'I thought it would be bad for your morale, Derek.'

That was one way of looking at it, though it was rather like a family doctor not passing on a consultant's diagnosis in case it upset the patient!

First, Mr Eady delivers a most important Opinion that is not shown to me. Then he is supposed to have changed his mind and I am given no notification of that either. Indeed, if he did change his mind, there seems to be no record of this most unusual *volte-face* by a senior member of the Bar. I should have thought such a rare occurrence would have been committed to paper.

I have since obtained a copy of the missing Opinion of Mr Eady dated September 20th, 1983. There was no way I could have ignored it five months before the trial. He foresaw the outcome of the case with devastating accuracy. The relevant passages are these:

This must clearly be regarded as a 'high risk' piece of litigation, which is likely to turn upon the jury's reaction to the personalities involved rather than upon any close legal analysis of the pleaded issues.

Accordingly, the recent payment into Court needs to be considered seriously, not because £10 represents a realistic figure (either for compensation or vindication) but rather because it does present one means of avoiding the considerable financial exposure now confronting the Client.

The trial is bound to take some time... even if successful there will be a very substantial solicitor/own client bill (irrecoverable from the Defendants), a large part of which has yet to be incurred. I should be very surprised if a jury were to make a large award in this case, and the reality is therefore (assuming a 'win' for Mr Jameson) that he will be out of pocket to a greater extent than if the £10 were taken out within the permitted period.

I need hardly add that, if he loses (and therefore becomes responsible for the totality of the BBC's taxed costs, including trial), the prospect for the Client is bleak indeed.

I have little doubt that the BBC regard their chances of success as being higher than 50 per cent, but certainly so far as Mr Jameson is concerned it would in my view be prudent to approach the case on the footing that he has no more than an evens chance of winning. Moreover, I would consider the prospect of his recovering a sufficient sum of damages to cover the solicitor/own client costs in respect of a trial to be remote.

In other words, heads I win, tails you lose. There was no more than a 50-50 chance of my winning and, even if I did, my financial losses would be considerable, which is exactly what happened, of course. I won insofar as the jury decided that the words were defamatory and was left with that bill for £75,000 costs. Libel litigation is most expensive, of course. Leading counsel, in a case of this kind receive a retainer of £5,000 to £10,000 and a "refresher" of up to £1,000 a day. Then there are the juniors to pay. It sounded highly refreshing to me.

Peter Carter-Ruck sent me a letter three months after the trial stating that he had always acted in my best interests and would have been entitled to his full fees, instead of making a substantial reduction, had he advised me to settle the case on derisory terms. As for that Opinion, he contended Mr Eady did not deliver it until the case had been pending for over two years, and in the

Court list for over a year. According to Carter-Ruck, when Eady said he thought it was a 'high risk' case, 'he had not then heard the broadcast in question and, when he did, expressed an entirely different view.'

The Opinion was dated September, 1983. Although requested by Peter Carter-Ruck and Partners, it was not shown to me. At the time I should have been reading it, those scornful words in an obscure satirical programme no longer mattered all that much to me. By now I was editor of the *News of the World* and the whole issue had become academic, as the lawyers say. All I wanted was out. I was long gone from the *Express* and knew it highly unlikely that Lord Matthews, as he had since become, would underwrite my costs.

As anticipated, when I went to see him with my troubles after the case he was most sympathetic. He appreciated that much of it concerned not me personally, but his newspapers. However, there was no question of him picking up the bill. Indeed he did not remember that the whole business began in his office four years earlier when I showed him the report of the broadcast. I remember telling Matthews at the time:

'Sound like a bunch of loony Trots to me, Chairman.'

'Yeah, I'm sure you're right,' he said, in his usual dour tones. 'Don't let them get away with it. Go for them. The least you want is an apology. Have a word with Edwards.' Andrew Edwards was the legal manager of Express Newspapers, a saturnine character who takes a dim view of the wicked ways of newspapermen, especially when they finish up on his desk. Carter-Ruck's pale yellow missives had landed there a thousand times. Naturally, he was the solicitor Andrew recommended to deal with the BBC.

'You can't go wrong with him, old man,' he said. 'The best in the business.'

Sensing which way the wind was blowing, one of my first actions on leaving the *Express* early in 1981 had been to tell Carter-Ruck to settle the case speedily on the best terms available. I could quite easily have picked up the telephone and called one of the top brass at the Beeb – most of whom I knew personally and professionally – and sorted it out myself there and then.

Peter made it clear that was not the way to do things. Must go through the proper legal channels, old boy, was the burden of his message. If we dropped the case now it would cost something like £5,000 in my own costs so far.

'Why should you pay £5,000 to be insulted', were his exact words.

Too true, I thought, especially as I am not working. Leave it to Peter. He's the expert.

And so it went on. Most of the time I had only the faintest idea what was happening, where these growing mounds of paper were leading us. By 1982 Peter's hypothetical £5,000 had grown to £7-8,000. We were up to £10,000 a year later and by the time we came to trial it was going to cost me £14-£15,000 to extricate myself from the tangled web spun by the lawyers.

The one factor that kept my faith alive was Peter's overwhelming confidence that this was a case that would never come to court. *We must call their bluff*, was his original theme. *This is most defamatory. Don't worry. I know the BBC. They'll settle out of court*. That was the gist of his argument at the time.

Late in the day, when the promised collapse of the mighty Corporation failed to materialise, he changed his tune. *Leave it to Counsel*, he assured me. *They will sort it out*. It seemed an unlikely proposition to me. Peter calmed me down. *That's the way these things are done, old chap*. That didn't happen either. A new approach. *Don't worry. They'll settle at the Court doors. I know the BBC.*

Imagine my horror on unlucky February 13 to see the procession of BBC executives high and low, accompanied by their high-powered lawyers, sail past me at the doors to Court 14, Queens's Bench Division, ready to do battle. More than ever, I sensed all was lost.

What puzzles me to this day is whether Carter-Ruck charged me for the Opinion he thought was too strong for my stomach. I cannot find it in his final account. In traditional style, that was presented as a single sentence covering five pages and adding up to some 1,000 words. You would have to be Master of the Rolls to make head or tail of it.

One line is crystal clear. The final total: £41,342.50 including VAT. Carter-Ruck assured me that it was a cut price job since I had lost. Had the other side been paying it would have been another £20,000.

That still left me owing the BBC £33,500 – Peter had told me during the trial with uncanny accuracy that the whole bundle would come to £75,000 – and I had not the faintest idea how I was going to pay that.

Most of all at this awful time I wanted to be done with Peter Carter-Ruck and Partners and those interminable sheets of pale yellow notepaper. I paid him his last instalment within days and thanked him for his offer to lodge an appeal for free. I was not very gracious about it, taking the view it was a meaningless exercise. At most the Appeal Court could only order a retrial. That could cost me another £75,000 – plus the costs of the Appeal.

All the same, he went through the motions of lodging an Appeal. Never say die, that's Peter. It must come from sailing those yachts.

The whole episode serves as a warning, as if one were needed, that libel is not for the ordinary citizen. It is a messy, complicated business best left to those with money to burn. In view of my experience, colleagues often ask whether I think they should take action against someone who has had a go at them. I tell them what was put to me over and over again in those torturous years: In libel, only the lawyers win.

I was down in the dumps for only a day or two. Fleet Street cheered me up by launching a Fighting Fund designed to take some of the sting out of that bill for £75,000. This whip-round was the brainchild of one of my dearest friends, Vic Giles, then associate editor of the *Star*, and one of the top art directors in the business. He put his skills to work by producing an advertisement in the *UK Press Gazette* proclaiming FIGHT FOR JAMESON! 'Many have been glad of his help in the past,' it said. 'Now is your chance to help him.'

There were those who took the view I brought it on myself and did nothing to help. One editor, a friend of many years, told his staff: 'He got himself into this mess, now let him get out of it.' Mercifully other editors were more compassionate – among them the rival I had fought hardest in past years, Sir Larry Lamb, former editor of *The Sun* who was now occupying my old chair at the *Daily Express*. Charlie Wilson, soon to become editor of *The Times*, was another great morale booster. Joe Ashton MP took me to dinner at the House of Commons.

The pounds and the pennies came in from near and far, from journalists and from ordinary men and women in the street who felt I had been wronged. A complete stranger in Monte Carlo sent £1,000. Many had brushed against me in my years as an editor. I still go through their letters on occasion when I need cheering up. My debt to them is immense. Altogether the Fund raised a badly needed £10,000. The biggest donation of all was from Lord Matthews.

Other support came from the most unlikely quarters. Sebastian Faulks wrote in the *Sunday Telegraph*: 'It is the irony of this case that in the eyes of everyone in court – lawyers, reporters, and, paradoxically, the jury – Jameson's extraordinary composure and dignity meant that he left the court on Wednesday night with his reputation curiously enhanced.'

Sir John Junor of the *Sunday Express*, never one to be regarded as a member of my fan club, wrote in his famous column: 'I suppose the BBC chiefs are now rejoicing at their success in crushing the man who by his own efforts raised himself from a poverty-stricken East End childhood to reach the top in Fleet Street. All I know is that, for my money, although Mr Jameson may have come out of the court case jobless, close to bankruptcy and maybe also close to tears, he comes out of it smelling sweeter by far than does the BBC.'

Pure essence of roses. Nevertheless, it has to be said that, like everyone else, John misjudged Aunty Beeb. Far from celebrating my demise, it was the BBC that came along and picked up the pieces.

To this day, everyone takes the view that I lost the case, thinking in terms of the money rather than the principle involved. The jury did reach the verdict that the words were defamatory, though not malicious, so I regard it as a technical victory. The thing that caused me most pain throughout was the suggestion that I was 'an East End boy *made bad*.'

To understand why it mattered so much we must go back to the beginning....

CHAPTER FOUR

All the little children

Good or bad, the East End certainly made me. The tabloid labels hanging round my neck – the *chirpy Cockney, the Cockney DJ, Cockney Del* – firmly cast me as a working class hero of those parts. The poor boy who made it. Tough, cocky, streetwise and funny. Cheeky chappie, lovable rogue…a bit of both. All very cosy and nothing to be ashamed about. Home-grown product of one of the greatest places on God's earth. Pity He sometimes forgot to water our corner of the allotment.

My problem is that I don't recognise myself in all this. *Typical, I am not. Archetypal?* – that's as big a joke as the trendies who flash the word around. Your actual Cockney Del was a maverick, a reject fighting to survive on streets ruled by bullies and bigots. People forget that I was born a bastard long before it became fashionable.

Fifty years later, I still have nightmares about that childhood. The setting is always a battlefield. Mud and dirt, people fighting, poverty everywhere. Those early years have dominated my life. That is why I laugh so much. It takes away the pain.

My very first memory says it all. The thought of it claws at my guts to this day. It is 1933 and I am clinging to my big bear of an uncle as he fights to escape from a trap at the end of an alley overlooking the railway lines. Sid has me on his shoulders up in the air, soaring and swaying, the earth rising and falling as he lurches around, arms flailing, trying to keep his balance. An awful wailing noise is coming from his lips and he is slobbering, as he always does at times like this.

We have run into a street gang looking for some light relief on their way home from school. They don't come any funnier than the man closest to me in all the world, one of my fictitious uncles. He is the local idiot, totally out of his head and known to most of Hackney as 'Silly Sid.' There are nine or ten of them in long shorts, pullovers and plimsolls, socks round the ankles. Jeering, spitting, swearing and lobbing tufts of grass uprooted from the railway embankment. The odd stone here and there for luck. *What a smashing game!*

Sid loves to take me out. He might be simple, but he is harmless enough left in his own world of madness. Ma Wren is always in two minds about it. She knows how easy it is for her idiot son to get into trouble. He wears her down until she grudgingly gives in.

'Can I take Dick out, can I take Dick out . . . the park, the park.'

'Oh, go on then, you're a bloody nuisance. Now listen to me! You be careful. Don't you go upsetting anyone and keep away from boys, the little buggers. God forgive me for swearing.'

She stands there, eyeing him doubtfully and calling on God's grace, as always. He never seems to listen, but she never stops asking. Now it is done. Sid has got me out of the house before she can change her mind. We tramp the street. Most of the time I am perched high on his broad back. Like every other toddler, I can badger, too.

Flyin' angel, Sid. Go orn, Sid. Give us a flyin' angel.

He stands me on a wall, turns his back and I clamber up. My legs lock round his neck and I clutch the top of his bald head, now and then gripping the grey hair that still grows curly on either side. A strange odyssey, this, a three-year-old discovering the world on the shoulders of Uncle Sid. By then he is already in his mid-forties. Still big and strong, but even so I have a child's intuition that there is something dreadfully wrong. Other grown men do not walk the streets for four hours chanting hymns while twirling a key round on a bit of dirty string.

One by one, two by two, all the little children . . .' is his favourite. Sid sings it tonelessly for hours, the key spinning in a circle the size of a dinner plate with the constancy of a metronome. What a sight on the back streets beyond the Hackney Marshes. A tiny tot with a mop of blond curls hanging on for life to the back of a nutcase. To the people there my big cuddly bear must have looked more like a gorilla playing with a doll. Which explains why the little children he loves so much have us up an alley, backs to the wall . . .

Silly old Sid, silly old Sid . . . Pooh, what a stink, Pooh, what a stink . . . who's shit himself, who's shit himself? Silly old Sid . . .

Oh my poor, sad, misbegotten, frightened Sid. He seldom swore since his dementia took a highly religious turn. Nor would he harm any living creature without provocation. His tangled brain could only distinguish good and bad and he always took the side of his friend Jesus. Now he has run into the boys he has been told again and again to keep away from. How is he going to get Dick out of this? Always Dick. When you stammer and cannot speak properly, Derek is a hard word to say.

'*Naiouw, naiouw, naiouw . . . bad, bad, baa, baa, baa . . . aargh, aargh . . . .*'

That dreadful dirge pours from him as he thrashes about trying to shield himself from the missiles while keeping me from crashing to the ground. I can feel the tears, the spittle and snot on his face as I hang on to his head to keep myself from falling. It was Lenny who saved us. Always Lenny to the rescue. Ma Wren would have sent him out looking for us when he got home from school. She knew it was a bad hour of the day. Lenny Frost, the nearest to me in age. My foster brother, one of the other waifs and strays. As dark as I was fair. Lithe, tough and unafraid. He was to protect me in a great many street encounters before we put away childish things like fighting every day of your life.

Our tormentors, the big boys of nine and ten, fell back in tribute to someone they knew none could match if he should happen upon any of them alone. So we made it home. Sid shaking his head back and forth in agitation, blood running down one cheek where a brick had caught him, his clothes covered in dirt. Me half-dragged along, clutching Lenny's hand. I got out of the way quick, fearing Ma's anger. Her concern would be for the hunters rather than the prey. Sid was not allowed to touch those who made a sport of his lunacy. 'You haven't been kicking again with those bloody great boots?' she would yell at him. 'If I've told you once, I've told you a thousand times . . . .'

It's only for your own good, Sid. They were always telling him that. I wonder if he knew it meant the lunatic asylum was beckoning. More than once he had been sent off to bed without food after outraged mothers had come to the front door screaming vengeance.

I can still hear them. 'The silly old sod . . . he's hurt my boy. He should be locked up! We're going to the police this time. Decent people can't go outdoors. You wait till my Fred gets home . . .'.

This was an early lesson for me that decent people are not always what they seem. They can spit on you, hurl abuse, throw bricks and bloody your head – then go and report you to the police. If you happened to live in Ma Wren's establishment at 53 Mount Pleasant Lane then the law most assuredly would be round looking for someone's collar to feel.

No doubt it was a fine house in Victorian times. A basement for servants with a large room at the front and kitchen and scullery leading to a sixty-foot garden backing on to the railway at the rear. Out there one solitary apple tree whose specky fruit was uneatable and a lilac bush allowed to flourish despite everyone's belief that it was unlucky. On the first floor the sacred 'front room,' normally reserved for Sundays and Bank holidays, with a bedroom and a tiny 'boxroom' behind it. Three bedrooms on the floor above and over them the attic – two cramped rooms with sloping ceilings under the eaves. At the front of the house stone steps led up to an imposing front door, though everyone used the basement steps down to the 'area' at the bottom of the house. The door here, opened by pulling a piece of string behind the letter box, led to a long narrow passage running the length of the house.

Mrs Wren had taken Number 53 as the young mother of two sons, Sidney and Harold. Like so many others over the years, her husband Fred, a cabinet maker, had come from the country to find work in London's teeming East End. In days gone by this had been one of the posher parts of Hackney. Upper Clapton, as it is called, consisted of rows of solid family houses built on a hill overlooking the green marshes beyond the River Lea, one of the more murky tributaries of the Thames. Horse-drawn barges plied the river night and day carrying the timber and wool that kept the East End at work. Furniture and clothing were to prove the salvation of tens of thousands of Jewish refugees who poured into the area at the turn of the century to escape their oppressors – and conscription – in Russia, Poland, the Baltic states and other parts of Eastern Europe.

The work and wealth they created in turn attracted other generations of poor from rural Britain and Ireland. By World War One, London's East End had become an overcrowded, sharply divided community of a dozen different tongues and religions. Like New York's East Side, it was this Tower of Babel, this melting pot, that was to make it famous as a place of laughter and tears.

Yiddish was the language most commonly heard on the streets. Even the gentiles who hated Jews knew the words of *My Yiddisher Momma*.

Mount Pleasant Lane already had an anachronistic ring to it by the time Mrs Wren arrived with her brood. It was going downhill fast. A great one for keeping up appearances, Ma took comfort from the fact that she occupied a whole house. At least the River Lea, which faithfully rose every spring and flooded all the houses at the bottom of the hill, stopped short before it reached Number 53. That put her a cut above them. Natural justice of sorts because, as she never tired of telling people, her father had been the Postmaster of Sandringham.

Misfortune soon followed the Wrens from the green pastures of Norfolk. Her husband died of consumption, as they called tuberculosis in the days it claimed tens of thousands every year. She was left alone in the big house at the top of the hill with two sons, one of them mentally deficient. Fred Wren, remembered as a quiet, ruminative man constantly ill with the dreaded dry cough, is supposed to have come to London seeking work. It was before my time, but I have a feeling the real reason was to escape the stigma of having an idiot son in a small village community. Ma Wren was never easy about it. She packed Sid off to Fred's spinster sister Ada, a piano teacher who lived nearby, at every opportunity. Asked what was wrong with him, Ma came up with different reasons to suit her mood. I would stand there with my mouth open at the most lurid of these tales.

'Well, you see,' she would tell some nosey parker, 'me husband and me went to the seaside for the day and Sidney wandered orf on his own. We looked everywhere. When we found 'im, some boys had dug a huge 'ole in the sand and buried 'im in it up to the neck. The water was already around his face, poor little fing. Another few minutes and he would have been drownded. It turned his 'ead, you know. 'e was always mental after that. Doctors couldn't do anyfing for 'im!' In another version Sid was caught in quicksands on the beach and sucked under. 'When they pulled 'im out, he'd gorn barmy,' she would say. Those were the polite versions. Indoors, at times when all hell was let loose, there would be dark talk of incest and family disgrace.

On these shaky foundations was born the house of Mrs Wren. Like the more famous woman who lived in a shoe, she was destined to have so many children that she never did quite know what to do. Without money and two sons to feed, she took the only option available – she turned the house into a shelter for lost souls. *Open all hours. Anyone with a hard luck story, apply within.*

'It was that or the workhouse,' she would say. 'Think I'd have been better orf in the workhouse!'

Altogether Ma Wren took in some seventy waifs and strays at 53, Mount Pleasant Lane. They were the perfect microcosm of the East End of those days. Young girls from the country, pregnant before they were old enough to know better, hiding away in the big city. Irish colleens with their babies kicked out by outraged fathers. Starry-eyed *shiksas* carrying the consequences of love affairs with Jews who could never marry them. Young families evicted by landlords who owned most of the property in those days. Babies dumped on the doorstep by distraught mothers. 'Please look after my —— until I get some money,' a pathetic note attached to the bundles would say.

Ma would never turn anyone away. Not that she was born a Good Samaritan, eager to succour the poor and the needy. Nothing so romantic. What really inspired her was the thought that somehow all these girls in trouble would pay their way so that she could send the rent man away smiling and keep the household going. Of course, hardly anyone paid on a regular basis. Some girls would send postal orders for 5/-. (25p) every week, then disappear for months only to turn up with 'ten bob (50p) off what I owe you.' At that they would take their baby and disappear forever. Other mothers would just simply vanish without bothering to collect the baby. Presumably they had met and married someone who obviously would not wish to know about a certain mistake back at Number 53. Some mothers would stay at the house with their illegitimate baby, going out to work in local factories and shops while Ma tended their offspring. Then one day, they, too, would marry and be off with baby. There were those who even wed the father, though that was rare. Most of them were married already and in those days divorce was very much the province of the rich.

Poor old Ma had a struggle keeping up with all this coming and going. One day a baby would be there, gurgling away in front of the fire, next day he or she would be gone. One week she would have £3 in her purse – a bonanza in those days – and the next she would be down to the pittance of her widow's pension to feed a dozen hungry mouths. Ma always managed somehow.

There was no welfare state in those days, no Giro cheques for fostering babies, not a penny to be had from anyone other than the flotsam and jetsam washed up on her doorstep. She could always 'pop' her wedding ring yet again in Uncle's – the pawnshop. Many times we had to take bed sheets down to Uncle's in the main shopping parade on Monday for a few coppers, then redeem them on Friday when someone in the house came home with wages. Or the ever resourceful Ma would make some money reading the tea leaves. Sometimes she would take in a lodger or two, ten bob in advance.

The only male guest who actually lasted the course in that crazy house was an eccentric character named Charles Rust, who found Mrs Wren after he managed to get away from Dr Barnardo's, the dreaded orphanage we were threatened with every day. Most Barnardo boys finished up in the Royal Navy. Charlie was different. He took indentures as a printer and his choice of a well paid trade frequently kept the whole house going. He was supposed to be a Communist, wore sandals without socks, did not swear or chase the girls and was forever going on cycling trips to Epping forest and the surrounding area. He even insisted on wholemeal bread. We thought him a right hoot, though we kept on his right side because he had money in his pocket and owned something loved by the whole street – a huge alsatian named Rex.

When I was caught napping in Fleet Street and nabbed for the *This Is Your Life* television programme, a guest from the old days recounted how I pinched a meat pie someone brought home for supper. It was only half the story. Charlie Rust would bring home a steak and kidney pie for Rex's supper. We used to sit there with our mouth watering as he took the dog into the garden for his feed.

'Can I give it 'im, Charlie?' we boys would plead. Can I, can I? Go'orn, Charlie, let's give it 'im.'

One day, I must have been six or seven, Charlie gave me the honour of feeding the dog. Out in the yard, I broke the pie in two, gave one portion to Rex and started eating the other. *Share and share alike.* Rex wasn't have any of that. He wolfed his down in one gulp, then jumped me for the rest of his supper. There was a fearful snarling and snapping as he pinned me to the ground. I had to surrender my last couple of mouthfuls before the adults discovered what was going on. I never liked the brute after that. A few months later he took a lump out of my leg riding on his back on the Hackney Marshes. I never told anyone about that, either. The wound, which should have been stitched, left an ugly scar on my right thigh.

We lost our compositor Charlie to a roly-poly girl named Daisy who he'd met on one of his nature rambles. She was twice his size and didn't wear make-up, but they loved each other dearly and eventually married and emigrated to New Zealand. He still keeps in touch. Sadly, Daisy passed on as this book was being written. They did their courting on a tandem. We used to laugh our heads off at the sight of them going off together. Charlie, a slight figure with a wisp of a moustache, bent over the handlebars. Daisy, big and sturdy, bringing up the rear. We would serenade them lustily with a song that could have been written just for Charlie:

'Daisy, Daisy, give me your answer, do,
I'm half crazy, all for the love of you,
It won't be a stylish marriage,
I can't afford the carriage,
But you'll look sweet, upon the seat,
of a bicycle made for two...'

This was the world of Ma Wren. Not exactly a fairytale, but certainly different. I can see her now, sitting in the big high-backed wooden chair by the grate, her bad leg up on a box. 'Oh, Gawd, they're driving me potty,' she would moan. 'I can't take any more. I just can't do it. What d'they think this is – bloody Liberty Hall?' There would be a hammering at the front door. The familiar sight of a nervous young girl clutching her baby in one of the big woollen shawls of those days. 'What the bloody hell does she want,' Ma would mutter as she shuffled up to the door. There she would break into a smile. 'Come in, dear, 'ave a cup o'tea. Don't stand out there in the cold. You'll catch yer death.'

CHAPTER FIVE

A mother of my own

P*ère inconnu*, the French call it. Father unknown. Sounds better that way. It was the only common denominator of the inhabitants of Number 53. I was born with the necessary credentials in the Hackney Hospital on 29th November, 1929. Ironically, the one person who did have a real father was poor demented Sid. It was to him I turned in those early years. He was the only adult who had time for a growing toddler. I would sit for hours at the big wooden table in the kitchen, playing with ha'pennies, bits of string, coloured glass, shiny stones and any other rubbish wormed out of his pockets. Collecting tat was his only means of existence. Not always visible, though certainly smelly on occasions.

'Now, what's Sidney got?' he would ask, untying the string round a baby's grubby bootie that held his money.

Roaming the streets, he would load an old hessian sack with bits and pieces that came his way likely to raise a few coppers, usually by bartering with the rag and bone men who were an everyday sight. Old ladies would emerge with a half-eaten loaf, a torn dress or their old man's worn-out trousers and press them on Sid. Other treasures he would 'find' in street markets or in the back-yard of shops.

Most of this forage was worthless, but he would secret it away all over the place – inside the house or garden, behind bricks in local streets, anywhere safe from 'the gels' at home. Since I was usually by his side, this made me a co-conspirator. I felt suitably important and would never betray him.

'Ow, Sid!' one of the big girls who made our life hell would cry as she discovered an old bike pump under her mattress. 'We don't want your bloody old rubbish in 'ere. 'Ow many times you got to be told, silly old bugger.'

There was no justice in it because, of course, Sid's treasure often fed us. Ma would wheedle a tanner out of him to buy bread and a bottle of milk. The girls, too, would suck up to him for money to fill their two greatest needs in life – cigarettes and stockings. It was always strictly on a loan basis. The money had to be back on Friday, pay day. Despite his incapacity, Sid could write after a fashion. He would note all these transactions in a penny note-book, licking a stub of pencil as he ponderously wrote the words . . . *Win, 6d, Elsie, 3d*. If they didn't pay back, there was no more money until they did – with a bit of interest. 'You may be daft, but you ain't silly,' they would roar at him. When they got too shrill he would fall back on his partial deafness and make out he couldn't hear what they were saying. 'Eh, eh? What's that, g-g-gel?' he would ask, cupping a hand to his ear. They would catch him unawares a few minutes later by saying quietly 'D'you want a fag, Sid?' His eyes would light up and they would pounce. 'You're not so bloody deaf now!'

'Are you deaf – or daft!' was an expression we heard a dozen times a day in that crazy house.

Sid was always all right with me. Growing up there, among all those screaming women, I felt safe on his lap. At least he never yelled at me. I remember he had hair growing from his ears and I would poke in my fingers to explore where it came from.

'Now, now, D-D-Dick. Now, now . . . who's a n-n-naughty boy then?' he would stammer, laughing all the while with his throaty voice.

My favourite treat was helping him make his fags. We would go out col-lecting dog ends wherever he could find them in the gutter – beside bus stops was always a good place – and he would spread an old newspaper on the table and make a pyramid of all the filthy, stinking dimps secreted away in various pockets. Sid would make a ritual of it. First tear off the saliva-stained mouth-piece, then get rid of the burnt end and peel away the paper to get at the tobacco left in the middle. He would make a separate heap of that. My job was to pack the tobacco in his cigarette machine. Sid would then flatten and shape it, take a leaf out of his fag papers and roll it into a cigarette. Usually he let me lick the gummed edge to finish the job. We then placed the finished cigarettes in an old tobacco tin that went everywhere with him, counting them one by one. On a good day he would hit the jackpot – ten fags! A tanner's ($2\frac{1}{2}$p) worth in those days.

Of course we couldn't play this game if any of the big girls were around.

They didn't like Sid and his dirty habits at the best of times. The sight of him spreading all those dimps on the kitchen table would send them right up the wall.

'You dirty, filthy, 'orrible pig,' Winnie would scream. 'I swear to God, I'll kill you one of these days if you keep bringing your muck in here!' Then she would sweep up whatever had offended her eye, perhaps an old newspaper or a lump of stale cake, open the back door and chuck it out. Sid would sit there, lip trembling, quietly whimpering to himself. Sometimes he would calm down by slipping up to the sacred "front room" to pound away on the keys of an old upright piano. Like many another retarded person, he had an ear for music and could play beautifully – usually hymns.

Elsie Wren and Winnie Pikeman were the two most permanent members of Mrs Wren's brood. They were of the first generation, both abandoned by mothers unable to face the world with the stigma of bastard babies. Elsie's mother, said to be in business in the Strand, turned up demanding her daughter when she reached the age of fourteen. Mrs Wren saw her off with a brolly. The two girls grew up together in Mount Pleasant Lane, sharing their early experiences – men, cigarettes and clothes were the main ingredients – and to all intents and purposes were just like sisters of similar age. Both were stunning. Tall blondes with flashing eyes and a taste for the latest fashions and make-up. Elsie was the princesss, the quieter of the two with long hair and a wistful expression when caught offguard. Winnie was more brassy, but still beautiful. Her main feature was translucent green eyes. A tigress with a temper to match. Winnie even scared Ma Wren. Once or twice a week, she would throw the most terrible tantrum. Men in particular would drive her potty. She liked the bad 'uns best. Handsome dudes, flashily dressed with two-toned shoes and hair slicked down with brilliantine. They usually finished up in her bedroom, rolling on the floor in a fight that shook the house. We would sit shaking with fear in the kitchen, waiting for it to go quiet. Then we knew everything would be all right. Winnie and her latest would come down eventually, full of the joys of spring. The trouble was that these affairs never lasted. Either she scared off the bloke or he was already married. Sometimes both. Then there would be murders. The violence that was to haunt my dreams fifty years later invariably started this way.

'Leave him alone, Winnie,' Ma would say angrily as Win took out her spleen on Sid. He was, after all, her *real* son. The other one, Harold, had taken off almost as soon as he was old enough to get through the front door, though he graced us with a visit at Christmas time. Left alone with Sid, Ma had to protect her own against the more dangerous madness of her adopted family. Presiding over that lot was like sitting on top of a volcano.

'You what!' Winnie would spit at her. 'You fuckin' old cow! Don't you tell me what to do, you bitch. I keep this house. Without my money, you'd all be in the fuckin' workhouse. Who bought the dinner in? Where's the food going down your gob come from, eh, eh? Answer that, you fuckin' cow. And don't you lot sit there looking at me like that, nei'ver. Get out of my fuckin' sight, the lot of you . . . Bloody Scum! We would sit there rigidly, terrified to accept her invitation because the first one up was likely to get her fist in their face by way of a parting shot. It was Ma's sorry lot to restore some kind of sanity to these little domestic occasions, to unfreeze the blood in our veins. The old girl was already in her mid-sixties and there she was trying to control a wild bunch forsaken by the rest of mankind. Once Winnie had Ma down on the kitchen floor, a carving knife pressed to her throat, spitting, screaming and cursing, threatening to do her in there and then. I swear only the arrival of Stan Shadbolt, one of the more constant of her boyfriends, saved Ma from a bloody death. It took him all his strength to wrest the knife from the crazy bitch. Nowadays she would be known as a psychopath. We could have called in a social worker.

For all that, Winnie had a heart as big as the house. She really did give away her last halfpenny if she felt for the person in need. Starved of food and affection, I was drawn to her strength and beauty. To me she was a goddess. When there was not so much as a crust on the table, she solved the problem in the time-honoured way. Winnie would appear with a strange man, take him upstairs and we would eat. On more than one occasion I was called up to collect the half-a-crown (12½p) from her at the bedroom door.

It was Elsie who got the worst of Winnie when she was looking for trouble. Their rows went on constantly and usually revolved around one pinching the other's ciggies, stockings or make-up. 'Those are my stockings you've got on, you cow,' Winnie would say for openers as she came tearing down in cami-knickers from her room, late for a date and breathing fire because she could not find any stockings without ladders in them.

'Oh no, they're not, Win. You lent me these last week and then said I could keep 'em because I let you have five Weights,' Elsie would come back.

'Oh, did I? Be a sport then. Lend us a bob and send Del up the road for a pair. Go orn, do us a favour. I'll pay you back.'

Sometimes it would work, and I would scarper off to buy stockings relieved that it had not ended in blows. Other times there would be much shouting, whining and tears as they argued endlessly about who owed what to whom. Elsie was terrified of Winnie's 'moods' and always came out on the losing end. That meant she gave a greater share of her wages at home and did more of the shopping and housework. Her answer to this was to nag, nag, nag – out of Winnie's hearing unless she was being provocative – about how she was being dumped on by everyone. 'It's always me who has to do things,' she complained bitterly.

It was through one of these rows that I discovered Elsie was my mother. Growing up in that hodge-podge of a home, with its comings and goings, it never occurred to me that I might belong to one of the big girls who stayed put. Until I was seven, they were all foster sisters to me. Elsie, Winnie, Ethel, Peggy, Doris, Kathleen, Vi . . . they all *seemed* alike. Kind and sweet at times, bitchy and terrifying when the mood took them.

Elsie always kept her distance. I had this feeling she didn't like me. She seemed to make a lot more fuss of Lenny Frost. That didn't bother me over-much. I fancied myself to be Ma Wren's favourite and even got on better than most with the temperamental Winnie, largely by offering to run errands for her. One day, sitting at tea – the main meal, taken in early evening – Winnie produced this jar of pickled onions with red chilli peppers floating in it. Fascinated by the colour, I wanted to know what they were. Winnie was never one to deny her sadistic tendencies, whether it was pulling wings off flies or feeding raw peppers to six-year-olds.

'G'orn, then,' she said, 'they're luv'ly. You eat one.'

I popped it in my mouth quick as a flash and took a bite on the thin red strand. A burning sensation, horrible. It must be poison.

'That's it, you little pig,' said Winnie. 'Eyes bigger than yer belly. You arsked for it, now you can eat it!'

I began to cry and Elsie intervened. 'Don't do that, Winnie. You know they're hot. He doesn't know what they are.'

'Spit it out,' she commanded me. This made me howl all the more. If I got rid of it in defiance of Winnie, I sensed all hell would break loose. And so it did. 'Give it here,' said Elsie, cupping her hand under my mouth. 'You eat it, pig. It's about time you learned some manners,' came back Winnie. They began pushing and shoving each other as Winnie tried to remove Elsie's hand from my mouth.

Bang! There was a crash followed by breaking glass. Winnie had resolved the argument by picking up the jar of pickles and hurling it at the wall. Glass lay shattered on the floor, pickled onions everywhere, vinegar running down the wallpaper.

'I'll murder you, you cow, if I'ave to swing for it,' she screeched while tugging at Elsie's hair. Elsie, by now crying herself, grabbed me by the hand and we bolted out of the house. We didn't stop to draw breath till we came to a bench on Millfields, a Leaside park half a mile away. Between sobs, she let it all come out. Her hatred and resentment over the way Winnie dominated life at Number 53, how she could have put me in a home – orphanage – and been free to go, but stayed on for my sake, to give me some chance in life.

'I'm only trying to do what's decent, and that's all the thanks I get. I'd be better off dead, not that any of THEM would care . . .' She repeated the words over and over again. I clutched her hand protectively, the realisation sweeping over me that Elsie, one of the big girls, was my mother. Not that it helped much. Here she was, wracked with grief, and it was all my fault. Several cigarettes and two hours later she was sufficiently composed for us to creep back into the house. All was well. Not a sound to be heard other than dance music on the wireless in Winnie's room.

At least I had a mother, which was more than could be said for the others. But why was she called Elsie Wren when my name was Jameson? I couldn't make it out. I continued to call her Elsie like everyone else – and did so until well into my thirties.

One incident stayed with me forever as a reminder of the barrier that always kept us apart. Dusk was falling and I was out on the street as usual, crouched down in the gutter playing gobs – fivestones – with some mates. I saw my mother, my beautiful blonde lady, approaching along the pavement. I looked up, ready to greet her. She saw me at the same time, paused an instant, then crossed the road so she would not have to acknowledge me.

In all her life she never once got over the guilt of having a bastard son. Nor did she ever tell me the truth about my father.

CHAPTER SIX

Bring on the angels

All human life was there at 53 Mount Pleasant Lane, as we say in newspapers. It was the perfect springboard for a future editor and broadcaster. Even those manic moments when our elders were ready to murder each other taught me a valuable lesson. By the age of seven I knew that people were prepared to kill for a cigarette. In their case hanging definitely proved a deterrent. Of course, it didn't seem much at the time. Nobody would have swapped our lot for an old boot. We rarely had enough of anything we needed, but were never short of debts and dirt, bedbugs and empty bellies. They were the staple of our everyday life. No wonder we were always laughing.

Beg, borrow or steal was Ma Wren's recipe for survival. Not necessarily in that order. She looked for all the world like the granny in Giles' cartoons. Short, squat, dressed in black to the ankles, hand on hips, mouth open in a roar. Up would go the casement window and she would bellow: 'Derr-eek! Come in for your tea, you little swine . . .' You could hear it the other side of the Hackney Marshes, a comforting sound that suggested all was well with the world.

'What's for tea, Ma?' you would say. 'I'm starvin' 'ungry!'

'Shit – with sugar on,' came the answer. It never failed.

For food we usually had to rely on the girls going out to work in neighbouring factories, laundries and tea rooms. They always got the dirty end of the stick. Long hours with low pay in the most menial jobs as waitresses, shop assistants and the like. The pay in the Thirties was less than £3 a week. It did not take much to persuade them to roll over in bed and not turn out for their lousy jobs. If no money had come in the previous Friday, apart from Ma's widow's pension of ten bob a week, we would be down to bread and marge by

Monday. Sometimes there was jam, or we might get away with dipping our bread into the sugar bowl. Lenny Frost liked sauce sandwiches. Brown sauce on marge between two thick doorsteps. On a good day we might have corned beef mashed up in potatoes and a great lump of suet or bread pudding to follow. Stews all the time, of course.

'Go round the butchers and ask him for twopenny'oth of bones and would he leave some meat on them, please.' Ma usually managed to get a cheaper cut of meat for a Sunday roast and that meant dripping for the bread later in the week. Friday nights it was round to the fish n' chip shop at the top of Southwold Road. Cod and chips, $4\frac{1}{2}$d ($2\frac{1}{2}$p). Now and again some Flash Harry taking out one of the girls would be dragged home carrying a brown carrier bag he had been persuaded to fill on the promise of delights to come. We would tuck into eggs and bacon, loads of fresh bread and mugs of tea while the girl eyed our benefactor wondering whether she had to keep that promise. It was always a feast or a famine, but much of the time we went hungry. Nowadays, sitting in West End restaurants, it tickles people to see me clear every last scrap on my plate and look for more. Now they know why. There were occasions when it got so bad that even Sid would be forced to turn out his pockets to prove he was skint. Lenny and I would then be called into action. We knew a dozen ways of making a bob or two on the streets, though we stopped short of picking up a tanner from randy bargees looking for a quick toss by the banks of the Lea. A better way was to stand outside Clapton station as the evening rush hour disgorged scores of City clerks on the line from Liverpool Street station.

'Gi'es ha'penny, Mister!' we would recite like a litany, hand stretched out each time a likely prospect stepped out of the station. It was hard going, with a success rate less than one in twenty. But eight ha'pennies made 4d – and that was a loaf of bread. Or you could buy yesterday's stale offering for 2d. Soak it in water, dry it out by the grate, as good as new. A bit musty, though.

In those days the streets were virtually empty of cars. A motorbike and side-car was the height of working class aspirations, and only young couples yet to marry and have babies could afford those. The horse and cart was still the most popular form of transport. That meant horse dung. Loads of it everywhere for those not too precious to be seen with bucket and spade shovelling up. 'There y'are, lady, just the job for yer roses,' we would say on the doorstep of some of the better houses. 'Only a tanner a bucket.' I recall one woman telling me to clear off and not dirty her doorstep. She got a bucket for free, all over her gleaming front porch.

The best earner was lighting fires for the Jews. Most of those early settlers in the East End were highly orthodox. That meant they were denied the comfort of a fire on *shobbas*, the Jewish sabbath that started at dusk on Friday. With their customary shrewdness, the faithful overcame this problem by employing us youngsters as *feuer goyim*. A tanner for a *goy* – a non-Jew – to light the fire. Easy pickings. Even better if you made a lousy job of it so the fire would be out in minutes. Lenny would be hanging around outside ready to go in and pick up another sixpence.

Tar blocks were another good source of income. They made smashing firewood, but collecting it was very dodgy. The wooden blocks came from tramlines under repair on the main roads. Trams and old-fashioned omnibuses were the main public transport in those days. We had to creep up behind the roadworks, find a pile of blocks and stuff them in a sack without being detected. They employed watchman with a special brief to catch thieving urchins like us. Nobody bothered about policemen in those days. The penalty if caught was a good hiding, often accompanied by a few kicks from huge working boots. My thighs were black and blue for weeks after one of these encounters. I never told any of the adults. It wasn't the done thing. Probably would have got another hiding, anyway. Twopence a bundle was better pickings than jobs like collecting empties for milk roundsmen on Saturdays – they paid only 6d for the day – or fetching tea and running errands for stallholders in the market. They would pay a bob (5p) if they had had a good day, otherwise a few coppers. Returning empty jamjars wasn't bad money – penny for the two-pound variety, ha'penny for a one-pound jar.

Remember we were beavering away making money to buy food while only seven or eight years old. Imagine a child of that age today collecting and lugging ten two-pound jars to the local sweetshop in paper carrier bags threatening to burst at any second. It wasn't all work. We still found time for fighting. Roaming the streets till ten or eleven at night was a constant tight-rope. You had to keep your wits about you so not to fall foul of gangs likely to pounce round every corner. All the various races kept to their own kind and claimed territorial rights over the streets where they held sway. There were orthodox Jews and poor Jews, Catholics and Protestants, Irish, Welsh, English, Scots and a few odds and sods like Greeks and Chinese.

On Mount Pleasant Lane we were divided into those at the top of the hill and the lower orders in the perpetually flooded Council maisonettes at the bottom – the Uppers and the Downers. Every so often, when one of our number reported a real or imaginary hurt, we would mobilise for battle. Our tanks were trolleys made from a plank, probably pinched from a building site, a wooden soapbox from the grocers and a set of pram wheels cadged from someone's mother. The front wheels were pivoted by a nut and bolt so they could be steered by rope fastened to the axle. The driver would sit in the box in front, head down and gripping the rope, and his mate would run like the clappers and push from the back, leaping on as the vehicle gathered speed. A bobsleigh on wheels, home-made for a few coppers. Behind would come the heavy infantry. Warriors mounted on scooters, similarly made from lumps of wood and ball-bearing wheels from roller skates. The artillery would comprise lads with catapults fashioned from a tree branch with thick elastic – tuppence a foot in the model shop – and a sling made from the tongue of an old boot. Then the rag, tag and bobtail that always follow armies on the move. Newcomers to the neighbourhood not yet judged suitable for enlistment plus a few cowards and malcontents expelled after being found wanting in earlier battles. Bringing up the rear were the nippers, some of them barely out of nappies, and the more daring girls. We were never short of them.

Ah, if only Nelson could have seen us! About thirty kids ready to do or die standing there on the brow of the hill, looking down across the railway bridge, waiting for the command from our leader, Billy Impetigo. We would sweep the enemy before us to the banks of the Lea that marked the very boundary of the East End. All would be still below. We knew those crafty Downers. They must be hidden behind front walls and fences, sticks and bricks at the ready, waiting till they could see the whites of our eyes. Imitating the warwhoops of Indian braves who held us spellbound at the tu'penny flicks every Saturday morning, we would go flying down the hill looking for trouble. Sometimes there would be a skirmish, thankfully with more noise than action, but as often as not the whole exercise would turn out to be a fiasco. No enemy behind the walls. We consoled ourselves by claiming they had all done a bunk. Chicken!

Looking back, I can only recall one boy being seriously hurt in these street encounters. Someone's crude bow and arrow cost him an eye, an accident that made him highly popular at school. Most of the time it was just bravado. We were like angry young stags pawing at the ground and claiming supremacy. The East End's strict code of behaviour was based on fair play and that meant most of the real fighting was on a one-to-one basis. Sadly these rules did not apply to anyone considered an outsider. To this day Cockneys are still highly suspicious of any but their own kind. Stanley Hyde, my best friend in the Thirties had the misfortune to wear spectacles. That made him different, an outsider, automatically dubbed 'Four Eyes' and the butt of many a cruel joke. One day a toughie named Lenny Burrows pushed him over in the pool of piss that had a permanent place in the school bog. Strictly out of order. Stanley was my friend, so that made it an attack upon me. I started a fight with Lenny that lasted the whole dinner break. Punching, wrestling, clawing, scratching and kicking, we fought our way across several roads, over some fields and finished on the Lea towpath. Then we did it all again in the opposite direction – with half the school following. God knows how they explained why they weren't home for dinner. I won on this occasion, probably because my temper proved tougher than his muscle. These encounters are concluded in a ritual going back donkey's years. '*Had enough? Had enough?*' you repeat again and again. Eventually your protagonist mutters '*Yeah, yeah!*' and the battle is done. Lenny became a good friend after that.

The outsiders who suffered most were the Jews. It fills me with guilt to recall the way they were treated, largely because they tended to be better scholars. Anti-Semitism was rife. Not only did they swot for exams and ask for homework, but – even more outrageous – they actually wore school caps. The usual ploy for some lout looking for a punch-up was to go up to a Jewish lad and say: ''ere! You killed Je-suss.' If there was no suitable response, usually the case, he would whip off the cap and send it sailing up a tree or over a wall, adding a couple of punches for good measure. Quite extraordinary, this, because in many classes the Jews were in the majority. In those days, when Hitler was no more than an ugly whisper and the state of Israel had yet to be born, the Jews still believed in the biblical philosophy *Turn the other cheek* . . . So they just put up with it in much the same way as the Asians who followed them were to do in the same East End streets decades later.

Not all the Jewish families were so forbearing. There were those who fought back like demons. We called them 'poor Jews.' Not necessarily because they were less well off than their cousins, but simply that we regarded being tough as synonymous with poverty. The closest friend of our own gang leader, Billy Impetigo (so-called because of his runny ears) was Manny Cohen, the best street fighter I ever came across. The Cohen family and others like them produced some of the greatest boxers ever in the East End. With my background, I was something of an outsider myself, equally at home with Jews, Catholics or Protestants at the Detmold Road Elementary School, a forbidding Victorian edifice near the Hackney Marshes. It was a rough, tough world and we had teachers to match. With a cane hanging from one of the pegs on every blackboard, they managed to knock reading, 'riting and 'rithmetic into us whether we wanted to learn or not.

I have edited newspapers, run training schemes, employed graduates of the top schools and universities in the land. It is rare for me to come across anyone with my command of English. That's why I scream with pain when the toffee-nose brigade call me Sid Yobbo, implying that I am an illiterate lout. My mother had the same standards drummed into her. I have never known her to make a mistake in writing. We went to the same school and both of us started work at fourteen.

W. S. 'Tiger' Hart was the master we feared most. He would stand on his dais, fist clenched, and hiss: 'Right! First one to make a sound, come up here and I'll knock him out.' We believed him, too. His great mission in life, like so many other teachers, was to somehow persuade us that knowledge was the key to success, our passport out of that bleak world.

It was an uphill struggle. The Victorian epidemic of consumption was on the wane. Other diseases, natural results of the poverty surrounding us, were still prevalent and sometimes killed. Diptheria, polio and scarlet fever were the worst. Many kids had iron calipers on their bowed legs, the telltale sign of rickets. School meals did not exist. Instead they shoved cod liver malt and free milk down the throats of the poorer children like myself to build us up. I scoffed all I could get my hands on. Vermin was another major problem. Regular inspections were held for lice and the worst cases had their heads shaven – about the most dreadful thing that could happen to a child. 'Nits!' The very word made us blanch. Teeth were the province of the School Dental

Service. Any tooth found decayed would be yanked out over a desk there and then without anaesthetic by so-called dentists in bloody rubber aprons. I grew up with four huge gaps in my teeth and a lifelong fear of dentists thanks to these butchers.

Most of the time we made a good impression at 53 Mount Pleasant Lane. Ma Wren liked to do things right. Her philosophy was what Cockneys call Fur Coat and No Drawers. So we might be hungry at times, but we were always kept clean and reasonably dressed. The boys wore long shorts with a rough flannel shirt in summer, long-sleeved jersey in winter. We never possessed suits or overcoats. Heavy boots with steel tips when there was money about, otherwise plimsolls. Many times did we repair our worn footwear with a sole cut out of cardboard. The girls had flannel dresses with cardies – cardigans — over a petticoat and sometimes a kind of corset called stays. All neat and tidy on the outside, dirt and vermin behind the lace curtains. The house was a huge slum. All about us the stench of decay. It was like living in a morgue reserved for the dregs of mankind. The floors were so rotten with mildew that gaping holes appeared everywhere. Peoples' feet had simply gone through the cheap oilcloth and the boards below. The furniture was little better. Apart from a few fine pieces acquired by Ma's late cabinet maker husband – I remember a grandfather clock, piano and a mahogany chest of drawers – most of it would have disgraced bonfire night. Backless, broken chairs, a black rexine sofa with half the stuffing out, a battered wooden table. There was a horror far worse than any of this. The house was being devoured by the curse of the poor – bedbugs. They marched by night in battalions to feed off our sleeping bodies after breeding in every crevice of the room. In the cracks of the peeling wallpaper, behind the skirting boards, inside the mattresses.

People talk about being poor, going a bit short, trying to make ends meet and find work in the good old bad days. I hear what they are saying and they have my sympathy. Inside, I'm thinking: *Poor! They don't know the meaning of the word . . .'* To me the depths of degradation, the lowest point in the compass of human squalor, is to sleep five in a bed – with one of the others peeing up your back every night – and wake up in the dark to feel your body covered in the bites left by these little red vampires sucking your blood. *That's poor!*

We never got the better of those bugs. At times we took the candle that lighted the bedroom and burnt the seams of the mattress, listening with delight to the crackle of incinerated bugs. Then we would place each leg of the bed into a discarded cocoa tin or the like filled with paraffin so their kith and kin could not crawl up the legs. Next morning we would still be covered in bites. We reckoned they marched across the ceiling and dropped down like dive bombers when over their target.

Everyone in those streets suffered. The Fumigation Department would be round with sulphur candles if anyone got scarlet fever and the School Medical Service shaved the heads of those found carrying lice. But even the bureaucrats stopped short of declaring war on the bedbugs. *When the lights go out, the Red Army's on the march*, we told each other. *Cimex lectularius*, a flat, oval bloodsucking parasite, half the size of the little finger nail, that has been attacking man since the time he was a cave dweller. They must have been at home in slums of the East End and were better fed than us.

No wonder Ma was locked in perpetual battle with the rent man. Mr Haddow was his name. He always wore a funereal expression with a black homburg and long overcoat to match. I think he called every week for the pleasure of a verbal duel with the old girl. He usually lost.

Mr Haddow's knock came faithfully around 5 o'clock on a Friday evening – anything but pay day would have been a non-starter – and Lenny or myself would go to the door to get the first round underway.

'Ma, it's the rent man!'

'Tell him I'm not in,' her voice would come floating up the passage.

'Come along, Mrs Wren, I know you're there. I've had nothing for three weeks. Give me a £1 for this week and something off the arrears.'

Ma would come striding to the door to stand before him, hands on hips, glaring belligerently.

'Are you deaf – or daft? I've told you I'm not in to rent collectors.'

'Now, now, Mrs Wren be reasonable...'

'Don't you *now, now* me! You tell those buggers at Donaldson's (the estate agents) that I've paid for this bloody pigsty a hundred times over. What are they going to do about the rain coming in, that's what I want to know?'

'Just £1, Mrs Wren.'

'Arseholes! You just give them my message.'

At that, she would slam the door shut and we would breathe again for another week. Ma always got away with it. People were evicted all around us in those days of private landlords. The rent for one floor of crumbling old houses was about £1 a week. Many thrown out of work in the depressed Thirties could not pay. It was a common sight to see a family on the cobbles with all their possessions, mum and dad ashen faced and the kids crying. Donaldson's were managing agents for Number 53. We never did discover who actually owned it. It was said to belong to the famous St. Thomas' Hospital. Perhaps that explains why they never did evict the old lady who lived in a shoe. She certainly had magic ways. Ma was psychic and much given to premonitions. One of her sidelines was reading the tea leaves for superstitious housewives who came fom near and far seeking reassurance. I would crouch behind a bit of curtain at the bottom of the kitchen dresser listening to them gabbing away. They would have a cup of tea, then Ma would give the grouts a shake and turn the cup upside down on its saucer. She would ask her visitor about her family and her troubles.

'Would it be good news you're looking for, dear, or shall I just tell you what I see?' she would ask archly. 'Oh, a ship, a tall ship. You're going on a journey. . .' Young as I was, it did not stop my noticing that the anxious ladies who paid a tanner for Ma's visionary powers had a much brighter future ahead than those who only gave her a couple of coppers.

Once I asked her what would happen to me when I grew up. *Tinker, tailor, soldier, sailor* . . . The kind of thing all little boys want to know.

'You'll be all right, duck,' she said. 'You're touched by angels.' She smiled and put her finger on the cleft in my chin. 'They always look after children who don't have daddies.'

I didn't realise it at the time, but Ma's soft words were to cheer me greatly in years to come. I was already beginning to wonder about the absence of men at Number 53, though had yet to realise that I was illegitimate. For a time I thought that Silly Sid was my father. He was, after all, the only man around permanently. Others came and went. Some lodgers, some lovers. All sorts of 'uncles' passed through our lives. Tailors, furniture workers, sailors, salesmen, boxers, crooks, con men. Few had any time for the young boy lurking in the corner, though they could be generous with their time and pennies if they were out to impress one of the girls. I was both fascinated and frightened by these visitors whose world seemed so much brighter than ours.

I remember one man with a West country burr and sideburns down to his chin who claimed to have sailed the seven seas. He talked of exotic places like Shanghai and the Malay Peninsula, filling my head with visions of pirates and heathens. 'Garn,' said Peggy, 'take no notice. 'e works in the docks.'

Peggy Crotty was everyone's favourite. A natural leader, she would scold and protect us, wipe our noses and bandage our cuts by spitting on a piece of rag. God knows where she came from. She was supposed to have been abandoned at Ma Wren's door, though a mother did appear briefly in later years. We had an infallible way of making Peggy cry. 'Ah, poor little fing,' we would mock her. 'When Ma found you on the doorstep, all yer little feet and 'ands were blue wiv the cold.'

She would wipe her eyes on her sleeve, give us a clout and get on with life, endlessly organising street games and keeping the young girls going for hours with skipping routines. The couplets they chanted went back centuries:

Salt, mustard, vinegar, pepper;
When the wind blows, we'll all go together.

There were no toys, other than those we made ourselves. The only Christmas present I recall ever receiving in those pre-war days was a six penny copy of Defoe's *Robinson Crusoe*, still a favourite book. Yet we filled the streets with wonder. There were a score of games to choose from, the boys usually separate from girls. Most of all they liked dressing up in 'borrowed' adult clothes and prancing around, aping their big sisters. The favourite for boys was *flicksies*, played with picture cards from cigarette packets. There were several variations. The most common was to stand a card up against the wall to allow the players to flick their precious collection of cards one by one until someone knocked it down. He then took possession of all the cards on the pavement. Marbles or *glarneys* and fivestones (*gobs*) were also popular games.

Of course there was plenty of mischief to be made. *Knocking down ginger* was the most innocent, though guaranteed to infuriate the adult world. It simply meant knocking on doors and running away. Sometimes it was possible to link several front knockers with cotton and rat-tat-tat on half a dozen front doors simultaneously. The sight of three or four neighbours appearing together and shaking their fists would delight us for days. We were smoking by the age of seven or eight, taking brave puffs at cigarettes pinched from machines in the high road. They would dispense two Woodbines and three red-topped matches for a penny. We soon discovered a penknife blade inserted in the drawer before it fully closed made it possible to empty the entire stock. Thus began a lifelong addiction. Another daring street sport was to aggravate the vendors who touted their wares on foot in those days. A piece of string across the pavement could send them sprawling with their heavy baskets. There's none so cruel as children. The streets were filled with the sight and sound of these poor folk trying to earn a pittance. *Cats' meat, cats' meat* . . . An old girl selling slivers of horsemeat on a wooden skewer. *Beigels, lovely beigels,* sang the little man proffering Jewish hard crusty rolls. *Muffins, muffins* . . . Junk men everywhere – *Ol' rags'n lumbah* – buying rubbish and praying for hidden treasure. Asians selling liquorice root and exotic sweet-meats, gipsies with home-made pegs and lucky heather, Africans weighed down by beads and bangles. Every day, the baker pulling his hand-drawn cart and Dick the milkman atop his horse and float. Mrs Pond, the chimney sweep. In summer, the Wallsie man came on a three-wheeled ice cream trike. Sunday barrow boys with cockles, mussels and winkles, tanner a pint.

We would be out there in the thick of it for hours, an eye always open for the chance to make a few coppers or get into scrapes. Love and hate, warmth and misery, trouble and laughter, hunger and plenty. A world of extremes where good and bad were doled out in equal measure. Ma was our minder indoors and Peggy reigned in the street. Ma treated her like a doll, spending hours twisting those auburn locks into ringlets with a long cylindrical stick while her victim wriggled and squealed as she combed out the knots. We boys were more likely to catch the copper stick, a wooden rod two inches thick used to stir up the stew of clothes she boiled in the scullery amid clouds of steam every Monday. It made a handy weapon to keep us in order – if she could catch us. We didn't worry about getting her 'aereated.' After all, she never obeyed the rules herself.

The worst crimes in the calendar were stealing from others in the house and swearing, particularly in front of girls. We also had to show respect for elders at all times and mind our manners. There we were, wondering where the next meal was coming from, but God help us if we put our elbows on the table or poked out our tongue at Peggy. We were also expected to speak properly. Contrary to popular belief, never in my life have I used expressions like *Cor luvvaduck!* and rhyming slang is mumbo-jumbo to this Cockney.

The best thing in the day was the *Daily Mirror*, then beginning its upward climb to become the world's top tabloid paper. We would fight over it the moment it came into the house, pulling the paper apart so each of us had a couple of pages. It took the drabness out of our lives and for me this was the start of a lifelong love of newspapers. I actually taught myself to read not at school, but on comic strips in the *Mirror*, Pip, Squeak and Wilfred, Buck Ryan, Captain A.R.P. Reilly-ffoull and later Jane and Garth were essential reading every day. The paper cost a penny.

We also loved the wireless, also in its infancy, though this was not always available. The accumulators that powered those early sets had to be re-charged every few days in the hardware shop. Tuppence a time was often more than we could afford. Harry Fox, Ambrose, Carol Gibbons and Henry Hall were band leaders who wowed the gals in those days.

As we got older, the ways of the adult world became ever more mysterious. The girls, the first post-Hollywood generation to defy convention and wear make up and smoke cigarettes, attracted men like magnets. We kids were left totally in the dark about their presence. Discussion of anything personal was strictly out of order. We weren't allowed to mention underwear, never mind sex. So it came something of a shock when Elsie presented me with a baby sister. Jean, a blue-eyed blonde like her mother, arrived seven years after my-self. Not to be outdone, Winnie had a baby daughter, Pam, a short while later. By this time I knew the business of babies was something to do with men, though it was not clear just what part they played. I had to find out. Obviously Pam's father was Albert Hall, a local decorator always in and out of the house who had courted Winnie in vain for years. Where did that leave Jean and myself?

The answer came by way of the errands I was constantly running for the bigger girls. Whenever something untoward was going on they would give me a written note to take to the shops. Naturally I always read it. They invariably specified: *Pkt. Mene san. towels, please.* This ritual suddenly took a strange twist. After the birth of Jean, the destination became not only the local chemist, but on several occasions a butcher shop in the high road. A Jewish kosher butcher. This time they read: '*Please could you let me have a couple of bob, Elsie.*' There would be embarrassed glances and much shuffling of feet as I passed the notes to the man nearest the door. They always finished in the hands of a tall, wavy-haired blond butcher in the corner. He would glance at me, take a florin from his pocket and pass it over without a word.

Rutz – Kosher Butcher said the sign above the shop.

A couple of years later I found the same name on a document while rifling through my mother's chest of drawers. It was an application form for a paternity order demanding child maintenance from the said Mr Rutz. This, then, had to be my father. Not that it mattered much. There was another application form with it in the drawer. For the committal of one Jameson, Derek, to Dr Barnardo's. Neither application received a hearing. A strange man the other side of Europe got in the way. His name was Adolf Hitler.

CHAPTER SEVEN

Beyond care and control

W hile others brushed away their tears, I sensed only adventure as we marched in threes to Upper Clapton railway station on the morning of Friday, 1st September 1939. Hitler's armies had invaded Poland and World War II was upon us. The formal declaration came two days later, a respite that gave the Government time to mobilise and evacuate the nation's children from cities and other areas likely to be blitzed.

Lenny Frost was four years older than me and we tended to go our own ways. On this occasion we stepped out together. I can remember holding his hand, an unusual gesture in keeping with the solemnity of the occasion as we stood in line awaiting the trains that would carry us into the unknown. People lined the streets waving hankies and yelling good luck greetings as we made our way from local schools to the station. I don't recall anyone from Number 53 among them. We were being taken off their hands, free of guilt or money. My feeling was that they were glad to be shot of us 'for the duration,' which soon became the euphemism for war. Around our necks on string hung the gas masks in square cardboard boxes that were to accompany us everywhere. Most children had a few spare clothes and possessions in cheap compressed cardboard cases and carried sandwiches and an orange or apple in carrier bags. There was a rash of navy blue gaberdine raincoats hastily bought since we were going away.

All I was interested in was getting aboard the train. Apart from one or two mile-long trips to nearby Walthamstow I had never before been on a rail journey. Nor had I seen much of the country outside a bus ride to Epping forest and a coach trip to the mud flats of Shoeburyness, near Southend. For some reason our destination on evacuation day was top secret. Please God, I prayed inwardly, let it be hundreds of miles from this place. A seaside town in the country would do nicely. In the event, the coast was declared a war zone and also evacuated.

To our astonishment, the steam train carrying us came to a halt only an hour later. 'Bishop's Stortford,' said the station signs yet to be blanked out for the war years. It turned out to be a sleepy rural town in Hertfordshire only thirty miles from the Hackney Marshes. 'What a swizz,' we told each other. We felt robbed. Young as we were, our heads were filled with warlike visions of fighters and bombers, tanks and machine guns. We knew that thirty miles was neither here nor there when it came to modern warfare. We might as well have stayed at home. Shepherded into a hall beside the station, we were given a mug of orange squash and a cake while billeting officers fussed and fretted about us, almost falling over themselves in their eagerness to strike an early blow against Adolf Hitler. A right bunch of berks, we thought. The idea was to break us down into small groups and take us out to find homes. All very well until they started separating brothers and sisters, friends and neighbours.

'Ere, Mister, I'm not going with that lot. I want my sister. My dad'll kill me! He told me to stay with Jim and Vi whatever happens.'

They sorted it out eventually, though many families were split up in the confusion. I had kept close to Lenny and we were together as an official took us along streets in our group, knocking on doors and asking people to take us in. There had been no time to make any prior arrangements.

'Mr. Chamberlain (then Prime Minister) has said it is everyone's duty to take evacuees if they have room to spare,' billeting officers imperiously told these country folk opening their doors on what they obviously regarded as roughnecks from London.

Lenny and I managed to get into the same house. A Mr and Mrs Lloyd, I seem to remember. They were kindly folk, though well into middle age and childless. Having two sharp-eyed, wary Cockney lads deposited on their doorstep must have been the greatest shock of their lives. Mrs Lloyd's first act was to produce tea and biscuits on a tray in the front parlour. That threw me because I was more used to tea out of a chipped enamel mug on a wooden table. She brought milk in a bottle and poured it into a jug beside the teapot. That did it. I had to go and open my big mouth.

'Here,' I said suspiciously, 'why don't you pour the milk into the cups from the bottle like everybody else?'

We never did get on. Lenny and I were soon in trouble, due to a shameful act on my part. Mr Lloyd was a builder's labourer, but his one great passion in life was his garden. He was out there for hours, digging and planting and pruning. One day he laid his seed potatoes out to dry until they were ready for the soil. I had acquired my first penknife from somewhere and spent a happy hour or so spearing the spuds with all the relish of a knife-thrower at the circus. Ted Lloyd was a quiet, gentle man and didn't say much. His wife Vera went right up the wall.

'You nasty, horrible, vicious child. You've ruined Mr Lloyd's whole crop of Edwards,' she railed at me. 'We're not keeping you after this.'

'I didn't, I didn't,' I kept lying stubbornly. 'It wasn't me, honest, it wasn't.'

'If it wasn't you, who was it then?'

'It must have been Lenny.'

It was, on the face of it, a small enough incident, a schoolboy prank followed by an attempt to cast the blame elsewhere. Yet that one stupid act eventually changed my entire life. For the better, I hope. In the row that erupted we were kicked out and I was parted from Lenny, more or less for all time. He went elsewhere and before long reached the magic age of fourteen – old enough to go back to London and work. It was in these strange circumstances that I came under the spell of Mr Ernest Hare, whom I knew vaguely as one of the teachers at my school. It so happened he cycled past the Lloyds' house on his way home. On the day of the potato massacre, Mrs Lloyd stopped him in the street and told him what had happened. He told her to send me out.

'Did you ruin those potatoes?' he wanted to know.

'Not me! I didn't do it.'

'Who did then, if it wasn't you?'

'I dunno, it wasn't me.'

'You're a liar.'

'I'm not, I'm not! It wasn't me.'

Wallop! His open palm caught me on the side of the face, sending me sprawling across the road. I lay there on the ground, too stunned to cry, utterly humiliated, totally defeated. It was one of those moments in life that are seared on the memory forever. I had asked for it and got it. All the same, the punishment was savage.

'Don't ever tell lies again, son,' Mr Hare said evenly. Then he mounted his machine and calmly cycled off down the road, leaving me there to lick my wounds. They were mental rather than physical. I think it must have been at that moment I took a subliminal decision somehow to make amends and prove myself to this man who had struck me down. I had found my substitute father.

Once again the angels must have been there to pluck me from the gutter. They handed me over to the care of perhaps the only family who could have helped at that dark hour. The Elliotts of Thorley Hill. They took me into their cosy three-bedroomed house and treated me as one of their own. It was marvellous. They even had a gadget on the walls where you flicked a switch and a heater came on. Electric fires, they were called – it was the first time I had seen such a thing.

Jock Elliott, head of the household, was football barmy. Out of work and with few prospects, he left his native Sunderland in 1928 with little to offer other than his skill as a shipwright and love of that round leather ball. Both served him well. By the time I arrived at the house, he had his own business as a small builder, ran Bishop's Stortford Football Club – and was making enough money to send his two sons, Maurice and Christopher, to the local public school. At his side was his wife Nell, one of the kindest women I ever met. Today Elliott – you see its board on building sites everywhere – is one of the giants of the construction industry with a turnover of £60 million. Chris is chairman, Maurice past chairman. Jock, over eighty and long retired, lives quietly with Nell. He still takes a close interest in the business that was little more than two men and a dog when I came knocking on his door.

It was a golden period, growing up alongside two sons roughly my age in a normal household. Jock, Geordie to the core and as hard as granite, saw in me the poor boy he himself had once been. Both he and Nell treated me like their own sons. True, I was useless at football, but at least my school had the right qualifications. It was an East End nursery for Tottenham Hotspur – the former Spurs captain, Eddie Baily, went there – and our team soon saw off Jock's beloved Stortford Town, depleted by wartime demands on its manpower. Jock simply recruited the school's best players.

Maurice was closest to me. We would go out for hours with the dog exploring fields and woods, finding birds' nests and looking for rabbits. All new to me, of course. These were Battle of Britain days and often we would lay on our backs in a cornfield watching three or four Spitfires and Hurricanes of the RAF darting in and out of waves of German Heinkel and Dornier bombers, streaking across the summer sky, London-bound like black ants. Once a German bomber shot up a railway line alongside fields where we were playing. I shoved Maurice in a ditch and jumped on him. It made me hero for the day, though fear rather than coolness must have inspired me to move so swiftly.

Best of all I liked to take my turn for a bath – something unknown in London – and sit by the fire in pyjamas with the boys talking over tea and toast about the war heroes of the day, the battles on air, land and sea, whether there would be any fighting left when we grew up. Jock loved to fire questions at us, no doubt to find out whether he was getting his money's worth at that public school.

'What's the capital of Australia?' he would want to know.

'Canberra,' Maurice shot back.

'Derek, your turn. Where's Rangoon?'

'Don't ask me, I dunno . . .'

I always played dumb. You learn young in the East End. It would not have made sense for me to appear to be as clever as Jock's own sons. The family were most surprised to learn one day that I had won a major schools' essay competition. Even more astonished years later when they switched on the 9 o'clock news on BBC1 to discover I had been made editor of the *Daily Express*. Jock used to kid me along when we were young. 'Don't worry, Derek,' he used to say. 'I'll always find you a job in the yard.' I should have taken him up on it.

It all had to go wrong, of course. No doubt, it was my fault. I could be moody and morose. The folks back home nagged at my mind, despite my earlier delight at getting away. Elsie occasionally sent letters with a postal order for 6d (2½p). They were few and far between. Many times I feared they were all dead. The red glow over London was visible on Thorley Hill as the Germans blitzed the city night after night. I felt guilty and resentful living in comparative luxury. The day came when Nell gently explained there was no room for me any longer. The boys were growing up and needed their own bedrooms. I was back on the move – downhill once again. This time I lived up

to the reputation we kids had with many country folk. Today Bishop's
Stortford is a bustling town, part of the London commuter belt. In those days
it was a small market centre frequently disrupted by Cockney kids running
riot through its sleepy streets. And I became one of the biggest tearaways of
them all. Being a bastard was a terrible burden to carry for the poor in days
gone by. Without the protection of money and status, you were vulnerable to
attack from all quarters. There was a kind of dark mystique about it. *The
Devil's work . . . sins of the father* and all that rubbish. In the East End it did
not matter much. Those of us living at Number 53 had protection in numbers
and, in any case, were too young to know the stigma we were carrying. It was
a different story among the country churchgoers. I had no chance with them.
The billeting officers dumped me on a succession of working class families
whose main preoccupation in life appeared to be hearing the wonderful story
of Jameson's heroic father. They would bring in neighbours, friends and relatives so that I could recount it all over again. One would say casually, as if just
passing the time: 'What happened to your father, Derek?' I had the story off
pat. Straight from *Boy's Own* paper.

*'He was in the first war, a pilot in the Air Flying Corps. Shot down more
than twenty Jerry planes. One day he and his mate got into a big dogfight.
Dad had a Piper Cub and he was alright, but flying back to base he realised
his friend was missing. He went back to find him. They must have been
waiting for him. Dad was never seen again. Killed in action not long before
the war ended in 1918.'*

That was impossible, of course. I wasn't born until 1929. What they knew
and were too coy to tell me meant I was branding myself as a liar without
being aware of it. Everyone could see the joke except me. No wonder they
kept moving me from home to home. The more they shifted me, the more
difficult I became. The end of my wanderings came with a Mrs Turner. By
the time I reached her abode, my reputation had preceded me. She kept me
with the dog in the garden shed. I was allowed indoors only to sleep in a tiny
room at the top of the house. I quite liked the shed. There was an old mangle
in there and my table was the shelf in front of the two rollers. Mr Turner kept
his tools hanging on the wall and naturally I helped myself when making the

69

model aircraft that were all the rage in those wartime days. Anyway, sod it, the dog loved me.

My undoing was the second refugee – as the locals called us – in the house. A Hackney boy from a doting Jewish family who paid visits and sent food parcels. Naturally he was allowed in the house and on several occasions, peeking through the kitchen window, I could see them enjoying a boiled egg each for breakfast. That made my bread and marge or dripping in the shed highly indigestible. There are some things you have to do in this world. One wintry day, as they sat chatting over breakfast in that cosy kitchen with its big Aga stove, I decided to demand my rights. It seemed to me that the war effort was being sadly abused if people like myself were denied rations laid down by Mr Churchill. I appeared on the kitchen doorstep and demanded my egg.

'There's no egg for you,' said Mrs Turner sniffily. 'When it's your turn to get an egg, you'll get it.'

'But I never get an egg,' I replied, 'If I did, I wouldn't be asking for one now, would I?' I added with childish logic.

'Don't you dare argue with me, you ungrateful little guttersnipe,' the good lady retorted. 'I know all about you,' she said knowingly, 'and your FATHER.' My father, late of the Air Flying Corps, always came up in conversations of a difficult kind with the adult world. He would have been proud of what I did next. I stormed into the kitchen, picked up Michael Levy's partially eaten egg from its cup, and hurled it at the kitchen wall. It hit the recess behind the cooker with a most satisfying *plop*! It was my last taste of family life in the country. *Beyond care and control* was the chief billeting officer's verdict this time. I was posted to a hostel for bad boys in the London Road. That had a good ring about it. It was a big, rambling Victorian house with a large garden occupied by the more villainous of my mates at school. I was king of the kids in no time at all.

CHAPTER EIGHT

The twopenny library

There were fourteen or fifteen of us, officially the most unruly boys in the school, aged between nine and fourteen. We were not all that frightening. Most were like myself, cast adrift from our own people and constantly shoved around by harassed officials. That was asking for trouble. Lenny Burrows and Billy Impetigo were there from earlier days. Our mascot was a tiny tot we called Ferret. There were also two or three Jewish lads, refugees from Hitler's Germany, who were in the hostel for no other reason than that they spoke with a strange accent and were thought by some to be spies. They probably were treated more cruelly by us then by the locals, particularly as we were under the lash of a German like themselves. Miss Hyman was her name. Matron in charge. Quite understandably, she was kindness itself to the refugee boys. God knows, they had suffered dreadfully and needed all the support they could get.

To the rest of us, she was the worst tyrant on earth. Tall, with grey hair swept back in a bun, she carried a thong of knotted leather bootlaces every-where. The slightest infringement of regulations, one word out of turn, and her home-made whip would strike like a snake's tongue. The back of the knees was her favourite target – we all wore shorts – though anywhere would do if you happened to be moving faster than her arm. Miss Hyman got the same response as tyrants everywhere. We drove her to distraction. Naturally we told anyone who would listen that she was a German spy. One trick of ours was to lift the blackout curtains late at night and flash torches so that people would think someone was signalling. We would ape her thick accent, then innocently claim to be sending up the German enemy if she was foolish enough to question it. No wonder she preferred to lash out first and ask questions afterwards.

By now I was thirteen. My age and reputation automatically qualified me as leader of this band of JDs – juvenile delinquents. As in all primitive societies, the only way anyone else could take over would be to beat me in fair combat. Easy enough, but nobody made an issue of it and so I found myself leader of the wildest bunch of tearaways in Bishop's Stortford. Miss Hyman was the main problem. Keyhold Kate we called her – after the character in *Dandy*, our favourite comic – because she had this sneaky habit of creeping up on us. How was I to run our illegal enterprises under the nose of this chosen defender of law and order? There was a simple answer, well known to anyone who has been in prison. I declared a state of armed neutrality. Provided matron left us to our own devices, keeping her nose out of our extra-curricular activities, I would guarantee her sovereignty inside the hostel. It worked a treat. We got on quite well together in this new spirit of mutual respect. For the first time the household chores were carried out with cheerful efficiency under my direction. She would actually come to me for help. 'Derek, haf the boys not clean der vinders?' she would ask. No sooner said than done.

Everything ran the way she liked it. Two boys on cleaning boots and shoes, two waiting on table, two washing up, two carrying the shopping, two dusting and polishing and so on. We each made our own beds and were responsible for our dormitory rooms. While still at school I could shop, cook, scrub, darn and run the entire household on occasion if Miss Hyman was poorly. I don't know what she made of it all, this sad victim of Hitler. She never spoke of herself. Kurt, one of the German boys, told me she was one of those tragic Jews who had been totally assimilated into German culture and never recovered from the shock of being cast out. The way she turned a blind eye to our villainy suggests that she, too, was not all that enamoured of authority.

Fagin would have been proud of us. We descended on the town centre like locusts, lifting goods all over the place, whether we had any use for them or not. The operation would be organised with military precision. One or other of us would wander around sniffing out prospects and we would weigh up the pros and cons back at the hostel. Just like the Hollywood gangster movies we adored so much. The street market with its wide open stalls was our favourite. Underneath them was buried treasure – black market and other goods reserved for special customers.

'All you have to do, Ferret, is crawl under that van and come out by the side of the stall. We'll attract the bloke's attention at the other end. Easy, innit? 'e'll never see you coming.'

One of us would approach, picking up goods like ribbon or hair grips we obviously had neither the intention nor the money to buy. The stallholder would eye us suspiciously. That was Ferret's chance. He would burrow under the van and get to the bottom of the stall with all the agility of his namesake. We didn't always get away with it. On several occasions someone would run out of luck and finish up in the juvenile court and be sent to approved school or even borstal. I myself was hopeless at thieving and most of the time craftily left it to my more enterprising associates. Once I almost got caught in a hardware shop. That put the wind up me for good. I approached the empty counter and, magpie-like, marvelled at the glittering objects that seemed crying to be taken. It turned out the assistant was kneeling on the floor rummaging about under the counter. Just as I lifted a padlock and keys, she stood up and spotted me.

'Help, thief!' she roared in the time-honoured way. With that, she wrapped both her fists tightly around my curls. I dropped the padlock, brought my arms up between hers and forced them apart. She took a clump of my hair with her as I bolted from the shop. I didn't stop running for a mile. For weeks afterwards I was expecting her to turn up for an identity parade. Nothing happened. No doubt they didn't bother because I had dropped the goods.

Most of the stuff we pinched was neither use nor ornament. Now and again Ferret would emerge with a box of combs or tins of shoe polish stuffed down his shirt, goods we could barter elsewhere. We even sold some of them back to rival stall-holders at prices too cheap for them to refuse. Other gear would be exchanged in the school playground for a couple of marbles or cigarette cards. I think Miss Hyman knew what was going on, but she kept the peace while remaining a fierce disciplinarian. There was an occasion when police came knocking at the door and engaged her in grave conversation. We sent Ferret out to earwig on them without being seen. It turned out they were looking for a pair of fur and leather gauntlets stolen from the driver's cab at a nearby bus terminal.

'She said she ain't seen them,' Ferret reported back. 'Told 'em she would keep her eyes peeled.' We all knew Billy Impetigo had been sporting the gloves for days, claiming he got them from home by way of his sister, who was billetted with a family in the town.

'Billy has gloves?' she said to me that evening after tea.

'It's all right,' I told her, putting my finger to my lips.

We made him take them back to the bus shelter that evening. It had nothing to do with the police calling. Nicking from shops and stalls was one thing. Stealing from your own kind was strictly out of order.

Some of our pranks were harmless enough, though the adults might not have thought so. I remember Mr Fuller, the ferocious old boy who taught us woodwork, clobbering me with a lump of two by one as he chased me around the work benches because we had organised a carpentry lesson of our own in the lunch break. Or *dinner*, as we called it.

Timber was a rare commodity in wartime days. We had dipped into his precious reserves to make a raft out of several planks. This we proceeded to sail along the River Stort running behind the cricket pavilion where wood-work classes were held. Mr Fuller caught us coming in to land and almost had apoplexy. Naturally, I got the blame.

'You varmint,' he screeched, 'it's swine like you that are causing this war.' *The thought of that kept us in stitches for days.*

The river was a magnet. We used to 'borrow' a rowing boat from the neg-lected boathouse of a riverside mansion at weekends and spend hours going up and down the water. Since it held only seven – and that was a tight squeeze – someone always got left out. On one of our trips, a disgruntled Ferret was left behind. We learned later he had gone up to the house, knocked on the door and cheekily asked Her Ladyship if he could borrow some paint.

'Why d'you want paint, young man?' she asked.

'So we can paint your boat, lady,' said Ferret.

They sent the river Conservancy Board man after us – on his bike. He came trundling along the towpath with a shotgun across the handlebars. 'Come in, come in, you kids,' he yelled at us from under his droopy moustache. Out in mid-river, his roars creased us with laughter. The madder he got, the more we enjoyed it. In the end, we abandoned ship. On the opposite bank, of course.

'Strewth, Ferret,' I rebuked him later, 'what've you got for brains – bleedin' blottin' paper?'

'Ah, well, Del, I was only trying to help the old gel, weren't I! Nuffink wrong with that, eh?'

School in wartime was a scrappy affair. Reading and writing were the main lessons, though we seemed to spend more time gardening than we did in front of the blackboard. *Dig for Victory* was one of the great battle cries of the day. Carrots, cabbages and spuds. What better to occupy the minds of two or three hundred youngsters in a school desperately short of resources.

We were all but forgotton at Bishop's Stortford. Few cared for the noisy, difficult visitors from London, even though our families back home were suffering the worst bombing raids of the war. I guess kids like me turned the locals sour. Their response was to call us *refugees* rather than *evacuees* and house us, grudgingly, in rooms, sheds and empty halls.

Detmold Road Elementary Boys School, that proud Victorian beauty by the Hackney Marshes, lost its identity altogether. Some of the teachers remained and we were all merged into our secondary school, Mount Pleasant Senior Boys, where I would have gone at eleven had the war not intervened. My class was assembled at the Baptist Hall in Portland Road, close to the town centre. It was literally just that – a redbrick church hall with a few side rooms and a modest courtyard outside. Kind as it was of the Baptists to have us – we were probably forced on them – they had little to offer. The building was never meant to be a school and we were desperately short of teachers, books and facilities. For tens of thousands like us, left high and dry in the exigencies of war, education had become a shambles.

Many of the boys and girls who set out on that adventure in September, 1939, had returned home within months, particularly as the so-called Phoney War at the outset dragged on. My foster brother Lenny was one of the first to go. Others drifted back as the war progressed. For me it went on forever. There was no loving summons back to Hackney. Bombs had nothing to do with it: I had not been wanted in peace and was an irrelevance in war.

I was to spend four and a half years in that dreary church hall. Half the time I never knew whether my tribe in London were dead or alive. The fact I hardly heard from them filled me with despair. I would send up angry prayers that Hitler had got them, lifting the agony of not knowing once and for all.

Then a letter would arrive from Elsie indicating all was well. That only made matters worse. It simply confirmed the long silences meant nobody gave two monkeys. Now my anguish would turn into suicidal depression. Many times I contemplated killing myself. Rejected, skint and always in trouble, that was me. Existence seemed totally futile.

Ernest Hare did not look like a man in the pocket of angels. Somebody must have sent him along to teach me there was more to life than raising hell on the streets interspersed with thoughts of death. He was a tall, lean character in horn-rimmed spectacles who seemed permanently enveloped in nicotine. He lit up every time he got out of the classroom, something we found most admirable. His passion was Kensitas cigarettes, a particularly virulent brand. Obviously a thinker, though he liked to laugh. Of course, he had a head start with me. I knew right away he was strong and decisive. He had shown it by knocking me across the street for spearing those spuds. Clearly a man to follow.

I formed a most unhealthy attachment for him. Both Thorley Hill, where I lived with the Elliotts, and Miss Hyman's hostel were close to the house he had taken with his family. It seems ludicrous now, but there were times in the Forties when I would wander about aimlessly in the street outside hoping to catch a glimpse of him. During holidays I would be in physical pain with longing to talk to him. The family must have understood. If they spotted me, I was invited in for a cup of tea and a home-made fairy cake. Mrs Hare, like a little robin, a roly-poly lady with bright rosy red cheeks, would make a fuss of me. I remember being terribly jealous of their own children, Michael and Pamela.

They must have found it odd, this gangling lad with the mop of curls who had a dreadful reputation thereabouts, shyly sipping tea and making small talk. I was always quiet and courteous, trying to behave like a respectable grown up in the hope of being invited back. Perhaps they were proud of the fact their dad had tamed me. I always kept myself clean and my clothes neat and tidy. The idea that to be poor means looking like a scruffy urchin straight out of the Bisto Kids is yet another stereotyped image foisted on the East End poor. I was as smartly turned out as anyone from a normal home, though most of my clothes were charity hand-me-downs. When the researchers from *This Is Your Life* asked Nell Elliott what she remembered most about the young

Jameson, she said: He was always so clean, always scrubbing himself.

It wasn't always easy. Billy Impetigo soon spread those dreadful sores around the ears that made his chronic skin disease, like the bedbugs, a trade mark of the poor. I was sent for treatment to Out-patients' at Bishop's Stortford hospital. The Sister in charge inspected my nails, told me I was filthy and slapped my face. Quite normal procedure, this, for someone like me, so I wasn't all that bothered. What she did next was pure sadism. For a half-inch sore on the lobe of one ear she cut off all my hair and shaved it with electric clippers. She then daubed both ears and the sides of my head with gentian violet paint commonly used in those days. I looked a right wally. The only thing to do was make the best of it. I got myself a flat cap and wore that until my hair started sprouting again. If anyone known to me came along in the street, I would raise my cap and say cheerily: 'Hello! How d'you do?' They would be brought up with a start by this pinkish bald head streaked with purple blobs, looking like a clown gone wrong.

It could not have happened at a worse moment because I had just fallen in love for the first time. Betty Stapleton was her name, but to me she was Shirley Temple. Honey-coloured curly hair, snub nose, freckles. She was from Eastbourne, which also sent its evacuees to Bishop's Stortford. Her mother ran a tea shop in the town – one of the few places where we London kids were welcome. God, I would have died for that girl. Little did she know it, but some of our most daring raids were carried out to make sure she was kept supplied with chocolates, lace hankies, socks, wristwatch straps, dusters, anything we could lay our hands on.

'What do I do with this?' she would say, holding up six yards of knicker elastic hoisted from the market?

'Aw, give it to your mum. Might come in handy in the shop!'

She must have thought I was quite potty. I would meet her out of school, standing there like some faithful hound waiting to be taken for an airing. Betty would tolerate me going as far as her gate and that was it. A year of total devotion and all I got for my pains was one snatched kiss. Adolescent girls at the time were not interested in boys of thirteen, especially those likely to turn up with a gentian violet head.

GI Joe was in town. The United States Army Air Force, as it was known in wartime, had taken over just about every rural corner of southern England to carry out mass bombing raids against the Germans. The Army itself followed later to prepare for the Normandy invasion. Uncle Sam's first conquest was not the Jerries. Rather the willing British, particularly the females.

The girls went crackers for them. Understandably so. Quite apart from anything else, there was a desperate shortage of men – husbands and sweethearts were all over the globe in the British forces. Those still at home wore rough khaki serge, usually with empty pockets. Most squaddies were on two bob (10p) a day. By contrast, the Americans in their smartly cut uniforms were loaded with more dollars than they knew what to do with. The folk back in American deluged them with goodies for themselves and the British allies they assumed were near starvation. It was like Father Christmas calling every day for kids like us. We soon found out how to gain entry into this magic world of plenty. My great love of the Americans, or Yanks as we always called them, started right here.

'Got any gum, chum?' was the password, thrown at every passing GI.

It didn't stop at chewing gum. They showered us with American candy, Hershey bars, Lifesavers, Choc-o-Nuts, glamorous ciggies like Camel and Lucky Strike, *Yank* and *Photoplay* magazines, comics galore with Flash Gordon, Superman, Dick Tracy, the Katzenjammer Kids and the rest. We Cockneys were specially privileged once the Yanks got the hang of what evacuation was all about. Well, almost.

'Gee, you mean Adolf has bombed you kids out of your homes! You don't know where your mom is! Say, that's too bad. Come on base Saturday pm and we'll see what we can find for you guys.'

Many had children or younger brothers and sisters back home and they loved to entertain us at parties hastily thrown together in Nissen huts on their airfields. There was no limit to their generosity. Candy, books, games, toys, something new called T-shirts, K-rations – they would have given us the socks off their feet had we asked for them. Naturally we would do a turn for them. Our Cockney songs and strange accent enchanted them as much as their speech did us.

'Hey, let's hear that again, you guys! *"Wor' back, gee back, 'ave anuvver look, Jack, you know wot I mean!"* 'Followed by a big wink and everyone would fall over laughing. Playing among these happy-go-lucky GIs, I used to think they were about the same age as ourselves.

Of course, the girls fared even better. But then they had more to give than Cockney street songs. We got early lessons in sex watching the Yanks going at it with girls in fields around town. The first time I saw two humans entwined was on a lazy Saturday afternoon in meads near the local castle ruins. A GI and his girl were walking along hand-in-hand, then suddenly sank to the ground out of sight. A couple of mates and myself crawled behind a hedge overlooking the scene and there it was, the moment of truth. Something we had thought and talked about endlessly happening before our very eyes. His bottom going up and down reminded me of a rabbit's white tail hopping through a meadow. Funnily enough, I knew the girl in her floral summer dress. Maureen, her name was. She came from a poor family I was once billetted on and had a husband in the Western desert. Like many girls at the time, she stained her legs with tan out of a bottle or gravy browning to simulate stockings, difficult to find in wartime. I used to watch her do it.

Playing Peeping Tom, face flushed and heart pumping, I could see where the tan ran out and the white of her open thighs began. Sex looked like something we ought to be trying ourselves, though I wondered at the time where love came into it since she was always showing people pictures of her soldier husband.

The ladies were not to blame. War produced a feeling of feverish excitement in everyone. Girls, girls, girls, bare-legged in the new shorter skirts, pining for their missing menfolk. Only too happy to fill the void, the Americans. Handsome, young, devil-may-care charmers who talked just like George Raft or James Cagney. Wildly generous with a new invention called nylons and steaks for mum and dad. There was always the excuse that we might be dead tomorrow – GI Joe, absent husband or the girl herself. This war embraced us all.

It astonishes me nowadays to read some of the nonsense written about World War II. The truth is that people here in Britain were never more happy. Only a fool would make light of the death and destruction that came with the war. Nevertheless, there was a buzz in the air, laughter in the streets. Sounds corny, but call it a sense of purpose. People felt they were needed by each other – and by their country. They walked proud.

My love of all things American was to have happy consequences. It completed my education. As I said, lessons in school itself were a rudimentary affair and we learned little beyond reading and writing. I wanted to know more about these Yanks and the land from whence they came. At last my anxiety to please Ernest Hare was rewarded. There was no public library in rural Bishop's Stortford at that time. Next door to the British Restaurant – a huge warehouse which served as a wartime canteen for evacuees and essential workers – was a small private library. Fee-paying and adults only.

I told Ernie – our name for him – of my predicament. He arranged to meet me outside the twopenny library after lunch. *Oh, happy day, the angels must have been there, too!* Without explanation, he took me inside, told the assistant he would vouch for me, and out of his own pocket paid for a season ticket allowing me to take out two books at a time. Forty-five years later that simple act still brings tears to my eyes. It saved me from myself.

As if he were setting homework, Ernie said we would discuss my reading material. We selected my first books. John Steinbeck's *The Grapes of Wrath* and *Studs Lonegan,* by James T. Farrell, two contemporary American novels that gave me some insight into what my life was all about. I learned that to be poor was a condition, not a crime, that there were great writers who could express exactly how I felt with passion and feeling. Even more miraculous, there were people on this earth to whom poor, misbegotten bastards actually meant something. Like a blind man suddenly given the gift of sight, I devoured every word, then went back for more and still more. Such was my thirst for enlightenment that in those last eighteen months at school I was reading five or six books a week. The great writers of the American Depression completely took me over. As well as Steinbeck and Farrell, I lost myself in the world of Ernest Hemingway, Theodore Dreiser, John Dos Passos, Sinclair Lewis, Upton Sinclair, Scott Fitzgerald. It wasn't all social revolution. There were brilliant thriller writers like Dashiel Hammett and Raymond Chandler and the classics – Dickens, Wells, Zola, Flaubert, Gorki, Twain. The best contemporary British, too, notably Graham Greene, Aldous Huxley, Evelyn Waugh and George Orwell.

It was not long before this literary explosion began to produce results. I entered an essay competition in support of one of those wartime propaganda drives designed to stimulate fund-raising on the home front. This was on the work of the Red Cross, something that would not have inspired me to read the entry form a few months earlier. I got hold of some brochures on this worthy cause, read the lot and sat down to write my essay.

My carefully researched words – first step in a lengthy career in journalism – carried off first prize in the under-fourteen age group, much to the astonishment of the whole school and much of Bishop's Stortford. *What? A kid from that dreadful school! First prize. Whoever heard of such a thing.* I was pleased to learn the results had been read out at Bishop's Stortford College, the public school attended by the Elliott boys.

Collecting the prize was one of the blackest days of my life, a collision between the world I was to leave behind and my new role of earnest young thinker. It was ten guineas' (£10.50) worth of book tokens, a tidy sum in those days, to be handed over by the Bishop of Hertford at a posh Saturday afternoon fête in the Castle Gardens.

The problem was I had no shoes, only a pair of scuffed plimsolls. Ernie Hare gave me yet another note for local Red Cross headquarters, where they doled out American welfare supplies. I feared the worst, having been there once too often in the past. Indeed, methinks I was their best customer. I should have explained the shoes were for an occasion to do with the good and kindly deeds of the Red Cross. Sadly, my tongue tends to freeze in the presence of do-gooders.

The lady read the note, sniffed and asked 'What size?'

'Six.'

'We haven't got anything in six.'

'But I must have some shoes. Please, lady, it's very important.'

'You're always in here,' she said. 'This is supposed to be for the war, you know, not the likes of you.'

She gave me a look as if I were something the dog brought in, sniffed some more and went to the back of the shop. She returned with a pair of shoes all right. Size six. Bright yellow girl's shoes. With square toes. 'That's all we've got,' she said, banging them on the counter.

God let me die. What am I going to do? I took them away, trying not to show my despair. Back at the hostel, a ray of hope. Try to cover that bright yellow with black polish. I did it once, twice, half a dozen times. It just did not work. The black polish would not penetrate the yellow dye of the leather. I was left with a pair of shoes looking like someone had spewed over them. They were marginally better than the worn out plimsolls. I had to wear them.

Perhaps nobody would notice. It seemed like hours before my name was called over the Tannoy at the fête. I hurt so much inside that my body was shaking. The lonely walk to the trestle table where the prizes were laid out seemed like ten miles. Every eye in the place must be on those square yellow shoes with black streaks. All those ladies and gentlemen in their summer finery.

The bishop shook my hand, then gravely handed me the book tokens.

'Well done, Jameson,' he said.

'Thank you, M'Lord,' I replied in the way they had told me.

Then I noticed he was wearing gaiters. *Bloody gaiters!* He looked like Pegleg Pete! And here am I dying a thousand deaths because some old cow at the Red Cross won't give me a pair of shoes. Sod 'em all!

I celebrated by spending the tokens on aircraft recognition books. Every last penny. They were required reading for lads of my age. Unfortunately the headmaster, Bertram Cartwright, did not always share our passion for the war effort. He congratulated me at assembly on Monday and told me to report to his study with my purchases.

'Aircraft recognition,' he said when I got into his tiny study. He made it sound like a particularly evil crime. 'What complete and utter rubbish! You disappoint me, boy.' Then he slowly dropped them one by one – there were five or six – into his wastepaper basket. He did not tear them up first, which I took to be an invitation to retrieve them when he was out of the way. I got them back in the dinner hour, much to the delight of my chums.

Mr Cartwright was one of the most unforgettable characters I ever met. He seemed to be about eight feet tall, was skinny with it, and wore an ancient pince nez. He looked for all the world like Will Hay, a favourite film comic of those days, and that is what we called him. With his drooping bow tie, pursed lips and tiny spectacles, Mr Cartwright would descend like the wrath of God on small boys like myself set on making mischief. 'Ah, I can see where you're going in life,' he would say to someone caught not paying attention. 'A lorry driver's mate.' It sounded like a pact with the devil. 'Empty tins make the most noise,' was another favourite expression as he knocked two heads together. Poor soul, he was like a captain without a ship running a school in that bleak church hall in the country. He wanted only the best for his boys and, like Ernie Hare, tried to teach us that learning was the only passport likely to take us out of the world of poverty and hardship. 'Eyes open, ears open, mouth shut,' he told us at least once a day, in his dry Staffordshire tones. Not that he ever practised it himself.

I spent the last term teaching some of my contemporaries how to tell the time. It was too late for them to learn how to read and write, but they might as well find out what the bloody time was! I divided the clock into two sections. First the minutes, then the hours. They soon got the hang of it. Nobody had bothered to explain it previously.

Now the time had arrived to go back to London. Ernie Hare had written asking that I be allowed to stay on at school. There was so much more to learn. Elsie gave me six months. I was fourteen in November, 1943, and left the following Easter. The money I got working would come in handy at home. By now my literary endeavours had persuaded me that I should be a journalist. Actually I wanted to be a novelist. However, it made sense to complete my education and get some writing skills before trying to emulate Hemingway. Journalism seemed a short cut to the ultimate object of writing books. It took forty-five years, but I have finally got around to it.

Mr Cartwright did not share my confidence. 'You haven't even read all the works of Shakespeare,' he said. 'How can you be a journalist?' He wrote on my leaving testimonial: *'Should do well in a shop.'*

Parting from Ernie Hare filled me with sadness. I gave him 20 Kensitas, but cheekily kept the four extra they put in a separate packet at the side with the slogan: *Four for your friends.*

'I guess we're friends,' I told him outside that redbrick hall where he had shown me the way out of the gutter. He raised his hand in a reproving gesture, then placed it behind my head and pulled my face into his raincoat.

'You'll make it, Derek,' he said. 'You have a great gift for words.'

It was the first time he ever called me Derek – and the last time I saw him.

CHAPTER NINE

Bottom of the heap

L ondon Transport's Number 6 bus, chugging its way across the capital from Hackney Wick to Kensal Rise, is not exactly a chariot of fire. Nevertheless, I leapt aboard the red double-decker with eager anticipation. This was Easter Monday, 1944, the first day of my working life. At last, I was going somewhere.

A fourpenny one carried me from Hackney Odeon to Ludgate Circus, dropping me a few steps from the stone portals of Reuters, the world's most famous news agency. All I knew about it at the time was that it was situated in Fleet Street and had something to do with newspapers. That was good enough for me. I was about to become a *reporter*.

Winnie had fixed it for me. Using her abundant talent as a manipulator of men, she lined up the post – as they called a job in those days – if only to prove that Del was as good as anyone else, despite what some boring blighters might say to the contrary. Naturally, I was with her all the way. She even found a suit for me to wear in the wardrobe of her current boy friend, busy elsewhere fighting the war. It was rather grand for my fourteen-year-old frame. A purplish-blue business job, double-breasted with sleeves down to my fingers. I looked like a kid going to a fancy dress party as Edward G. Robinson.

'I'm looking for Mr George Gates,' I told the man in navy blue uniform with gold buttons in the front hall of Reuters.

'Not here, sonny,' he said. 'He's the Timekeeper.'

'I'm supposed to be learning to be a reporter,' I told him importantly.

'No,' he said kindly. 'That's not George. You best have a word with him. Outside' – he pointed to the door – 'first left, first door on left.'

By now, my confidence was fast disappearing. Winnie had said I was going to be a reporter. Something was dreadfully wrong. Outside, I almost scuttled across the road to catch a Number 6 going the opposite way. The hell with it, perhaps the commissionaire had not understood. I went up the side street, found the agency's back door and was directed to the office of Mr Gates.

'Jameson, that's right. Start today. Eight-till-five, hour for dinner, 27/6d (£1.37½p) a week, get your pay from me Friday afternoons.'

Dark, stocky George Gates rattled it out the minute I gave my name. He stood by his time-stamping machine at a wooden bench in a big, bare office. Other benches lined the walls at which two or three elderly men were putting parcels into large leather satchels. These they passed to a dozen or so lads of my age laughing and talking to each other as they stood around waiting.

I feared the worst. Obviously this was the servants' quarters and these were delivery boys about to make their rounds. It seemed an unlikely way to become a reporter. Perhaps you have to start at the bottom. At least it was Fleet Street. My head was in a whirl.

'Right, let's get you started,' George cut in on my thoughts. 'We'll find you a satchel. D'you know St James' Park? London Transport, Passport Office, the embassies.'

'Yeah, I know that,' I lied. It was all Dutch to me, but it didn't seem right for an aspiring reporter to admit he did not know his way around the big city.

'A bob that, there and back,' George said, shoving a shilling in my hand. 'Hour and a half, you've got.'

So began the first day of a career that was to span four decades. An outdoor messenger in the Dispatch Department of Reuters. Out in the street, one of the boys marked my card. St James's Park was the area between Victoria and Westminster, home of London Transport headquarters and the other places George had mentioned. Go round the corner to Blackfriars station, get the District or Inner Circle line going west.

'Good bloke, George, 'e's given yer the best start, see,' he explained. 'Do it in an hour, easy, and you'll make fourpence on the fare.'

I soon learned the ropes. Those first months as a messenger taught me how to find my way around London, most useful in later years. I was just one more recruit in an army of messengers employed by Reuters in wartime days. The agency was the major clearing house for world news. A shortage of mechanics and spare parts limited the teleprinter machines that poured out war reports to newspapers, radio stations and Whitehall offices. The rest received the news by way of a duplicated hand service. We messengers delivered it to foreign embassies, lesser government departments, journals and magazines, commercial offices and any other subscribers not rated important enough to have a teleprinter spewing out tapes in their offices twenty four hours a day.

It was strictly a dead-end job. Most lads did two or three years, then were off into the Forces. We were so low in the pecking order that entry to the main building was forbidden. We were confined to the dispatch department and an adjoining alley behind Fleet Street. It seemed a desperately long way to the top. Winnie had slipped up somewhere.

Though I didn't know it at the time, my benefactor was a dashing Jewish bookmaker named George Pearson, one of Winnie's wide circle of male acquaintances. George was to die horribly a few months later. He climbed on the roof of his house in a storm to fix tarpaulin over a gaping hole left by one of Hitler's bombs. A gust of wind caught him and he fell to his death in the concrete area below. George had a sister, Vicki, who was a secretary at Reuters. This was the lady who kindly got me the job. We never met, though she went on to become a senior executive on women's magazines. I wonder if she knows it was her good deed in 1944 that gave me a start in Fleet Street?

Like all boys of my age, my main preoccupation outside work was to keep up with the progress of the war. We devoured the papers and glued our ears to the radio following the decisive battles then raging, moving the marker pins on our wall maps spelling out the splendid news that Nazi Germany was being squeezed to death. The First U.S. Army and Second British Army landed in Normandy on D-Day, June 6, almost to the hour that Allied troops took Rome on their push north in Italy. In the east, Red Army troops had made spectacular gains and were knocking on the doors of Warsaw on their triumphant way to Berlin. All the same, Hitler was not finished yet. He ordered every German soldier to die where he stood rather than give ground. One week after D-Day, he launched a secret weapon that once again placed bomb-scarred London right in the frontline: the pilotless flying bomb.

In their usual fashion, the bureaucrats at home promptly bungled the situation by trying on one of the biggest cover-ups of the war. For days news of this fearsome weapon was kept from the public, but we boys out and about on the streets soon realised something desperate was going on. The first flying bomb actually fell on the night of June 13 in the Roman Road area of Bow, in the East End, where one of our fellow messengers lived. Six people were killed.

'It's a Jerry secret weapon,' we would tell people knowingly. 'Nuffink to worry about.'

There had been no heavy air raids on London since 1941 and now bombs were going off all over the London area day and night without any warning from air raid sirens. Within days, they were coming by the hundred, bringing heavy casualties and massive damage. Winston Churchill reckoned we Londoners were proud to share the same perils as men at the front.

Naturally, we boys found this late flurry of German activity highly exciting. We would stand on walls watching the black devils arrive. First a tiny dot in the sky, swiftly getting bigger as they reached the London area at a speed of 400 miles an hour. So long as we could hear the angry roar of their jet engines all was well. The second the engine cut we would drop like a stone to the ground, awating the dreadful thud telling us the ton of explosives had gone off.

Hitler called his new horror toy the V1. Cockney-style, we soon found better names for it: Doodle-bug or buzz bomb. By the time the British and Canadian armies overran their launch sites in September, some 8,000 of them had been launched against the London area, killing more than 6,000 people and seriously injuring another 18,000.

There was worse to come. Within days of the last doodle-bug falling, a far more stealthy and frightening killer joined the Battle of London: the V2 rocket. This time there was no flame to be seen belching from its rear, no strident buzz, no sound at all. All twelve tons of it silently sliced through the sky at 4,000 miles an hour, exploding a one-ton warhead on target three minutes after launch from rocket sites in The Hague.

Information about this extraordinary example of German scientific skill, prototype of the rockets later to conquer Outer Space, was kept from the British public for two months, despite the fact the damned things were going off all over the place. Far more deadly than the buzz bomb, they were to kill 2,700 people and seriously injure 6,500 others before our troops reached their bases. About 1,300 were aimed at London, though many fell short.

Once again, we lads on the streets quickly realised the Germans had another secret weapon, far worse than anything known previously. All through that winter of 1944–45 we had stories to tell of walking along streets when suddenly there would be a deafening bang and a pall of smoke rising skyward. The closer you happened to be to the explosion, the greater the fear that next time it could have your number on it.

My worst moment came delivering messages in the lobby of Australia House, in the Strand in Central London. Six or seven of us behind its solid thick walls were bowled over like ninepins as a rocket went off with a roar 300 yards away at the junction of the Aldwych and Kingsway. I got under a table and stayed there, scared out of my wits, until the building stopped shaking and the dust settled.

By the time I got into the street the emergency services had cordoned off the area. I ducked under the tape and ran like the wind back to the office in nearby Fleet Street, not daring to glance back at the carnage behind. The rocket had landed outside a crowded post office on a busy Friday lunchtime. Nearly 200 were said to have perished, but these German hits were never officially reported in case morale was affected.

Bureaucrats always favour keeping people in the dark, producing the opposite result to that intended. Wild rumours and baseless speculation are far more dangerous than the truth. That particular rocket fell within fifty yards of the Air Ministry, then based at the bottom of Kingsway, which encouraged spurious stories that the Germans were able to land rockets on specified targets with pinpoint accuracy. There was talk of a million women and children having to be evacuated from London. Some families left the capital in a second mini-evacuation. Most stayed behind, preferring to call Hitler's bluff. We knew our lads would get to his V1 and V2 sites before he could break us.

All the same, Hitler's threat to life and limb were as much an incentive for getting an inside job as my dreams of becoming a journalist. I found the key to the door by becoming super efficient. The time allowed for our rounds was always generous, not least because we were likely to run into diversions and other problems arising from the bomb debris that littered almost every street in the inner city. By rushing everywhere, jumping on and off buses, taking short cuts and avoiding the temptation of milk bars and tea shops, I was able to deliver my messages and get back to base in half the allotted time. That meant I was always first in line when there was extra work to be done. The price of this highly commendable service was that Chief Gates, one of the most friendly of men, should tacitly support my efforts to win promotion. The day soon arrived when he asked me to stay on after work for a chat.

'I've had hundreds of lads pass through here,' George said. 'You're the best of the lot. You can stay here, join the staff, be an overseer in no time at all. More money, steady job. Or you can go upstairs and take your chances.'

My good friend George wasn't too keen on 'upstairs.' That was where the journalists and office workers hung out, some of whom took delight in treating messengers like dirt. One of his jobs was taking round the newspapers so he had plenty of experience of toffee-nosed twerps in white collars and ties. He obviously wanted me to stay here in dispatch, join the 'staff,' which meant becoming a recognised employee, and go on to greater things below stairs.

'Sorry, Chief,' I said. 'I've got to get into the editorial. It's what I've always wanted.'

'Okay, son, thought you'd say that. Nine o'clock Monday. Fourth floor. You're going up in the world. Let's hope it lasts.'

Life had changed greatly when I got back to Mount Pleasant Lane. For starters it was now number 51, not 53. Ma Wren, my mother, Winnie and the rest had been bombed out three times, which explained in part why I was so often kept in the dark in Bishop's Stortford. Nobody had got hurt in the Blitz, though the damage was sufficient to move house and receive war compensation. After being shunted around various temporary homes, they had somehow managed to get the house next door to where we grew up.

Lenny Frost was there, working for the local butcher shop before going into the Parachute Regiment. Eventually, he courted and wed a local girl, Margaret, and they have lived happily ever after with their son, Paul, in the new town of Harlow, not far from Bishop's Stortford. Len had been a late starter at reading and writing and I never liked to ask whether he had got the hang of it. Years later, when I moved from editorship of the *Express* to the *Daily Star*, he said: 'I prefer the *Daily Express*. It's a much better read.' I was delighted to learn that Margaret had taught him. They are among my favourite people.

The war had brought stability to the lives of the girls. Winnie had settled on a rascal named Roy Marchington, an Army deserter who was skulking in the scullery when I got back home. One day there was a knock on the door and I answered it to two military policemen in their red caps. They rushed past me into the house. No trace of Roy downstairs, so they raced to the upper floors. Roy was in the loo, reading the *Mirror*. He should have stayed there. Instead, he panicked and bolted down the garden in his shirtsleeves, across the railway line, through some allotments and over a fence to the adjoining road, straight into the arms of two more redcaps. They had worked out his escape route in advance. He got a heavy sentence, but was pardoned after the D-Day invasion on the promise that he would behave.

Roy later married Winnie and they emigrated with her daughter Pam to Australia. They were not happy there. Dying of cancer, she phoned me after a 40-year silence to say going to Oz was the worst thing she ever did. I don't think she would have settled anywhere, poor Winnie. She was the most frightening woman I ever met, though at times so warm and generous you could have died for her. Such was her guilt that she would pray aloud during air raids.

'Oh, God, please God, spare me, don't let me die,' she would rave. 'I promise to be good, promise, promise . . . I'll never do wrong again, I swear it.'

When the buzz bombs were roaring over the Hackney marshes, she would coax me into the cupboard under the stairs where she slept and wrap herself around me, shaking with fear. This was most disturbing for a 14-year-old, specially as she wore only cami-knickers and reeked of Californian Poppy. It was just as well Roy had gone back to serve king and country.

My mother, Elsie, was still working and cleaning and shopping, keeping the household together as Ma Wren grew older and more infirm. Sister Jean, honey blonde and sweet with it, was now eight and growing up into a beautiful young lady. At war's end, the right man came along for Elsie in the shape of sturdy Bill Barrett, an infantryman returning home after serving in the frontline virtually non-stop for five years. They married, had a daughter, Marilyn, and settled down in Hackney. Bill went out on the night shift for the next forty years in the publishing hall of the *Daily Mirror*.

Peggy Crotty, who now called herself Pat, had married a quiet, handsome Armoured Corps soldier named Len. Returning to his unit from their weekend honeymoon, he fell off his tank under the tracks of the vehicle behind and was killed instantly. She was a widow at twenty. At the end of the war she married a riproaring Cockney sailor named Stan Kemp and they brought up three children in a Council flat behind Shoreditch church. In his day, I reckoned Stan to be the best spoons player in the East End and persuaded the late Russell Harty to invite him on television. Sadly, Stan's heart was not in it – they had just heard Peggy was dying of cancer. She passed over a few years ago. 'The bravest woman we ever nursed,' said one of the nuns at St Joseph's Hospice. That was my Peggy, all right.

She died on a Monday. I was off duty that day, being editor of a Sunday paper, the *News of the World*. At about 2 o'clock in the afternoon my body was suddenly wracked by terrible pains. I lay on the bed writhing in agony for something like two hours. Then the pain totally disappeared. It had lifted, as if by magic. The phone rang at 5.30 and I said to Ellen, my lady: 'That'll be about Peggy. She's died.' It was her son to say she had succumbed that after-noon. I had known for weeks she was gravely ill, but had no idea she was that close to death.

It was cancer that claimed Ma Wren, too, just months after my return. She was a great character right to the end. One of her last acts was to start smoking. 'I've seen you silly buggers spend enough money on them,' she said, 'I might as well have a go myself.'

She wasn't too keen on the idea of Reuters. Ma thought *news agency* was the same as *newsagents*. What upset her was that she had bullied the manager of the local Co-op into giving me a job as an errand boy. 'You want a decent job with a chance of making something of yourself,' she told me. 'If you don't like the Co-op, what's wrong with the Post Office? You don't want all that travel-ling.'

Ma lived to be seventy seven. She suffered dreadfully in the last days until Winnie persuaded a doctor to give her something that put her into a final, peaceful sleep. I crept down in the night and wept over her body, lying there in an open coffin. Winnie heard the muffled noise coming from the front room and nearly had a heart attack.

We gave Ma a good funeral, her beloved Co-op's best. It was only proper because many times she had fed us with the 'divi' – the rebate on purchases given by the Co-op every quarter. Within minutes of returning home from the cemetery, they were all going hammer and tongs again. Ma's posh son Harold, the one who visited at Christmas time, was trying to slope off with the grandfather clock his father had made. He and Winnie played tug of war with it on the front steps.

'You bloody swine,' I screamed at them, tears of anger running down my face. 'Ma's not cold in her coffin yet.'

It was only left to do something about Sid, whom she had kept beside her through thick and thin all those years. He had become increasingly difficult as Ma got older, acquiring a paranoid obsession from somewhere that he was being done out of money left to him by old Aunt Ada, the piano teacher. Dick the milkman, who had kept him in pocket money for years for collecting empties, ran out of patience when Sid hit him over the head with a bottle, demanding his mysterious bequest. He wouldn't have anything to do with him after that. Still worse, Sid used to earn a few coppers pumping the bellows for the organ at the local Congregational church. One Sunday evening in the middle of evensong, he emerged from behind the organ loft, marched up to the minister and shook him vigorously demanding payment.

The day came when we told him he was going on holiday. Sid knew differently as they took him off to the mental hospital at Colney Hatch, site of the notorious Victorian lunatic asylum. Tears ran down his cheeks and he sobbed silently as he left us for the last time, carrying his bits and pieces in a cardboard suitcase. 'Thank God Ma is not here to see it,' I told myself.

CHAPTER TEN

How's your spelling, laddie?

Colney Hatch would be an apt description of the big, bustling Reuter editorial office that was to be my place of work for the next fifteen years. In the closing stages of the war it had a direct line to every major city of the world via its own correspondents or domestic news agencies abroad. On top of massive coverage of the Allied war effort, it was the prime source of information about what was going on inside the territories occupied by Hitler. Foreign bureaux included neutral listening posts like Stockholm, Lisbon and Madrid. Reuters also monitored every Nazi broadcast through its own radio station at Hadley Wood in Hertfordshire.

Every hour of the day, thousands of words poured into headquarters at 85, Fleet Street by cable, radio, telephone and teleprinter. Editors known as copytasters rapidly assessed the news value of the incoming file. Red-hot news of major significance would be dictated directly to a teleprinter operator and within minutes transmitted to every newspaper and radio station of any importance across the globe.

Lesser news would be passed to sub-editors for processing and fed into the teleprinter network, which included desks embracing different areas. The General Desk laid down the basic world service for British newspapers and the BBC. Regional desks received this file plus additional copy of particular interest to their region. Attached to these desks were various subsidiary units like the London staff of Commonwealth news agencies and Forcereuter for British Service newspapers.

Reuters is to news what Lloyds of London is to insurance. Old established, highly respectable and very British. It was, in fact, founded by a German bank clerk. Paul Julius Reuter, a Jewish convert to Christianity and contemporary of Karl Marx, came to London in 1851 to establish a commercial news service which relied upon a wondrous new invention called wireless telegraphy. By 1925, his brainchild was under control of the Press Association, Britain's foremost domestic news agency, and these kissin' cousins shared Lutyens' impressive building in Fleet Street. The PA sold Reuters to British newspapers as a non-profit-making cooperative in 1941. In later years some major Commonwealth news organisations were invited to join the board.

The agency ultimately became the treasure trove at the end of the Fleet Street rainbow. In my day, it was strictly the poor relation, forever going cap-in-hand to the owners seeking an increase in the fee paid by subscribers, depending on their size and circulation. All it had going for itself was an immaculate reputation as the purveyor of pure journalism. Reuters' trade mark was fast, accurate and impartial news. It had to be. The clients embraced every shade of political, religious and social thought on earth.

On my very first shift on the inside, I found myself alone and totally in charge of the editorial – the air raid siren had sounded and everyone evacuated to the basement. Normally nobody bothered, but the new V2 rockets put the wind up everyone. One had gone off nearby and they were reputed to fall in clusters. Being the new boy, I was told to stay upstairs and keep my ears open.

George Bowler, a little man with a big reputation as a trainer of amateur boxers, ruled over some fifteen editorial messengers. Our duties were simple and boring. We were there as dogsbodies to look after the needs of the journalists, particularly their unquenchable thirst for tea. My first job was 'blueing up.' That meant interleaving double-sided carbons into sandwiches of flimsy typing paper so sub-editors could produce six or eight copies of a story simultaneously for internal distribution. Eight hours of that left you covered in a sticky black film. Another dreary job was tearing the tapes – ripping copy off the teleprinters and placing it in wire baskets for the attention of editors. Then we had to race round the editorial delivering copy to the different desks as well as running errands for anyone who ranked higher than a messenger.

The whole place buzzed with frantic activity. Up to two hundred deeply involved people on a floor the size of a football pitch. Bells ringing to signal important bulletins, editors alerting desks to major newsbreaks, telephones ringing, lights flashing, typewriters clattering, teleprinters clicking away, carrying the story of the war to every corner of the earth. All this in an atmosphere of intense competition. Reuters felt honour-bound to get the news out before its two American agency rivals, Associated Press (AP) and United Press (UP). One of our jobs was to ferret around in friendly offices that took these wire services and check the comparative times of major stories.

A cheer would go up as the senior desk editor excitedly gave his subs such stirring news as: 'Reuter two minutes ahead of AP and four minutes on UP with Churchill's arrival in Paris.'

It was not merely a question of being first. There is a tradition in newspapers that the story published should come from the agency that delivered it ahead of the others. The Americans are more punctilious in this respect than the British. Some of our papers credit 'Reuter' or 'AP' at the end of a report, but most of them ignore it completely. These attributions were more common in wartime days because readers wanted to know the source of the news they were reading.

By now, I was getting to know journalists, those easygoing characters whose way of life enthralled us so much. We messengers most admired the war correspondents, who would sit around the office, feet up and drinking interminable cups of tea, in between hair-raising assignments to the war fronts. At Reuters they came from a dozen different countries, though there were not many British among them. Reporters over here did not qualify for exemption from the forces.

My favourite was Jack Smyth, a softly-spoken Dubliner whose red hair and wild ways made him a great favourite with the ladies. He was captured by the Germans after dropping at Arnhem with the 1st British Airborne Division in its disastrous bid to secure a bridgehead across the Rhine.

'Jaysus, they sure gave me a hard time,' he told me once. 'There was I, in a British Army officer's uniform, telling 'em I was a neutral Irishman and demanding to see the nearest Irish ambassador.

'Well, they were having none of that. "How many parachute troops under training in Britain?" That's all they were interested in. How the hell was I to know, me an Irishman?

'"Half a million," I'd say. 'Twas the wrong answer, of course. They gave me a hell of a pasting. Then I'd be dragged in again. "How many parachute troops under training in Britain?"'

' "Twenty thousand." '

'Wallop! That was me for it again. Apparently 20,000 was even more ridiculous than half a million.

' "Jaysus," I'd tell 'em, "if I knew the answer, wouldn't I be telling? It's not worth losing my teeth for! I'm an Irishman." '

Of course, he would never have told them. Not lovely Jack. He volunteered for the Pacific war immediately he came home from a German prison camp, gaunt and pale, and got a world scoop with the suicide of the Japanese warlord, General Tojo. He did it typical Jack style – by wooing Tojo's former secretary.

Back in Britain, he taught me much about my chosen profession – Jack was one of the greatest reporters of all time – and I mourned with many others in Fleet Street a few years later when he and his wife were drowned. Their car ran into the Liffey on a stormy night in Dublin. By then he was head of the national Irish News Agency.

People like Jack filled us with delight, taking the drudgery out of 'blueing up' and running errands. We had our diversions. One of my tricks was to get a bob's worth of tea in a big enamel jug in the canteen, top it up with hot water in the Gents, then sell it for twopence a cup. I could make a bob in minutes that way, enough for tea and toast and the bus ride home.

When things were quiet we would spend hours playing tu'penny ha'penny football on the desk tops. Four pins made two pairs of goalposts, two old pennies and a halfpenny the players and ball. The idea was to strike the penny with the base of a comb so that it hit the halfpenny, which was then supposed to ricochet into the goal. The champion was Pete Mancini, whose family owned Mick's, Fleet Street's famous all-night café. It is still there. Another caper was to aggravate drivers of huge lorries constantly arriving at local offices with newsprint supplies. As soon as the driver started up, we would crouch and run like the clappers behind the front wheels, emerging triumphant before the back four hit us. Anyone refusing the challenge would be labelled chicken and banished from civilised pursuits like tu'penny ha'penny football.

One day as we sat there enveloped in carbons, the ancient bellboard above the desk rang imperiously, rattling the replica bell in the porthole labelled *Editor*. The usual groan went up. Nobody ever wanted to run errands for

THE top man of them all. Walton A. Cole, a huge Scotsman, put the wind up us kids. His commands were always short, sharp and difficult. 'I'll go,' I said. Anything to get away from those bloody carbons.

'Twenty cigarettes, laddie,' he said in his usual peremptory fashion, planting two half-crowns (25p) in front of me. Sounds easy, doesn't it? Hell, it was the worst errand of all. Cigarettes were like gold dust in those closing days of the war. You could tramp the streets for an hour looking for a telltale queue that meant the tobacconist had some to sell. Then you had to stand in line for anything up to twenty minutes. When the magic moment arrived and you got to the counter, the odds were that all the decent fags would be gone. Count yourself lucky to find ten Black Cat or something perfumed of rare origin.

This time, I was lucky. Those oval things, Passing Cloud, Mr Cole was very partial to those. Might give me the change. I plonked them down on his big desk at the far end of the editorial, taking my time finding the loose coins in my pocket. He waved them away. Then he actually spoke. Most unusual.

'Why is it, every time I ring the bell, you appear, laddie?' he barked in that short, clipped Falkirk accent. How dare he! I didn't hesitate for a second.

'Because every time you ring the bell, the other lads say: "Let the old bastard wait – he only wants cigarettes"!'

He guffawed at the thought and looked at me warmly. 'How would you like to work for me?' he asked. 'All the time. Have a desk up here.'

'I'd love to,' I said. I had expected to be fired.

My long journey through the night was over.

Being discovered by Tony Cole was the best thing that happened to me. He was an extraordinary man, the genius who steered Reuters into the postwar era and laid the foundations for its spectacular success. He tirelessly travelled the world, masterminding reciprocal news and information services and developing Reuters as the foremost wire service.

In the closing stages of the war, he was very much the brooding giant presiding over the feverish activity going on around him in the London editorial. He would sit for twelve hours at a time behind his desk, looking the double of the late King Farouk of Egypt, soothing and coaxing one minute, spitting and snarling the next.

97

He never had much to say to me, but there were times late at night when I would find him sitting there, a solitary figure with just one desk light picking him out in the gloom at the administration end of the big newsroom. I would ask him if he wanted anything and we would exchange a little small talk.

'How's your spelling, laddie?' he wanted to know at one time. 'Get yourself to night school. Learn everything you can. English, history, shorthand, typing . . . the lot. Without those, you'll have no chance.'

I took him at his word, telling him proudly that I had enrolled at night school as he had recommended. That was good enough for him. From that day forward he took great interest in filling the gaps in my education, asking questions and throwing words at me. I remember the first.

'How d'you spell epitomy, laddie?'

'Spell it? I've never heard of it!'

'Look it up, look it up. That's what dictionaries are for.'

Joyce Hewlett, his devoted secretary, joined the campaign. Her dictionary was on permanent loan to me and she got hold of a typewriter so that I could practice at my desk. I was even allowed to type letters for two of the executive assistants, John Lucas and Hilary Green.

It was during one of our late night chats that I told Tony Cole the time had come for me to leave Reuters. I was desperate to become a junior reporter, to learn the business in the traditional way on a local or provincial paper. I could not spend the rest of my life making tea and running errands – or even becoming a typist.

'Aren't you giving money at home?' he wanted to know.

Yes, I was, but I would have to manage somehow. Perhaps get a second job in the evenings.

'Rubbish,' he said. 'A good journalist means working twenty four hours a day if necessary. And you can't afford to go out into the provinces and send money to your mother.'

He thought hard, staring at me through his spectacles, weighing me up. 'Tell you what,' he said. 'We'll train you here. There's no reason why not. You won't earn much, but you'll learn to be a journalist in the best school of all.'

Those angels again. They must have been beside me as I walked on air along the most exciting street in the world. At sixteen, I was to be a Fleet Street reporter.

Oddly enough, the other lads thought I had taken leave of my senses. I had been due to go up to 45/- (£2.25) a week as an editorial assistant, as messengers were called when confirmed in office. My wages as an apprentice reporter would be 37/6d. (£1.87). Nor did they rate my attachment to the academic life. They were out most nights chasing the girls and pursuing the new jitter-bug craze. Much as I secretly envied them, my determination to make a success of life was the stronger pull.

For some reason, the one man I had expected to support me totally was very sniffy about the Editor's decision to turn me into a reporter. Sidney J. Mason was the chief news editor, in charge of all correspondents, including those in the London bureau. They worked for the UK Desk, which covered British news for the rest of the world. This is where I was to be trained.

Sid, as everyone called him, always wore braces and a thick leather belt as a kind of badge to let everyone know that he had once worked on the London docks. A short, grizzled man, he was rough, tough and straight to the point. 'I'm not going to make it easy for you, son,' he said. 'This is a hard business and there's no place in it for people who can't deliver the goods. If you're not up to it, you're out.' True to his word, he never once did anything to smooth my path.

I went and took my place diffidently at the end of the reporters' desk, trying to appear purposeful while the chief reporter, Ronald G. Bedford, was busy working out the day's news schedule and sending reporters on assignments. He had promised to get to me as soon as possible.

Sitting there looking important was my undoing. I caught the eye of Muriel Penn, an evil-looking spinster whose bane in life was young lads like myself. Her job was airmailing so-called Situationers of background news to clients around the world. She had been there for years. We reckoned she must have been Baron Reuter's girl friend.

'Get me some tea, Jameson,' she rasped, reaching in her handbag for money.

'Sorry, Miss Penn, I'm er, er a reporter now and don't get tea any more.' I stood in front of her, blushing scarlet and covered in confusion.

'You'll do as you're told, young man, and now,' she shot back.

'Come here, son!' Thank goodness. Sid Mason, spotting this little scene, had intervened. I went over, telling him in an outraged whisper: 'She's asking me to get her tea. Bloody cheek!'

He gave me a hard look. 'You heard her,' he said. 'Do as you're told. And that goes for today, tomorrow and always. Then argue about it afterwards. Go and get that fuckin' tea!'

I took her money without a word, went up to the eighth floor canteen and fetched back the mug of tea, bristling with resentment and humiliation, tears in my eyes. I went back to my chair wondering what next. Perhaps my career was over before it had even started. 'Over here, Jamie,' said Ronnie Bedford, patting the seat beside him.

'It's all right,' he said reassuringly. 'I had a word with Sid. It won't happen again. You know Ma Penn. She's just trying it on.'

I felt better already. He started my lessons there and then.

'The first thing to get in your head,' he said, 'is that a reporter has to keep his eyes and ears open all the time. Miss nothing. You've got to adapt yourself to every situation as it comes along, be prepared to do anything, go anywhere, talk to anyone. Your feelings don't come into it.

'If you've been up all night, haven't eaten and are soaked to the skin, never mind. You can worry about that some other time. The only thing that matters is getting the story – if there is a story to be got. Often it doesn't exist, but you don't give up on it until you're one hundred per cent certain. Otherwise, some other bastard will get it and you'll have the pleasure of reading it in a rival paper.'

A great talker is Ronnie. The kind of man you could listen to forever. Quite extraordinary, really, because he was born with handicaps that would have destroyed most of us. He is undersized, has only partial vision and a speech impediment brings a husky lisp to his Yorkshire burr. Yet Ronnie was delivering the *Barnsley Chronicle* on a pushbike at 14 and here he was, ten years later, chief reporter of Reuters' London bureau. True Yorkshire grit. Ronnie is one of Fleet Street's great professionals, loved by everyone. He went on to become science editor of the *Daily Mirror*, a job he held for thirty years until his retirement.

That first day he asked me whether there was a story I wanted to write. 'Don't tell me now, think about it. When you're sure, come and talk. It's got to be a story here in London that is going to interest people overseas. We'll see. Just now, read the papers. Every paper, every day, right through. A journalist has to know what's going on in the world. That's his job.'

A reporter never forgets his first story, any more than a musician his first gig or a surgeon his first operation. The one I came up with concerned a fifty-yard strip of sand that had been dumped to create a rather forlorn beach on the north side of Tower Bridge. Someone told me the Port of London Authority planned to remove the sand as it interfered with shipping. Ronnie looked dubious.

'The thing is, Ronnie,' I told him. 'This is the only beach the poor kids of the East End know. Apart from a coach trip to the mudflats outside Southend, I never saw the sea until I was fifteen. To kids like me, this beach *is* the seaside.'

He brightened at that news. 'Great,' said Ronnie. 'A real human story. Slum kids deprived of their playground by the bureaucrats. Write it like that, the way you told it to me. Only get in all sides of the question. Perhaps it is a danger to shipping.'

'Can't be, can it?' I said. 'Been there for years.'

'Okay, prove it. Talk to the experts. It's a good story. Don't spoil it. Take your time.'

I think Ronnie made me write and rewrite that story fourteen times. 'No, nothing like that,' he says nowadays, 'more like thirteen times.' In that one tale were all the essential elements of sound reportage. It had to be handled in true Reuter fashion. That is copybook style, the way reports should appear in all newspapers.

In these days of fierce competition, reporters sometimes are encouraged to 'help' the story along a little, twisting facts to make them fit a preconceived and preferably sensational pattern. They find gimmicks to 'liven up' the copy and it's just too bad if the angle they are chasing is out of context with the basic facts.

I am frequently clobbered for the misdemeanours of others because of my tabloid affiliations. Few people realise that I cut my journalistic teeth in the purest school of journalism, where nonsense of that kind is regarded as heresy. There is nothing wrong with bright, lively, even sensational journalism. However, it should always be fair, accurate and objective.

My Tower Bridge beach story was contentious, so it had to be balanced, representing the views of the authorities as well as the children. What was expert opinion on the supposed threat to navigation? What did the local council say? Have we talked to any of the children and how much does it matter to them? Get the thoughts of local youth leaders. Describe the scene in a way that will hold the attention of readers in Timbuctoo. Probably they have never heard of the Tower or the Thames.

Back and back again I went to show Ronnie my words picked out with two fingers on the typewriter. All the time strengthening the story, filling in missing details here, finding some better quotes there.

'Always remember this, Jamie,' he told me. 'Every story must have a time, a place and a reason. You, the reporter, have to answer five questions in the reader's mind: *Who, what, when, where* and *why?*'

Ronnie taught me everything I know about journalism, much of it in the tortuous progress of that first story. It took about a week to produce. 'Fine, fine,' he finally pronounced. 'Put it on the wire.' It was actually published and months later I got a cutting back. From a paper in Java. As for the beach, it was closed down and the sand dredged away, never to be heard of again.

My transition to the professional classes came shortly after the greatest explosion of joy ever witnessed in the annals of mankind. VE Day on May 9, 1945, marking the end of the war in Europe, will never be forgotten by those who took part in it. Though there was still unfinished business with Japan, nothing could hold back the tide of emotion greeting the news that Hitler's Third Reich had been crushed.

Appropriately, London was centre of the world stage that day. Britain had been in the thick of the fight from the start, standing alone after the fall of Europe, and the capital had borne the brunt of the Luftwaffe's attempts to destroy us from the air. Now the civilians who stood up to the dangers at home joined the men and women in uniform on the streets for the biggest party of all time.

We youngsters from Reuters worked in relays, putting in a few hours at the office and then rushing out to joint the millions thronging the centre of London. With our knowledge of the back streets, we were able to establish a base at the corner of St James' Park overlooking Buckingham Palace. There we could watch the whole world pass by and catch a glimpse of King George VI, Queen Elizabeth and the two princesses coming on the balcony every few hours to wave to the delirious crowds below.

If anything, it was a mass love-in. Strangers clutched at each other, kissing and giggling, exchanging swigs of brown and pale ale and the occasional whisky. Anyone in uniform was greeted as a returning hero and carried shoulder high by crowds laughing, crying, singing and screaming as they roamed the streets seeking fresh excitement.

I was covered in lipstick. Like other randy teenagers on the loose in that mob, it was a real bonus to be able to grope and passionately kiss pretty young girls without fear of a slap around the face. We would stagger back to our headquarters beneath a tree at intervals with more and more adolescent fantasies to recount. Most were tales of being raped by drunken nymphomaniacs.

All the same, I felt an imposter, as out of place as a pickpocket at a Sunday school outing. We were the war's lost generation. Too young to fight and fornicate, but old enough to know what was going on. Yet we became the main beneficiaries, staking out the best jobs while our elders were away doing their duty. I have often pondered the thought that, but for the war, I would never have been given my chance as a trainee reporter. So it was with some relief that we finished up in the early hours in the Reuters canteen, singing our heads off as Ronnie played jazz and wartime favourites on the piano. One of his many accomplishments is that he is a brilliant pianist.

My delight at making it as a trainee reporter made me a good scholar. I soon became part of the news desk team. There were about a dozen reporters covering Britain for the foreign press to supplement the basic news file provided by Reuters' sister agency, the Press Association. This meant much of the time we specialised, reporting stories that the PA did not handle in depth if at all.

I remember my first major assignment was to join the team covering the talks that led to independence for India. Moslem and Hindu leaders were at each other's throats and had come to London separately to argue their case with the Attlee Government. Gandhi's man, Jawaharlal Nehru, wanted a single self-governing dominion of India. His opponent, Mohammed Ali Jinnah, demanded Partition and a separate state for his Moslems. In the end, he won and became first President of Pakistan. Millions were slaughtered in the racial conflict surrounding this issue.

Naturally, every word, every move at the London conference leading to Partition was followed with fanatical interest back in the sub-continent. I was on the squad delegated to shadow Jinnah and let the world know every sigh he uttered. I still shudder at the memory of trying to match my puny 100 wpm. Gregg shorthand to his supercharged oratory. He would rattle away nineteen-to-the-dozen and, unfortunately, rarely finished a sentence. 'We demand the right of free ... and I will tell you why are we here today in London?' he would say.

Hours later, I would be sweating blood transcribing my notes in a telephone box while a copytaker at the other end kept asking awkward questions like: 'A "free" what, old boy? Why is he in London? You've left something out!' I was terrified that one word in the wrong place might cause a bloodbath back in India. Fortunately, the leader of our team was Monty Taylor, an urbane Englishman who had been everywhere, seen everything. 'Get the context, dear boy,' he would drawl. 'Long as it sounds right, they'll never know the difference. Let's go and have a G&T.'

The news desk was full of characters like Monty. They were a cosmopolitan bunch in keeping with Reuters' global traditions and included former war correspondents like Jack Smyth, adjusting to the slower pace of peace in austerity Britain. We also had a handful of displaced persons, Reuters men expelled for supposed offences against the regime in the countries they were reporting. Foremost among this group was a Yugoslav war hero named Monty Radulovic, six foot tall and good looking with it. With his black eyes and olive skin, he looked a darker version of that other hero from the Yugoslav mountains, Josef Tito.

The trouble was that Monty and Yugoslavia's leader did not see eye to eye. One mention of Tito's name and he would spit on the floor, though we taught him it was best in Britain to *look* as if he were spitting rather than actually doing it. Monty was as Royalist as Tito was Communist. He escaped from the Germans occupying his country and stole a submarine in Trieste with some compatriots and sailed to Alexandria. None of them had been in a submarine before. Monty joined the British Army, had a heroic war record, and was among troops who linked up with Tito's forces on the liberation of his homeland. Translated into Reuters' correspondent in Belgrade, capital of the new People's Republic of Yugoslavia, it was not long before Monty and President

Tito fell out. He had to flee his country once again.

Tito, of course, was still best known in Britain as the great partisan leader of wartime days. Among his admirers was one Alfonso Mauri, a fiery Spanish Republican who had fled Franco's Fascist regime at home to settle in Argentina as Reuters correspondent in Buenos Aires. Sadly for Alfonso, General Peron did not like Republicans any more than Franco. Before long he, too, was expelled and now sat at a desk in London next to Monty Radulovic. It was like throwing a lighted match into an oil drum. They got along fine as reporters and even became good friends. But the rest of us would craftily manage to bring politics into the conversation. In seconds they would be going hammer and tongs, arms waving, abusing each other in their halting English.

'I tell you, Mauri, you Communist! Do not say "No!" Say "Yes, me Alfonso Mauri is Communist. I proud to be Communist." Then Monty spit on you, spit on Communists!' Towering over the short, curly-haired Spaniard, he would have difficulty remembering our strictures against spitting on the editorial floor.

'Monty, you very silly person,' Alfonso would say, raising his eyes heavenward. 'I think you nice man. In the head? Nussink! Like wood. I very sad for you.' He would stand there, quivering with anger, tapping his skull. The rest of us would be falling about.

Poor Ronnie Bedford had to play mother hen to this lot. Since Monty and Alfonso were still getting the hang of reporting in English, and my own command of the language had far to go, he had to play teacher as well as chief reporter. 'You've written this with the left boot,' he used to complain. But he didn't mind, really, and joined in the fun.

Once, he got the pair of them writing a story on Big Ben, which had come to an abrupt halt for some reason. Monty made the phone calls, Alfonso went to the library for the background. Their first version read something like this: *Big Ben, clock at famous House of Parliament of London, go tick tock for 123 years. Today she stop. Perhaps she getting old, say people.*

Ronnie would stoop over his typewriter, eyes inches from the keys, rattling away to knock our poor efforts into shape before they went on the wire. He told Monty and Alfonso that their Big Ben story had been published in the Cairo newspaper *Al Ahram*. The Yugoslav got hold of a copy from somewhere and kindly presented it to his partner. Alfonso carried it proudly in his wallet for weeks until he showed it to an Egyptian he met. The cutting turned out to be a list of entrants to Cairo University.

These were the happy days of my reporting apprenticeship. I could not have had a better guide. What Ronnie lacked physically, he more than made up in other ways. I have never met anyone so aware of what is going on around him. He sees, hears and knows all well before the people around him and makes light of his infirmities.

So curious is he about everything that he once took me to a Spiritualist church in north London to find out what they were all about. There was an ancient lady medium preaching, the words pouring from her in what was described as the voice of a Red Indian who lived two hundred years ago. At the end of this psychic demonstration she filled the church with flying doves. The congregation oohed and aahed in wonder. I couldn't see a thing. I nudged Ronnie. 'Damned if I can see anything,' I said. 'What about you? Can you see any doves?' He came up close to my ear. 'If you can't see anything, what bloody chance d'you think I've got?'

Nothing lasts long in our peripatetic profession. The sad day came in 1948 when Ronnie landed himself a plum job at the *Daily Mirror*, then the world's biggest selling tabloid newspaper, and we lost his marvellous company and professional wisdom. It was soon time for me to move on. Having done the requisite spell of reporting, I was transferred to the General Desk to learn the art of the sub-editor.

Sad to say, I was very much under a cloud at the time. Like many another adolescent hothead, I had blown all the chances people put my way. In time I would deeply regret turning my back on the goodwill and support given me by Tony Cole and others. There and then, I had no doubts at all about my new mission in life. I was now a Communist.

CHAPTER ELEVEN

The Red menace

With my background, it was inevitable that one day I should become a Communist. In 1946, my head was filled with the valiant wartime deeds of the Red Army and, like many another, I still had an affectionate regard for Uncle Joe Stalin. Here in Britain, Clement Attlee's postwar Labour government was tackling the ravages of war and there was a revolutionary spirit in the land.

I've always been for the underdog. 'Blessed are the meek, for they shall inherit the earth,' was the biblical exhortation that made most sense to me when I was forced to go to church and Sunday school as a kid. My heart goes out to people hurt by life, the poor and needy and those crippled in mind or body. The Russian revolutionary poet Mayakovsky said it all for me with these words:

Man's dearest possession is life, and since it is given to him to live but once, he must so live as to feel no torturing regrets for years without purpose; so live as not to be seared with the shame of a cowardly and trivial past, so live that dying he can say: 'All my life and all my strength were given to the finest cause in the world – the liberation of mankind'

Heady stuff guaranteed to turn a young idealist's head. A pity I didn't know at the time I got hooked that Mayakovsky committed suicide at 36, disillusioned with Stalinism.

In any case, such lofty sentiments were far from my mind as a 17-year-old. I was happy enough making my way as a trainee reporter, working on English, typewriting and shorthand at night classes and finding time every week to spend an evening in the Territorial drill hall as a volunteer with the Army

Cadet Corps. I thought the khaki uniform might wow the girls.

It was the thought of young ladies said to believe in free love rather than the dialectical theories of Karl Marx that took me to the Hackney headquarters of the Young Communist League (YCL) one rainy evening in 1946 when I had nothing better to do. The *YCLers*, as they called themselves, had been outside night school that week handing out leaflets inviting students to a social.

They welcomed me with open arms. Sad to say, it had nothing to do with sexual liberation. What made me special was that I was a very rare fish indeed in the Hackney YCL – the first among them who was not Jewish. Although Communists were supposed to have pulled the chain on religion, denouncing God and all his works as the opium of the people, the fact was that just about every Communist in London's East End was Jewish. Many belonged to orthodox families who did not mix with gentiles. Even the hall where we met belonged to the local synagogue. To find a *goy* coming through the door was quite a sensation.

In time, I was to learn that their Jewish religion was stronger than their Marxist faith. Most had been drawn to Communism out of fear and hatred of Fascism and anti-Semitism, which had always existed in the East End. It also gave them a link with Russia, land of their forebears. They still observed Jewish holidays and dietary laws, worked in shops, factories and offices run by their own kind and married only within the religion. The subsequent oppression of Jewish dissidents in Russia must have shocked them deeply.

I found myself enrolled not in some clandestine group about to start the revolution, but rather as the maverick member of a narrow, cloistered and middle class community. What mattered most was not the overthrow of capitalism, their own bread and butter. It was making a good marriage.

There was a girl named Thelma, whose father was in the stationery business. She was Myrna Loy to me and I chatted her up like crazy. One night two of the comrades took me to one side and pointed out gravely that my designs on this young lady could only bring grief to her family. They expected her to marry a nice Jewish boy.

On another occasion, a friend named Walter Grunfeld invited me to his home for tea. We were chatting in his living room when the door opened slowly and a tray was pushed into the room on the floor. A meal was laid out, chicken liver, *gefulte* fish, *chrane*, the lot. There was no sign of the person behind this Jewish feast. I asked what was going on. 'My family welcome you to our house,' Walter said. 'They cannot greet you as they consider you unclean.' Non-kosher, that is, not dirty!

So, Hackney's Communists, supposed to be the most militant and active in the country, were in reality little more than a Jewish social club. But they had to go through the motions, which meant their revolutionary activities bordered on black comedy. One of the first campaigns I became involved in was to demand a ladies' lavatory on Hackney Downs, some local playing fields. We flooded the area with crudely printed leaflets complaining that the nation's youth was being cynically exploited, that there was a grave short-age of amenities. *Is this really a land fit for heroes to live in?* we asked. Apparently, all would be well if Hackney Borough Council built a ladies' loo on the Downs. When the leaflet failed to produced results we decided on revolutionary action. We would stage a demonstration in the Council chamber while a meeting was in progress. It happens all the time in these days of the loony left, but was a rarity in the Forties. You cannot stand up in the middle of a meeting and start making speeches. What you need is a short, snappy slogan. The aldermen and councillors of Hackney must have been most bemused to see a bunch of us stand up chanting: 'Ladies' loo, loo, loo, loo . . . ladies' loo, loo, loo, loo.' They're probably still working it out.

Then there was the occasion when YCL leaders decided to launch a campaign against conscription. The term of national service was eighteen months, later extended to two years, but we Communists dare not oppose it entirely in case we were accused of being Soviet pawns. So Party headquarters came up with the idea that conscription should be limited to twelve months. Once again a slogan was needed, as laid down by the great teacher, Lenin. *Not a Day over a Year.* Nobody outside our own ranks had the faintest idea what it meant, but it sounded okay. I was given the job with another comrade of painting these fighting words on a bridge over a road in Bow. To be on the safe side, we waited until one o'clock in the morning before clambering out on to the perilous perch with our cans of white paint. He on the left, me on the right. All went well for ten minutes or so, until our lookout below began flashing his torch to warn us of trouble. We scarpered. He had seen a police car. For years afterwards, people in the East End puzzled over the letters sprawled across the local landmark: NOT A DA OVER A YE.

Daft as it seems today, I was getting more and more involved in YCL activities and was still no closer to finding true love. It wasn't for the want of trying. Any fly on the wall from Fleet Street who crashed one of our Bolshevik
secret meetings would have been most surprised. We spent hours in
committee plotting and planning not insurrection, but trying to organise our
non-existent sex lives. There were always fierce debates on the best place to
find girls.

'Now then, comrades, is it going to be Box Hill for the ramble this Sunday,
or do we try Epping Forest again? There were some smashers in that cafe last
time.'

'What about the girls from Islington YCL? They've got some real crackers
and the blokes are dreadful, covered in spots, most of 'em. Can't we find out
where they're going and get in there!'

'How about this in the *Daily Worker*: "Ramble led by Manny Yospa. Coach
by Charing X to Welwyn. Followed by grand tea, social and dance. Inclusive
cost 7/6." Should be able to get our leg over there.'

'You're all talking rubbish. There's only one way to find a girl. Speak to her
nicely, invite her to the pictures. If that goes all right, get invited to her house
for tea.'

'Bloody bourgeois!'

'Fascist pig!'

'Running dog of imperialism!'

'Who d'you think you are – Clark Gable, yet!'

The girls on the committee listened to it all with amused tolerance. These
were the days before feminists arrived with their talk of sexism and equality.
Most of us married local girl comrades, anyway.

My own day soon arrived. One look and I was smitten. Jackie was her
name. Dark, passionate, with impeccable credentials. Her father was from
Russia, a lifelong Communist. He had recently died, probably from injuries
received in an air raid. Her mother was French and strong in the faith. I lost
no time inviting Jackie to join me outside Dalston Junction station that
Saturday afternoon to sell copies of *Challenge*, the YCL organ. On a good day
we might shift five copies and claim a great victory for Socialism.

We fell in love in the afternoon and into bed that evening. Her mother
thoughtfully had gone to the pictures. It was the first time for both of us. So

desperate was our need, one for the other, that we exploded in an orgasm simultaneously. The most stupendous, wonderful, earth-shattering experience of my entire life. Jackie felt the same. We wrapped ourselves in each other on her narrow single bed and never wanted to let go.

I was seventeen, too young to be sensible, sex-starved and hungry for love. Perhaps they are the same thing. Jackie was two years older than I, sensitive and highly strung, eager to find someone she could cling to. Two lost souls coming together and nothing was ever going to hurt us ever again. Or so it seemed. Her mother Rachel was to make one of her frequent visits to her family in Paris within a few days. She was reluctant to go, sensing that Jackie had grown up like her sister Jeanne and brothers Rene, Charles and Johnny. Jackie was the youngest by thirteen years.

'Promise me, both of you, no mischief while I'm away,' she pleaded. We gave our word, only to break it almost as soon as we put her on the Number 38 bus to Victoria station.

It had been an impossible pledge. We could not keep our hands off each other. All that long, hot summer of 1947 we were crazy for sex, blind to anything but the need to possess one another. Any time, any place. Once, I recall, in a rickety lift in the trade union office where Jackie worked. I left the gate open on the top floor while people waiting below yelled up the shaft. We were like hungry children who had stumbled on a candy store. By the time Madame Schtyk returned home three months later Jackie was pregnant. We had heard vaguely of French letters, but that was the extent of our sex education.

We contemplated abortion and even got as far as a back street operator's kitchen, a place smelling of cabbage so repellant that we bolted without a word. I was quite happy to marry and become a father. It seemed the right thing to do for a bastard like myself. Jackie was not all that pleased, but agreed to marriage readily enough. We wed at Hackney town hall in November, 1947. Ronnie Bedford and Jack Smyth came from the office and Jackie's mother, brother Charles and a school friend, Muriel Dobkin, completed the party. Ronnie took a picture, we had a drink in some tatty local pub, and that was it. We spent our honeymoon at the Curzon cinema. A French film, naturally.

Barbara Nicola Jameson was born the following March. A bonny, brown-eyed girl with an adorable personality. Her mother was never less than difficult and her father always too preoccupied to be much use. For all that, she grew up good and strong. Today she is married to John Sidgreaves, a British Telecom engineer, and they have a grown up daughter themselves, Paula. Barbara is sales executive in a factory outside Manchester.

Jackie and I never really got it together after the wedding. Shotgun weddings are not to be recommended unless bride and groom are certain of each other. Jackie always had the feeling that she was cut out for a glittering career in something or other – she was never sure what – only to have her hopes dashed by early marriage.

Although she was nominally Jewish, there was no religious problem. The immediate family were totally non-orthodox and the father had been a dedicated Communist. I moved into the mother's slum flat in Dalston, then a poor Jewish area of Hackney, and was surrounded by warmth and love. 'What a nice Jewish boy,' the old *bubbalahs* (grannies) used to say as they sat at their doorstep and I walked past pushing Barbara in her buggy.

It was the first time I had actually felt part of a family.

All in all, it was a great relief to be married and standing on my own feet. The only person who did not seem to like me was my wife. It didn't seem to matter. I was young, stupid and busy elsewhere. Trouble was beckoning at Reuters. This Communism lark was threatening my entire future.

Russia's brave defiance of Hitler's invading armies brought a dramatic change in the fortunes of the British Communist Party. The war made it respectable. Membership reached record figures and sales of the *Daily Worker* exceeded 100,000, though much of that was due to the genius of its racing tipster, Cayton. The comrades were not able to bask in Uncle Joe's reflected glory for long. By the late Forties, Anglo-Soviet friendship was rapidly evaporating. The Iron Curtain had fallen over Europe and East-West relations were chilly enough to be labelled the Cold War.

Communists are masters of political expediency. They do not waste time weeping for the past. The chance to win the hearts and minds of the workers had been and gone. A direct appeal for support in the present climate was a lost cause if ever there was one. Not to worry, we told each other, history is on our side. What next then? We must fight for peace and defend the Soviet Union against the warmongers.

So began a remarkable campaign of infiltration from within. The object was to rally support for the so-called peace-loving democracies among millions of sympathisers who so recently had been cheering Soviet victories in the war. Since they were not going to join our ranks, we would embrace theirs and win them over to our cause. Any organisation not directly opposed to us was considered fair game.

We descended on their meetings with a plan of action carefully mapped out, usually with the help of Party members on the inside. We would find out who might be relied upon for support, talk persuasively to those open to influence and, most importantly, stir up trouble for those "reactionaries" in office we knew would be dead against us. When the moment was right, we would pounce – and take over the lot in the name of democracy. We never declared ourselves as Communists.

The number and complexity of organisations infiltrated in this way was staggering. Many were ripe for picking and passed under Party control – "won for peace" – in a matter of weeks. Others might need softening up and working on for months, if not years. Some never fell at all, thanks to an entrenched leadership who spotted our dirty tricks and took counter measures. Our best weapon was the lethargy of members who could not be bothered to vote in elections or even attend meetings. Communists were never less than "active" members, always eager to serve and willing to turn out in all weathers. Organisation, propaganda and tactics were our middle names.

Our prime targets were trade union and Labour party branches, Co-operative groups and the anti-nuclear lobby and peace movement. There was no sense of doing anything wrong or underhand. These were public organisations, open to all, and we simply went in and wooed and won them over to our point of view. A Tory or Labour supporter might do the same. We just happened to be better at it.

I remember taking over the Hackney Labour League of Youth in a fortnight in this way. It could not have been easier. The Labour party allowed its youth movement only limited powers, which naturally upset what passed for young militants in those days. We knew from friends on the inside that a critical debate was coming up on the issue of the League having equal voting rights with adult members. Wide-eyed and innocent, we joined in time to propose a motion of no-confidence in the management committee. It was passed and a new committee elected *pro tem* on the spot. The members were those who had supported the emergency resolution. All of them our supporters.

Sometimes, we swooped on the innocent just out of force of habit. We created havoc in this way in 1947 at a famous and old-established youth club in the East End presided over by Sir Basil Henriques, a juvenile court judge forever being quoted in the papers for his pronouncements on delinquency among the young.

We found a desultory organisation, largely run by do-gooders, where the main activity seemed to be ping pong and dancing to a battered old gramophone. It took no time at all to sort that lot out. We got several members on the committee by proposing a programme of debates, community service, summer holiday trips and so on. Sir Basil, realising late in the day that his club was the subject of a Communist takeover bid, tried to intervene. Angry words were exchanged and I remember one of our young girls, a real toughie from Stepney, prodding him in the ribs and saying ' 'ere, Basil, wot 'ave you ever done for the people, eh?'

The joke was that having taken over these organisations, what were we supposed to do with them? There are only so many resolutions to be passed calling for democracy in Greece, an end to Yankee imperialism and better pay and conditions for shipyard apprentices on Tyneside. One night's debate under Communist rules would be enough to send anyone to sleep. In any case, we had other fish to fry and would be off to do it all over again, leaving our new-found friends to sort out the confusion we left behind.

At least they were now on our list as 'progressive.' We could always go back there to sell some literature, organise a collection for the latest lost cause or get a quick resolution passed which might make the columns of the *Daily Worker*. Since we did not openly advertise Communism, we were quite happy to attach our various pseudonyms to more and more organisations. *Peoples*, *democratic*, *peace-loving* and *progressive* were the words much in vogue in the late Forties.

The same process was taking place in other countries and all these activities came under the umbrella of the so-called Peace movement. It was certainly

Communist-led and probably inspired by Moscow, but many people far removed from any *ism* supported it for the very sound reason that they preferred Picasso's dove of peace to the drums of war.

It wasn't long before Fleet Street was on to our crazy progress through the various leftwing and anti-war organisations. Those suspicious of Russia saw the peace campaign as a Kremlin plot to subvert the West. Taking a lead from the odious Senator Joseph McCarthy, the Reds-under-the-bed brigade in Britain began to get the jitters.

The Republican from Wisconsin, who made the term McCarthyism synonymous with witch hunt, launched an inquisition into Communists, left-wingers and fellow travellers from 1947 as Chairman of the Senate Investigations Committee, pledged to root out subversion in all branches of American life.

Dire warnings about Communist infiltration soon spread to Britain, America's staunchest ally, as the Cold War whipped up real fears among millions of people that World War III – the nuclear holocaust – was in the offing. The only question was when would it break out.

Reuters was in the frontline just as it had been in the war against Hitler. It had exchange deals with the Soviet news agency Tass and other Communist outlets and monitored broadcasts behind the Iron Curtain. The major proportion of the news file in the postwar years concerned East-West relations, divided Europe, the threat of nuclear war and Chairman Mao's victories in China. The Korean war was not far away.

With both sides of the great divide waging a massive propaganda campaign, Reuters was vulnerable to any suggestion that it might favour one against the other. What made this delicate balance particularly dodgy was the existence of a band of Communist sympathisers on the Reuters payroll. One false move by any of us and the agency could lose all its lucrative contracts with the Americans.

We really were nothing to worry about, merely a small group of like-minded people who were suspicious of American intentions just as others feared what the Russians were up to. Only three or four were actual Party members. The others fitted neatly into the category of fellow travellers. There could not have been more than a dozen all told.

Some referred to us in whispers as the major Communist cell in Fleet Street outside the *Daily Worker*. We never thought of ourselves as anything so grand. We did not hold private conclaves, secret or otherwise. The nearest we got to a plot was when the bigger Party group covering all members in Fleet Street met to discuss tactics to be adopted at the monthly meetings of the Central London branch of the National Union of Journalists, our main arena of operations.

Much of the time this concerned nothing more sinister than proposing a resolution for the release of some liberal editor who had fallen foul of the rightwing regimes across the world. That would immediately inspire a counter-blast from the *Daily Telegraph* lobby, who would want to know why we were not fighting for press freedom in Poland or Czechoslovakia. We would also rally support to pack any meeting where elections were taking place to make sure our people won as many seats as possible. The other side did exactly the same thing so it all worked out fair and square in the end. True, the Communists tended to win most seats, but then they did most of the work and had the constitution necessary to withstand hours of debate on such vexed questions as democracy in Greece.

The same boring verbal duels between left and right would go on inside the Reuters Chapel of the NUJ. As in the Branch, the Communists and their supporters ran for office on the Chapel committee. Most of us occupied the key position of Father of the Chapel at some time or other. We won support not through some devious Red plot, but because we were inclined to thump the table more vigorously than others in negotiations over pay and conditions. That was the limit of our militancy. There was never any attempt to call a strike or disrupt production – which happened all the time in Fleet Street two decades later – and any thought of interfering with the sanctity of the Reuters news file was strictly taboo.

I was rapped over the knuckles once for threatening a strike in talks over photographers' pay with the Newspaper Publishers Association, the proprietors' organisation. At that time Press photographers were the Cinderella of the profession. Although they were expected to crawl through the proverbial field of mud to get pictures, often risking life and limb, they were paid less than reporters.

'Unless you meet our just demands for parity, there will not be another picture taken in Fleet Street from this afternoon,' I stormed. The bosses tut-

tutted and called for an adjournment to consider their position. My colleagues rounded on me. 'How dare you,' said one supposed firebrand, 'who gave you a mandate to threaten a strike? Your behaviour has been disgraceful.' The NPA team filed in a few minutes later, smiled sweetly and said we had made out such a good case that they had decided to give photographers equal pay.

My disgraceful behaviour won me the sobriquet 'The Red Menace' in those years. It always puzzled me in more recent times that nobody remembered that other Jameson when I went on to become senior executive and editor on several newspapers. That would have been a better story for *Private Eye* than 'East End boy makes bad.' I did have a narrow squeak in the Seventies at a posh reception thrown by the *Mirror* at a Labour Party conference in Blackpool. I was drinking a glass of sophisticated Muscadet while making small talk with two of the top men in newspapers, Sir Edward Pickering, currently Rupert Murdoch's senior editorial executive in Britain, and Percy Roberts, until his retirement managing director of Mirror Group Newspapers. Who should stroll up to join the chat but Ken Morgan, director of the Press Council. 'Ah,' he says, turning to me, 'it's the Red Menace.' Ken had known me in his previous life as secretary of the NUJ. I made a hasty excuse and left.

These earlier activities as a young revolutionary certainly were well known to my bosses at the time. There is little doubt they transferred me to sub-editing duties so that I would not get into mischief in the name of Reuters outside. There had been one or two hair-raising episodes that must have given them palpitations.

One of my jobs as a reporter had been to cover riots on the site of the Ridley Road street market in Hackney. In 1946, a group calling itself the Association of British Ex-Servicemen began holding meetings there to condemn atrocities against British servicemen in Palestine by terrorists fighting for the establishment of the state of Israel. The association were thinly disguised Fascists. They sang the Nazi *Horst Wessel* song, harangued the Jews and were addressed by Sir Oswald Mosley, leader of the prewar British Union of Fascists.

Communists and Jewish groups in the East End were having none of that. Every Sunday night saw a pitched battle, with bricks and bottles flying through the air, as thousands of police tried to keep the two sides apart. In the thick of the fray on one particularly bloody occasion, I came face to face with the senior police officer in Hackney, a Superintendent Satterthwaite.

'This is outrageous,' I screeched at him. 'These horses are knocking down women and children. 'You're supposed to be here to keep order!'

He was not going to argue the point. His answer was a short, sharp shove from the shoulder that knocked me flying. For a second I expected to finish under the hooves of the aforementioned horses. I was badly shaken, and made much of reporters being savagely assaulted by police. I think Reuters justifiably took the view I was not all that innocent.

Another time, I got what was supposed to be the first interview with Sir Oswald Mosley since he decided to show his face in public again. I spotted him in his familiar trench coat tucked away in a shop doorway watching the mayhem. 'I deplore the violence,' he told me, 'but people must have the freedom to speak.' I phoned over the story, returning to the fray with a smirk on my face. The other reporters spotted I was on to something. After a decent interval, I said loftily: 'See that bloke in the doorway of Grodzinski the bakers? That's Mosley.' They rushed over and were back just as quickly. The laugh was on me. 'That's not Mosley, you fool,' said my old night school pal, Bernard Shrimsley, covering the riots for the Press Association. 'That's Tom Hopkinson, former editor of *Picture Post*.' Oops. I flew the half-mile to the phones at Dalston Junction station. 'Quick,' I told the copytaker, 'kill Mosley story and substitute following: *A hoaxer posing as former British Fascist leader Sir Oswald Mosley fooled reporters today at the scene of ugly riots...*' Well, he looked like Mosley.

Once, I was spotted by four Fascist heavies and chased a mile down Cambridge Heath Road into Mile End Underground station. It was that or a battering. I realised my last minute on earth might come if they reached me as a train came into the station. Mercifully there was no sign of them as I took the train to safety.

The riots gave me a rare opportunity to hear the two greatest orators of our time in action: Mosley and Harry Pollitt, the former boilermakers' union leader who was general secretary of the Communist Party. Both addressed the faithful in 1947 at fringe meetings in the Ridley Road area.

It was an emotional moment for Sir Oswald, his first open air speech since his years of internment for supporting Hitler and subsequent exile in Paris. Protected by a line of police four deep, he stood on top of a van and harangued the crowd. Much as I opposed him, I sensed his mesmeric qualities. 'The old gang...you know them...the politicians and time-servers, the money-lenders and lickspittles...have betrayed this...our great country.' Slow and rasping, pausing every few seconds for maximum effect, he delivered a thinly veiled attack on Jewish capital in true Nazi style. He sounded like Adolf Hitler in English.

Pollitt's speechmaking was different, though just as effective. He spoke much faster in a no-nonsense Lancashire accent, pouring scorn on opponents with humorous asides. 'Comrades, they tell us to count our blessings. The trouble is that the working people of Britain, the old age pensioners, the young lads learning a trade, the people that matter in this great country, have no blessings left to count.' He would start speaking in low, confidential tones, as if letting his audience in on a great secret, then rise to a quickfire crescendo to hammer home his point.

Both of them were superb speakers, matched only by the great Winston Churchill at his wartime best. They make today's politicians look wimpish. Whatever happened to political oratory and hellfire preaching in this great country of ours?

I went to get some fatherly advice from Harry Pollitt at Party headquarters in King Street, where thick pebble glass shielded the faithful from being over-looked by porters at Covent Garden market across the road – or anyone else who might be interested. My mentor at Reuters, Ronnie Bedford, had delivered an ultimatum: Career or Communism.

Harry asked me about myself, how I got started in journalism, what I was doing politically and in the union. He didn't waste time thinking about my dilemma. 'Well, you've got no choice, have you, lad?' I still didn't know what he was going to say. 'It's got to be your career. You can't come this far and throw the lot away. Communists lead by example. You must finish what you have started. Learn the business properly, become a good journalist. You can worry about politics later.'

Ronnie must have given me up for lost when he came on crusading articles I had written in the columns of the YCL weekly *Challenge*, a twopenny journal designed to spread the gospel among the young. They were carried under bylines that fooled nobody. First it was Derek Jamieson, rapidly switching to Roy Jameson when people began asking what was a Reuters reporter doing writing vitriolic articles in the Communist press? Looking at them today, I can't imagine why anyone could have been that upset – unless it was the purple prose. They were awful. This is how a 1946 piece on Mosley began:

> *WOULD the men who did not return from the hell that was Dunkirk; the men who finished their lives at the bottom of the murky waters of the English Channel, or the men whose lives were snuffed as a candle flame high up in the cold clear space of the sky fighting in the days of the Battle of Britain, think kindly of the fact that the British Labour Government tolerates the renewed activities of the man who introduced the brutal, cold-blooded tactics of the Nazi regime in Great Britain – Sir Oswald Mosley?*

No wonder Harry Pollitt told me to concentrate on my career! In the event, Ronnie's fears and Harry's advice were pre-empted in the Kremlin by Joe Stalin himself. In 1948, he suddenly expelled President Tito's Yugoslavia from the Comintern, the federation of Communist states. It was the beginning of the end of my Red period. One day Tito was our great Partisan hero, the next he was a blue-rinsed dilettante, lackey of the imperialists. We were supposed to turn all our ideas upside down at a nod from Moscow and applaud the wisdom of our beloved leader. Stalin clearly was a despot.

Others felt as I did, though some waited eight years until the Soviet repression in Hungary before they finally broke with the Party. A few have kept the faith, accepting the Leninist tenet that the end justifies the means. 'You cannot make an omelette without cracking eggs,' is how he put it.

I dropped out of YCL activity and did not join the Communist Party, as was expected as comrades got older, though I continued to be active in the NUJ. People assumed I was still a sympathiser. I was going through severe withdrawal symptoms – you do not lightly drop an emotional attachment like Communism – and said nothing. Such was the anti-Communist hysteria of the time that all the comrades were twitchy, fearing spies and traitors in their midst. It was no time to exchange confidences about a crisis of conscience. I had nobody to tell that the light had failed.

At Reuters, the man we looked to for leadership was remote and unapproachable so far as I was concerned. Lawrence Kirwan, wartime group captain in the RAF, was the senior member of our group by virtue of the fact that he was a senior executive, one of the duty editors responsible for news output. A striking man, with greying temples, he was a born leader. It was no good going to him with my doubts. In any case, he did not like mixing politics with work. Lawrie was strictly a Communist by example. He parted company with Reuters eventually, joining the Hungarian news agency in London, and went on to become President of the NUJ.

Philip Cutler was the noisiest of the bunch. He was a small, round man with pallid complexion, rimless glasses and a shrill, squeaky voice. Phil, too, had a remarkable background. He had been a colonel in British Intelligence stationed in Washington during the war. The story was that he had turned to Communism out of disgust over an Anglo-American propaganda offensive being mounted against the Russians while they were still busy fighting Hitler's invading armies.

I remember Phil's soulmates cringing with embarrassment at the reception he gave news that the Chinese Communists had opened fire in 1948 on a Royal Navy frigate, HMS Amethyst, in the Yangtse river.

'That's right, blow 'em out of the water,' he roared, rubbing his hands with glee. 'That'll teach the bastards.'

Not the most discreet way to behave in the atmosphere of suspicion and mistrust of those days. The Cold War and its ugly progeny, the McCarthy witch hunt, meant that gradually all those in any way sympathetic to Russia were ostracized. In April, 1949, Britain and the rest of western Europe joined the United States in a military alliance designed to contain the Soviet Union. Such was the prevailing mood that many saw the formation of NATO as an inevitable preliminary to war. If America sneezes, Britain catches cold, was a popular saying in those days. It was no time to be a Communist.

The great purge reached Reuters when one of our supporters did something we had been religiously avoiding for years. She doctored a speech by one of the Western leaders. I believe it was President Truman. An error of omission, not commission, as the lawyers say. In sub-editing the speech, she deleted some Cold War reference. Nothing very dramatic, but enough for the long knives to come out.

Called before the bosses to give account of herself, she broke down, confessed all about the Fleet Street group, named names and begged forgiveness. The blacklist had arrived. We began to be picked off one by one. I don't think anyone was actually fired. Nothing vulgar like that. It was simply made clear they would be better advised to take their services elsewhere.

Some faded away, leaving journalism altogether. A few recanted. The majority got jobs on Party publications like the *Daily Worker* or working for the Communist world's news outlets in London. Phil Cutler and Gwyn Davies, a poetic Welshman who had been a senior sub-editor at Reuters, finished at the Soviet news agency TASS. There they joined the Street's best known Communist, the affable, cricket-loving Harry Cousins, secretary of the NUJ's Central London branch.

A friendly whisper in my ear told me my name was on the blacklist. It was too late to magic up Tito and plead a change of heart, quite apart from the fact that Judas has never appealed to me. Instead I found a swift and cunning way to avoid the executioner's axe. I sent off a card to the Ministry of Labour stating I no longer wished to exercise my right as an apprentice to be deferred from conscription.

Please call me up for National Service.

Above

Ma Wren and some of her brood living at 53, Mount Pleasant Lane. This is the only picture of the remarkable Mrs Wren (*far left*), wrapped up against the wind. It is 1937 and we are on our first and only trip to the sea – a coach outing to the mudflats at Shoeburyness, Essex. "Aunty" Winnie has my sister Jean on her lap. Behind her, my mother Elsie with two of the other girls, Violet and Peggy (*right*). The two little boys lost are my foster brother Lenny and me (*far right*).

Left

Peggy and Winnie are dressed to the nines, Forties style. This is the close of World War II and they are off for a night out, though still mourning Peggy's first husband, killed when he fell off his Army tank.

SOUVENIR
of

1940

COPYRIGHT XPDOGRAPH

Top left
A rare picture of me as a boy, taken
soon after the outbreak of war. I
have escaped the slums and am
discovering country life as an
evacuee in Hertfordshire. It was not
cows and chickens that astonished
me so much as everyday things – like
milk jugs and electric fires.

Left
Short back and sides, smart shirt and tie. Who says all slum kids are scruffy urchins? Here I stand over my two younger wartime "brothers," Maurice (*left*) and Chris Elliott, who were to grow up and take over the giant Elliott building and construction consortium founded by their father, Jock Elliott. I was invited to join at the bottom, sweeping the yard, but was desperate to become a journalist. Object achieved *above*, I sit (*right*) looking keen in my first week as a reporter in the bustling Reuters newsroom. I was to spend 15 years here, eventually becoming a senior executive.

Right
Wedding party on the steps of Hackney town hall. Married at 17 to Jackie, a revolutionary of Franco-Russian parentage. Family and friends pose for a picture before we go off to the cinema for our honeymoon. Daughter Barbara arrived four months later, not long before daddy flees into the Army to escape an anti-Communist purge.

Below
Playing with mother and daughter on Hackney Downs on one of my frequent trips home. Before long, I volunteer to serve abroad. There seems little point in being a soldier on a commuter line to Aldershot.

Opposite
Standing outside the High Court with Ellen, having lost the libel action against the BBC over an item which dubbed me "an East End boy made bad."

Cash to the JAMESON FIGHTING FUND 31062794 Midland Bank, 60, West Smithfield London ECIA 9DX

FIGHT FOR JAMESON!

Change the jeers to cheers

The price of defending his ability, reputation; even his intelligence has been disastrous. The jeers that Jameson endured were jeers aimed at editorial people throughout the newspaper industry. HIT BACK! Help Jamie pay off the lawyers . . . The bill is colossal. Many have been glad of his help in the past. NOW IS YOUR CHANCE TO HELP HIM!

'*I brought this case to show that honesty, integrity, decency and fair play do exist in Fleet Street*'

DEREK JAMESON, Law Courts, February'84

Above
A helping hand from Fleet Street as disaster strikes. I am out of work and left with a bill for £75,000 after bringing a disastrous libel action to answer a Radio 4 satire lampooning me as "an East End boy made bad." Old friends rally round and launch a fighting fund through advertisements in the *UK Press Gazette*. It raises £10,000.

Right
Sons number 3 and 4 – Ben (*left*) and Dan. Despite the breakdown of my marriage, I am very close to my two boys by Pauline and see them regularly. Here we are out together on a charity gig. Barbara and Peter, my children by the first marriage, are also never far away.

Top left
Hail the chief! A fond farewell in
1973 for retiring *Mirror* boss
Hugh (now Lord) Cudlipp in
Manchester's Midland Hotel and
I catch the great man's eye by
keeping the troops in order as
chairman of the boozy
proceedings. It is my greatest
solo performance – and I am
rewarded by being promoted
Northern editor of the *Daily
Mirror*. Now I am just one step
away from the top of the ladder.

Top right
Marriage number 2 in 1971 to the
delightful Pauline, known to the
Mirror as the Madonna. She had
refused my proposal, but agreed
after reassuring words from the
great Marje Proops. At a
boisterous reception in Fleet
Street, three top *Sunday Mirror*
men look on approvingly – (*from
left*) deputy editor Joc Grizzard,
editor Michael Christiansen and
assistant editor John Knight.
Sadly, the marriage was
not to last.

Right
A childhood fantasy comes true –
in 1977 I become editor of the
Daily Express, sitting in the chair
of the legendary Arthur
Christiansen. It has been a
bumpy ride to the top. Now
I have made it. Across the road
from my window is the alley
where I began work as a
14-year-old messenger.

CHAPTER TWELVE

S/22172890 Jameson. D. Cpl., RASC

I loved the Army, every last barmy minute of it. From the moment we conscripts reported for medical inspection and documentation in a draughty drill hall at Whipps Cross, on the eastern outskirts of London, it was obvious that National Service was going to be pure farce.

August, 1949. World War II had been over four years. Now the Cold War was threatening ultimate conflagration and Britain still had massive commitments across the world. Conscription had started in 1939 and was to continue until 1960. The last of the 5,300,000 men called up in that historic epoch were demobilised three years later.

There were some three hundred of us crowded into that drill hall on the first day. The call-up was compulsory for men from eighteen years so most looked as if they had barely started shaving. Against them I felt almost ancient. Having been deferred, I was two years older than them, married and a father.

Visions of seeing the world, bell-bottom trousers and a girl in every port made the Navy first choice of the vast majority of us signing on that first day. Most of the others wanted to join the boys in blue in the RAF. A nice cushy number, we reckoned. Few were falling over themselves to get into the Army. Too tough and too much bullshit. Even worse, some joker out there might take a potshot at you.

Everything possible would be done to meet individual wishes, our call-up papers had assured us. Unfortunately, they were not looking for sailors or airmen when our day arrived. Each and every one of us finished up in the Army. In my case it was the lowly Royal Army Service Corps, now disbanded, which looked after supplies and transport. The RASC also provided the Army's clerks and pen pushers so anyone with shorthand and typing was an automatic choice. I was to meet many fellow journalists in the months ahead, most of them well choked. They felt a glamourous civvy street job like ours should have merited a commission in some fancy regiment, not typing rosters in a dreary office.

The medical inspection lived up to its reputation as a music hall joke. We had to queue up with nothing but a small towel to cover our essentials, dropping it when we got in front of a medical officer so he could carry out a minute examination. I discovered with surprise they really do cup your balls in one hand and tell you to cough. Naturally there were one or two virgin soldiers among us reluctant to reveal all. They were slow taking off their clothes and some kept on their trousers.

'Come along, come along,' roared one of the drill sergeants supervising proceedings. 'Get 'em off! The MO's not shy. He's seen it before. He promises not to laugh.'

In the middle of this hubbub a sergeant came along with a sheaf of papers in his hand calling out my name.

'You haven't put anything down for father,' he yelled when I made myself known, indicating the form in his hand.

'Haven't got a father, Sarge,' I said quietly.

'No father? What do'you mean, *NO FATHER*!'

I felt everyone must have heard him by now and told him through gritted teeth: 'I am illegitimate.'

'Oh, oh, sorry, my fault, beg your pardon,' he said in a whisper.

I knew then that it was going to be grand to be a soldier. If a drill sergeant could apologise to a sheepish recruit, that said a great deal for the army. Two years in khaki never changed my view, only reinforced it. Without any doubt, the British Army is one of the greatest institutions I ever encountered. Funnily enough, the same sergeant had another problem minutes later when I sat before him for still more form filling.

'You've written "none" against religion,' he said.

'That's right, Sarge. I don't have any religion.'

'What are you, agnostic?'

'Not at all. It's just that I've never been baptised.'

'So you're not agnostic or atheist?'

'That's right. I've got nothing against religion, but I just don't happen to belong to any of them.'

'Right,' he said. 'Church of England!'

I looked suitably astonished at the Army baptising me on the spot in a regimental drill hall in Whipps Cross. 'That's for your benefit,' he explained. 'Put down anything else and you'll be on cookhouse duty every time there's a bleedin' church parade.'

Army life in earnest begins in an induction centre at North Camp, Aldershot, where we are confined to barracks for fourteen of the longest days of our lives. Beguiled, browbeaten, brainwashed into something that bears passing resemblance to a soldier. Hour after hour every day on the drill square, learning how to look the part. *Attention!* Stand still, that man. Don't move a muscle. Arms tight to sides, thumbs against trouser seams, stomach in, chest out. *Stand at ease*, blessed relief, legs twelve inches apart, arms behind back, palms entwined. *Stand easy*, move, talk, scratch your bum, but keep those feet still and no smoking. *Quick march, thirty six paces a minute*, fingers curled with thumb on top, swing arms shoulder high, chest out, chin in. *Salute*, everything that moves, palm flat, right arm longest way up to forehead, shortest way down. Plus all the variations. Jogging *at the double*, the funereal *slow march*. How to *right turn, left turn and about turn*. PT 6.30 every morning, games Wednesday afternoons. Rifle drill and weapon training would come later.

Our instructors are regulars, drill sergeants from the Brigade of Guards and other top regiments. All of them have been through the war and bedazzle us with the campaign ribbons on their chests. Real soldiers teaching a bunch of young, unruly civilians how to walk tall. They also play mother and father to lads who have never been away from home and don't know how to peel a spud or make a bed.

We are introduced to foul muck called blanco, a clay-like substance that has to be dampened and made into a paste to smooth on every surface of our webbing equipment. In training that means the whole shebang every evening. Large and small packs with straps and ammunition pouches and the belt and ankle gaiters worn at all times. On top of that little lot we burnish every brass button, badge and clasp and bull up two pairs of boots until the toecaps are mirror bright. Knife-edge creases have somehow to appear like magic in our heavy serge uniforms. To the uninitiated, these daily chores take two or three hours. Every morning all kit is laid out on the bed in perfect symmetry for inspection. Right down to the last neatly squared sock, everything has its official place in a tableau that probably goes back to Wellington. Blankets and sheets are folded into a sandwich on the palliasse, the webbing equipment draped around it. God help anyone who presents a blanket half-inch wider than its neighbour. This is regarded as tantamount to mutiny.

Reveille at 6.00. One minute the sleep of the dead after all that work and exercise, then total madness as the orderly corporal descends hollering, banging the iron bed frames, ripping off covers and threatening dire penalties for those who refuse to stir.

'Feet on the floor, feet on the floor. C'mon, let's have you. Move, move, MOVE. Anyone still in bed on the count of five is for it. One, two, three, four, FIVE!' By then even the most comatose manage one foot on the floor.

Then, the bleakest moment of all. Thirty half-asleep, irritable recruits struggling to get to one of four decrepit basins for a wash and shave in cold water in time to be on parade for physical jerks at 6.30. Breakfast at 7.00, then a mad scramble back to the barrack room to get kit laid out and please God the bastards don't poke their nose into brasses left untouched the night before.

'Stand by your beds!' comes the order from the lance-corporal who traditionally occupies the end bed. We stand there, butterflies gnawing at our stomachs, as the orderly officer and sergeant of the day enter briskly on their rounds, eager to find transgressors. The officers we hate most of all. They are second lieutenants, conscripts like ourselves, obviously selected for a commission on the basis of accent and class. In those days, any officer of working class origin must have developed a cut glass accent at grammar school. Perhaps sensing our hostility, the National Service officers treat us like dirt.

'Sergeant, this man is a disgrace,' they would drawl in the languid manner adopted by subalterns. 'Put him on a charge for dirty kit.'

As often as not, he would poke his swagger stick into his victim's pile of bedding and tip over the lot so that everything is sent flying on to the highly polished floor. We stand there, rigid, burning with anger, unable to flicker an eyelid by way of protest while some poor sod just one week removed from his mother's loving care is treated like a child molester because blanco has smudged his brass.

'Sir!' roars the duty sergeant, reaching for notebook in tunic pocket. He will take the man's name, have him listed on Company orders for an offence under Section 40 of the Army Act, in that whilst on active service he did fail properly to maintain his kit, and the commanding officer or his adjutant will dole out seven days' fatigues, known as jankers. That means reporting to the Guardroom for a week of hard labour. Extra drill, cookhouse duty, scrubbing floors, heaving coal. He will stagger back to his barrack room every night at 10.30, time for lights out, and clean his kit in the washroom by the light shining through the window from the street lamps outside. If he is lucky, his closest mate will have done it for him.

There is no justice about it. In theory, you can appeal all the way up to the colonel commanding the battalion, but only a fool would try to buck a system going back centuries. For it is quaint old customs like these make the British the greatest soldiers in the world. The psychology is simple. Do as you are told, do not answer back, and you will survive. Probably have a few laughs, too.

It works a treat. If a tough coalminer from Durham is prepared to put up with some wally from Surbiton with a pip on his shoulder spreading his kit all over the deck, then he'll accept anything. Anyway, that second louis probably had it even worse when *he* was in training. Shot or shell, desert or snow, hell or high water, the British soldier simply gets on with it. That's what discipline is all about.

A perfect example is Morris Benett, the man who gave evidence for me in the libel trial. He was my managing editor when I was running the *Daily Express*. Morris won the Military Cross as an infantry captain in Italy during the war. He fought the battle of Long Stop Hill, commanding a badly battered company that held up two crack German divisions at a narrow pass for several days in 1944.

Morris doesn't talk about it much. He was badly wounded at the time. Exercising my editor's prerogative, one day I insisted on knowing why he had dared take on Hitler's Panzer Corps against such fearful odds.

'Well, we were told to stay there, so we stayed,' he said. 'To be perfectly honest, I was a bloody sight more terrified of my colonel than I was of the Germans.'

My own Waterloo was the fault of two pairs of boots, soldiers *not* for the wearing of. As well as learning basic drill, we were at the induction centre to be kitted out. When it came to boots, they had run out of my size nines in black. I was handed two pairs of officers' boots. Very nice, too. Unfortunately they were brown. Now you cannot have private soldiers marching around in officers' boots. No chance. Our platoon sergeant, a Sgt McConnell of the Scots Guards, spotted them the second I stepped out of the Quartermaster's stores.

'Brown boots,' he said. The narrow slits that passed for his eyes opened momentarily. 'BROWN BOOTS! We can't have nasty specimens like you walking about in BROWN boots, can we?'

'No, Serg'nt,' says I.

'Well, what are you going to do about it?'

'I dunno, Serg'nt.'

'Of course you don't. You lot never know anything, do you? Wouldn't know your own name if we didn't stick it on a label round your necks, would you? WOULD YOU?'

'No, Serg'nt.'

'No, what?'

'No, Serg'nt, I wouldn't know my own name if you didn't tell me.'

'Quite right. Now listen carefully. This is what you are going to do. Go down to the NAAFI dinner time and you'll find they have a good line in black dye. Get yourself some of that. At boot inspection tomorrow I want to see those 'orrible brown boots turned into nice shiny black boots, just like magic. Right?'

'Yes, Serg'nt.'

'Yes, what?'

'Yes, I'll get some black dye and dye my boots black.'

'Right! Ten o'clock tomorrow. You've got all night to do 'em.'

You've got to be joking, I'm thinking to myself. No way am I going to dye these boots black. I *like* brown officers' boots. If they want to issue me with brown boots, I'll wear brown boots. It's not my job to dye the fucking boots. If they want me to wear black boots, let them issue me with black boots.

Anyway, we've not been paid yet. How do they know I've got money of my own to spend on bloody dye. They can get stuffed.

As I told my mates, I was all set to pass on these brave thoughts on to Sgt McConnell at boot inspection the following day. However, the sight of those gimlet eyes and tight lips under his peaked cheesecutter cap would have put the fear of God into Henry Cooper himself.

'They're still BROWN!' he spluttered.

'Ah, yes, well, Serg'nt, you see I thought . . .'

'You WHAT?'

I beat a hasty retreat. 'No black dye in the NAAFI, Serg'nt!'

He gave me a long look, then barked: 'Right. Get some the minute it comes in and let's have those boots black.'

I prayed he wouldn't check, but God doesn't smile on cheats. Sgt McConnell jumped on me first parade after dinner. The bastard had been down to the other ranks' NAAFI to find out whether they had any black dye. My luck! They had a shelf full of the stuff.

'What did I tell you to do?' He stood before me like the Lord Chief Justice passing life sentence on a pickpocket.

'Told me to dye my boots, Serg'nt.'

'And then what did you do?'

'I lied to you, Serg'nt.'

'Yes, you did lie, didn't you, you idle, useless, little toerag! I ruin my dinner worrying about why the NAAFI has no dye for our brave soldiers and what do I find? I'M TALKING TO YOU!'

'Black dye, Serg'nt.'

'Yes, BLACK DYE. Buckets of it. Pisspots full of it.'

'Sorry, Serg'nt. I thought . . .'

'Thought! THOUGHT! Lying vermin like you are not allowed to think. Do you take my punishment, or do you want to go in front of the CO?'

'I'll take your punishment, Serg'nt.'

'Right! Latrine duty every single morning you are in this camp.'

That is how I came to spend my first two weeks in command of the company shithouse. Not the best job in the world, cleaning up the nauseating mess of some ninety recruits. Many had the runs thanks to a mixture of sheer fright and their first taste of Army grub. The eight cubicles and wall of urinals looked like a Gents in a second-rate football stadium after a Cup tie. Putrid would be too polite a word for it.

I didn't mind all that much. My Communist past helped. I was serving people all right, on my knees, head halfway down a filthy lavatory bowl. It also got me off the first drill parade of the day and there were great opportunities for a fag and a chat with the skivers and scrimshankers who inevitably hang around the bogs of this world. They taught me a lot.

Time to think, as well. I decided the only way to survive in this man's Army was to go along with the system, not try to beat it. To laugh, not cry. Most of all, to get a stripe up there on my sleeves. That was the essential passport to a better world for the serving soldier. Nothing concentrates the mind so much as unblocking a bog choked up with pages torn out of *Dandy*, *Beano* and the *Sunday Post* in the absence of paper, toilet, WD, military personnel for the use of.

I managed to dodge other drill parades by getting myself classified as illiterate. It was all the fault of tests we had to undergo to discover where we fitted best in the military machine. Standing around a bench, we were each handed a jumble of metal and wire and told we had sixty seconds to turn them into a padlock. It worked in every case except mine. I was left with seven bits of metal in my hand. The instructor told me to report to Hut 5D at 10.15 next morning.

We sat there in the Nissan hut while a kindly, bespectacled sergeant in the Education Corps handed out sheets of lined paper, just like school. 'Now I want you to write a composition,' he said. 'My first day in the Army. That's simple enough, isn't it? Think about it, take your time, and write down your impressions of this lot.' He didn't sound too happy about it. Obviously one of us, a National Serviceman.

By NAAFI break I had filled five sides with a none too subtle dig at the lunacy we had gone through, not least the brown boots. Most of the others seemed to be having a bit of a struggle getting down their name, rank and number. We handed in our papers and went off to the canteen for morning break. On our return the RAEC instructor wanted to know who Jameson was. I put up my hand and he beckoned me to his table.

'What's this?' he said in an outraged whisper, pointing to my essay.

'It's what you said, Serg'nt, my first day in the Army.'

'What d'you do in civvy street?'

'I'm a journalist in Fleet Street, reporter and sub-editor.'

'This is a class for illiterates,' he said in shocked tones. 'How did you get in here?'

I told him about the sad tale of the padlock in the aptitude test.

'That's crazy,' he said. 'It's supposed to be a check on mechanical efficiency, not writing skills. What d'you want to do? Go back out there,' he gestured towards the square outside, 'or stay in here?'

I wasn't proud. 'Stay here,' I told him with great conviction. Sadly, it didn't last long. I was quite happy that we were all going to learn how to write a letter home, but that Sgt McConnell began to get to know us after a few days. The lads soon let out there was a reporter among us. He had words with the Education Corps man. Why was he harbouring a journalist in a class for illiterates? There was no answer to that. Well, not in those days, anyway. I was back on the square in no time.

The welcome mat was already out three weeks later when we were posted up the road to 2nd Training Battalion, RASC, at Dettingen Barracks, Blackdown, near Aldershot. They had been told to look out for me for several reasons. Being twenty years old and married, I was something of a father figure to many of the lads. Then there were my adventures in the bog and attempt to pose as an illiterate. On top of that, I was a real live Fleet Street reporter. Naturally, I didn't bother to explain the sub-editor bit.

The battalion's job was to turn out hundreds of Army clerks for units all over the world and to complete our military education by route marches, exercises, rifle drill, weapon training and map reading. Whatever a man's trade, whether he be a clerk, cook or bottle-washer, the Army expects him to be a soldier first, fully trained so that he can take up his rifle and fight with the best of them. Since conscription was meant to last only 18 months, training had to be completed in twelve weeks.

It came easy to me. I had learned weapons and drill in the Army cadets, already knew shorthand and typing and always made the most noise at lectures, especially when current affairs were under discussion. So it came as a surprise to nobody at the end of the course when I was invited to join the permanent staff as an instructor. That magic stripe, guaranteed to protect the bearer against latrine duty forever, was up on my arm three months after call up. It was soon joined by another. Corporal Jameson! Now it was my turn to do some shouting.

My job as an instructor meant looking after a platoon of recruits for the eight weeks they were at Blackdown following basic training – a great relief for them after the horrors of Aldershot because most of us were National Servicemen who shared their view that the Army was midway between pantomime and a horror story. Mind you, we were loyal soldiers of the king. We ranted and raved in true military style, threatened and coerced in search of glory as the top rated platoon and never doubted that the RSM stood on the right hand of God.

Nevertheless, we never forgot we were human. We didn't charge anyone if a happier alternative could be found. We taught them how to get their barrack room jobs done without too much pain, the best way to score a weekend leave pass, how to fiddle their trade tests. Most importantly, not to go under, to laugh at it all. Vicious bullying nowadays seems to be as common as mud on Army boots. In my day never did I see an NCO lay so much as a finger on a soldier – that would have brought a serious charge of assault – and nor did we swear directly at a recruit. By all means call him dozy, useless, scruffy, thick, idle, insolent, misbegotten. But never swear at him. That was taboo, though you might not think so watching war films on the telly.

Training battalions involving young soldiers always attract plenty of drama. We were no exception. The brutal regime got to many who had lived sheltered lives at home. Every conscript remembers the early days when the sobs of weaker brethren disturbed barrack rooms after lights out.

'Who's that bawling?' the cry would go up from some bighead.

'Corp!' – for the corporal in the end bed – 'there's someone here wants his dummy. Can you come and give him a cuddle?'

Eventually, all would be quiet, though likely as not there would be another outbreak within minutes. It is strange and disturbing, the sound of grown men crying to themselves in the middle of the night.

Then you had the rebels, the hard cases seeking to prove they were tougher than the system. The lost, the lonely and the damned – the Regimental Sergeant-major was mother and father to them all.

Non-commissioned officers are the backbone of the British Army. Officers have little direct contact with other ranks, as the lower orders are called, and in my day they were more than happy to leave the NCOs to run everything. They had an active social life in the mess and strictly rationed their appearances to parades and inspections. Adjutants responsible for administration and quartermasters looking after supplies were the only officers who could actually be found *working*. A battalion's success and efficiency depended primarily on the RSM, most important NCO of all.

RSMs are legendary characters who have reached the top rank as senior warrant officers by virtue of lengthy service, an ability to roar loudly and strike terror in every heart and a fine appreciation of what makes their fellow men tick.

'Psycho-lology, that's what it's all about, Claude,' my first RSM told me. Nobby Clark, his name was. A short man by Army standards, he strutted about the place like a bantam, chest out, arms swinging, always on the alert for unsoldierly conduct, as he called it. He wore oxblood boots, a kind of halfway house between ours in black and theirs in brown.

I asked him once why he insisted on calling me Claude.

'I don't trust you jokers who read 'n write,' he said.

There was the occasion when one of our head cases – the lads reckoned he used to go jogging in the woods at night in the nude – climbed on to the roof of his redbrick barrack block and threatened to jump to his death below. A cluster of squaddies stood gaping in the forecourt while the room corporal hung out of a window pleading with him to come inside. Up comes Nobby Clark, pace stick under his arm, and takes it all in at a glance.

'Jump, you idiot,' he roars through cupped hands. 'Jump!'

The rookie took one look at the RSM and clambered back to the outstretched hands of the NCO. He was taken off to the BMH, British Military Hospital. Apparently he was about to go on sentry duty and had not cleaned his equipment. That's psycho-lology, all right.

Another time, I'm in the armoury booking out the Lee Enfield .303 rifles that my platoon members will protect and preserve for the rest of their Army lives. The registration number every rifle bears has to be logged against the regimental number of its new owner. Great care is exercised when weapons or ammunition are involved. Everyone is aware that they can kill.

My lads are outside, looking sheepish. They have never handled a rifle before. Some have them tucked under arms, others between their legs. One or two are holding them like a cricket bat. An utter shambles. I get an urgent summons. 'The RSM is coming.' Someone has spied Nobby Clark heading their way nineteen to the dozen. He is there by the time I get to the door. He is in a benevolent mood, realising they have yet to learn rifle drill.

'Ah, just got your rifles, I see,' he said. 'Now then, lads, remember this and mark it well. In the British Army, the rifle is a soldier's best friend. When you go to bed at night, I want you to sleep with it under your pillow.'

'And, if its gets in the way of your head, then you'll move your head!'

With a curt nod at me, he was gone, leaving a few bemused soldiers wondering how they are supposed to sleep with a rifle under their pillows.

Life could have been worse. I was home in London most weekends, and there were friends to visit in Surrey at off-duty moments during the week. Playing nursemaid to recruits gave me and my fellow instructors plenty to laugh about. We pulled some diabolical tricks on each other. I remember a competition to see which platoon would donate most blood to the local transfusion service. The others were astonished to learn every member of my mob had volunteered. What they didn't know was how I had wangled it.

'They've got these great nurses,' I had told my lads. 'You don't feel a thing when the needle goes in because they put their hand inside your thigh as you lay there on the couch. There's a cup of tea and cake afterwards and the platoon that does best will be sure of a 48-hour pass.'

I wasn't sure about the thigh, but knew my lot were coming up for a weekend pass. There was a satisfied smirk on my face as I marched my full platoon to the mobile transfusion clinic. I stood them at ease. 'Just a little prick,' I said guiltily, then went inside to report our arrival. Stone me! Talk about he who laughs first. When I got back outside no less than seven of them, nearly a third, had crashed to the ground in a faint at the thought of the needle. They were all hard cases, too. Nothing was going to get them in there after that.

Despite the fun and games, it seemed crazy to me to spend my Army life going backwards and forwards between London and Aldershot like a City commuter. I wanted to see something of the world. The company commander thought I must be barmy, a married man applying to go overseas. I told him my marriage was shaky and it would be better for both of us if I served abroad. It wasn't far from the truth. Jackie was not too happy about her husband popping up every few days, obviously enjoying life immensely while she was left to bring up our baby daughter alone. In a matter of weeks I was posted to the Army Training School in Austria.

This was the postwar Austria of *The Third Man,* zithers playing in the cafes and a spy round every corner. Or so it seemed. The training school was at Lendorf, a village outside Klagenfurt, capital of Carinthia in the southeast corner of Austria. To the north of us was the Soviet zone of occupation and in the east the borders of Czechoslovakia, Hungary and Yugoslavia. We were there to defend democracy against that lot!

It was almost worth volunteering for service abroad just for the trip by troopship from Harwich to the Hook of Holland, then by train along the Rhine and across Austria. Three days of scenic splendour leading to a luxury barracks built to house SS Headquarters in Southern Europe. I had a cosy room of my own in the shadow of the Dolomites. Three lectures a day on clerical duties and current affairs. The rest of the time I could wear civilian clothes and come and go as I pleased. To the victor, the spoils. We lived like the aristocracy. Weekends in idyllic hotels reserved for British forces or on tourist trips to Vienna or Salzburg. For outdoor types, water polo on Lake Worthersee or skiing in the mountains. Fags were a bob for a tin of fifty, we were paid in Mickey Mouse vouchers called BAFVS worth double the exchange rate, forty schillings to the pound. The front row of the famous Klagenfurt Opera cost the equivalent of $7\frac{1}{2}$p!

The natives were friendly enough, though we knew most of them had worshipped Adolf Hitler, the all-conquering Austrian who became leader of Germany. The grand houses occupied by the families of British regulars, many of them from slums back home, were confiscated Nazi property. By 1950 we were hailed as the only thing standing in the way of the Russians and treated accordingly. Everyone smiled and local *gasthöfe* put up English menus offering steak, eggs and chips, bacon butties and cups of tea. The local beer comes in two shades, dark or light. About the farthest most of us got with our German language lessons was to learn how to order *dunkel* or *lichtas* beer.

Anyway, there were always girls to translate for us. Lili Marlene must have begun her career 'neath the barrack gate in Austria. Every night they stood waiting outside the barracks, comely lasses with peaches-and-cream complexions eager to acquire a British husband and passport to take them away from bleak, shattered postwar Europe. Some expected nothing more than a trip to *chocolata* hill, where they had given their all only a year or two earlier for a bar of chocolate to feed their families. By now the rate was up to a tin of fags. The statue of a fiery dragon stood in the Klagenfurt town square. The locals say its tail wags every time a virgin passes, though nobody had seen it move since the British arrived. We doubted whether they had said the same of the Germans.

Being married, at first I resisted the temptation of easy sex. Infidelity was not all that popular before the permissive Sixties. In the end, I got fed up hovering around the APO, Army Post Office, eagerly awaiting letters from Jackie that rarely arrived. My theory that a parting would be best for both of us had worn thin within weeks. She was making me pay for it by not responding to my frantic declarations of love in lengthy letters dispatched every two or three days.

Trust me to get tied up with a contortionist. Elle wrapped her lithe body in knots twice nightly and three times on Saturdays at a Klagenfurt fairground. I regret to say it wasn't done as a demonstration of athletic prowess. More a striptease in which the punters do not actually see the girl. Elle cavorted around in a pair of white panties behind a screen illuminated by a smelly oil lamp. The shadows were sensational. She could be a cobra unwinding one minute, go-go dancer the next. When she stretched out her forefinger, slowly curling it as if beckoning the onlooker, every man in the place thought he was on a promise.

In the event, it was Joe Muggins who collected Elle after every performance, gripping her arm firmly and marching through the fairground crowds trying to look tough. Every second I expected a bottle on the head to let me know what Austrians thought of British squaddies pinching their girls. 'Ooh, Derek,' she would say, 'do not go so fast. I will have a glass of beer, I think.' She never realised we were at death's door.

We met on a park bench. I sat there making out to be reading an Austrian magazine, which I held upside down. She watched this performance for several minutes, looking perplexed. Then she realised it was a come on. 'You are British,' she said. 'British, crazy pipple. Ja?' I wasn't going to argue with that. She looked like Audrey Hepburn.

Elle didn't want a British passport. She already had one. She had married a

Welsh sergeant after the war and gone back to Merthyr Tydfil with him. The family welcomed her as one of their own. In the working men's club most nights, the men drinking pints and playing darts, the women wittering on about babies and three-piece suites over Babychams. Snowballs on Bank holidays. Friday was pay day so they all had baths and one of them went for fish and chips. Usually Elle. It wasn't much of a life after the Dolomites. After two years of Babychams, Elle told her David one day she was going home. 'I didn't think you'd make a go of it, love,' he said. 'Will you be all right now, back there?'

It wasn't a very satisfactory affair. For all her contortions, Elle wasn't into sex much. She seemed to like it only if I handed over a 100 schillings after she told me hard luck stories about being poor. Apparently taking your clothes off behind a screen pays very little. It is more a labour of love. I sensed there was another man around somewhere. She would rattle away in Deutsch to her mates and a certain Wolfgang seemed never far from their thoughts. What knocked our romance on the head finally was a spot of compassionate leave I took to find out whether Jackie was ever going to speak to me again.

CHAPTER THIRTEEN

Scissors and spies

Nearly three months had passed since I heard from Jackie. Her last letter questioned whether there was any point in going on with our marriage. She was fed up, sick of being left to look after baby while I lived it up on the shores of the Worthersee. The CO looked suitably grave as he read it. 'I think you should go home,' he said. 'Sort it out once and for all. She doesn't seem to appreciate you're here serving your country. Fourteen days' compassionate leave.'

Jackie hadn't even take the day off work when I got home. Waiting to greet me was her mother, by now highly suspicious of the antics of her soldier son-in-law, and a note telling me to collect Barbara from the local day nursery. We finally made it up in bed. There's nothing like a good cuddle to bring about a reconciliation. I held Jackie in a bear hug and promised all would be well once I got out of uniform.

'I'm counting the days,' I said. 'We all have demob calendars and cross off every day we have left to serve. It's not much longer now.'

Then I blew it in spectacular style. Elle had challenged me in that incredible accent of hers – a mixture of German and Army slang English delivered in sing-song Welsh – to write to her while I was in London. 'Elle just your Osterreich bint,' she said. 'You home, civvy street, with *frau* and muckers, soon forget poor little Elle, isn't it?'

'No, never,' I protested. 'I wouldn't do that to you. I'll write to you. You'll see.'

Write I did, not because of the promise so much as my resentment that Jackie had gone off to work, leaving me to while away each precious day of my leave with the old girl. While she was busying herself around the flat, I sat down at the kitchen table and wrote to Elle, giving the game away by looking furtive every time Ma-in-law passed by.

Jackie had not been home from work ten minutes before she summoned me into the bedroom, the only place where we could find any privacy. 'You bastard,' she screamed as I shut the door, 'you've been writing to a woman.' In her hand, she held out a sheet of blotting paper. I took the blotter without a word, studying the writing on it with a puzzled look implying it had nothing to do with me. Clearly visible, back to front, was the imprint 'Darling Elle.' In those days before the Biro people wrote letters with fountain pens, blotting the words frequently to stop the ink smudging. The old girl had twigged me. I was right up the creek, and only myself to blame.

It got a bit heated after that. I was soon on the bus to pay a call on Q (Movements), Royal Engineers, at Liverpool Street Station asking if my trip across Europe could be advanced three days. It could. I was grateful the sergeant did not ask whether the ugly scratches on my face had anything to do with this most unusual request. Servicemen usually want their leave lengthened, not cut short.

The Medloc Express – *Medloc* was the acronym for Middle East Lines of Communication – was running back to Trieste almost empty. I managed to find a lady soldier, an ATS corporal named Yvonne, to share my troubles. Her advice was to write to Jackie confessing all. Put it down to loneliness and not hearing for months, she advised. Yvonne warmed to her subject with such enthusiasm that she forgot to get out of her gently rocking sleeper at Dusseldorf, where she was stationed. She finally decamped at Munich. An Engineers lance-corporal wrote 'Munich-Dusseldorf Single' on Army notepaper and assured her it was valid on any West German train. I gave him two hundred duty frees for his kindness.

Elle carried the can for my marital misfortunes. I wrote to Jackie trying to explain and promised to unravel myself from my contortionist, a tragic victim of postwar disruption who had come to rely on my support. I went round to the room Elle shared with another girl to tell her it was all over. She wouldn't let me in. I heard sounds in the room, but all fell silent as I hammered on the door. Must be that Wolfgang, I thought, much relieved. A brief farewell on the back of a postcard and that was the end of the affair.

Well, not quite. Women always seem to be at their most loving when the bird has flown. The next day, sitting in the NAAFI, one of the lads brought the cryptic message 'Your bint's outside.'

I said a sheepish hello, took her arm and walked to the park bench nearby where we had met. She sat there and began to cry, pushing me away as I tried to comfort her. 'It's not you, darling,' I said. 'I'm married, you know. I've got a little girl. I had to tell the wife because I wasn't going to hide you, not you, not my lovely Elle . . .'

I'm mumbling away, the usual facile excuses, when suddenly Elle rummages in her handbag and produces a pair of large scissors. Oh, God, I thought, she's going to stab herself. That's men for you. It was me that got it, under the ribs on the right hand side.

'Christ,' I said, 'you stupid cow, you've stabbed me.'

I shot up, looked with horror at the bloodstain growing larger on my shirt, grabbed the scissors from her hand. 'Get out of here quick, and take these with you, otherwise you'll be in big trouble,' I told her. 'If anyone asks, I'll say I had an accident with my bayonet.'

It wasn't much. The tip of the scissors pierced my shirt, but penetrated the skin only a fraction. I didn't need medical attention. There was plenty of blood, though. Now I had two long scratches on my cheek and a wound in my side. Imagine two women caring that much about me! I felt quite chuffed. All the same, it must have taught me something. I kept away from Elle after that.

The time had come for stocktaking. My best bet seemed to be to stay in camp, reading, listening to music and avoiding any further romantic entanglements. Perhaps Jackie would sense from my ardent letters that I truly wanted forgiveness and would not err again. There's also a limit to how long the body can stand up to the drunken regime of a wandering soldier. Every evening in the *Gasthof Heinrich* drinking endless pints of *lichtas beer* with cherry brandy chasers, an hour or two of dalliance with *meine schatts*, a four-mile trek back to camp, crashing into bed as late as 3.00. First parade was 7.30 in the morning.

I remember one night collapsing in a field and waking up on a misty morn to the eerie sound of a hundred people snuffling and snorting. For a second I thought this must be death. As my eyes became accustomed to the early light, it dawned on me that I had spent the night in the middle of a herd of recumbent cows.

At the training school, I was the only National Service instructor on a staff of old sweats, which made me natural leader of the opposition to bullshit and bureaucracy in all its military guises. Virtually all the soldiers sent to us for advanced training were conscripts so we shared common cause.

One of the RSMs I encountered was an old cavalryman named Van Spall, of Dutch East Indies origin and, like all of his breed, a splendid character. The lads called him 'Abdul,' a dig at his nutbrown complexion, though naturally not to his face. Coming out of the NAAFI, two or three of us spotted him half-mile away, the other side of the square. 'Look out, Abdul's about,' said some wit. Back came his voice, with a roar like a wounded bull: 'I'll give you Abdul.'

I pulled a marvellous stunt on him with one of the Ukrainian displaced persons who did all the dirty work in the camp, collecting rubbish, cleaning up, gardening, cookhouse fatigues — all the jobs that back home would have gone to squaddies on jankers. We called this particular bloke Ivan. His job was to collect the dustbins in an old cart drawn by two huge dray horses. For five fags, he would let out an ear-piercing Cossack cry and leap from his seat on to the back of one of the poor nags.

Every Friday afternoon, RSM Van Spall took the young officers' parade, an obvious ploy by the colonel to keep conscript subalterns on their toes. We used to watch them in action, keeping well out of sight, just for the pleasure of seeing those arrogant buggers suffer a little. Since they were officers, the RSM had to suffix his orders with the odd 'Sir,' which made it all the funnier.

'You're several minutes behind the rest,' he would tell some sweating second lieutenant who had missed a step. 'One thousand glorious years of British military endeavour, then you had to come along, Sir!'

Or with deep sarcasm: 'Are you wearing a scarf, Sir, or is that your hair I'm standing on?'

In the middle of this lot I let Ivan go. Twenty fags it cost me instead of the usual five. Straight across the square the old cart trundled. Just at this point the RSM wheeled round to see what was happening, Ivan did his Tarzan bit. 'OoohaIAIOeeeh.' You would have thought the Red Army was coming. There on the square, holy ground, the officers began to laugh. So did half the garrison, tucked away in the shadows.

I was in headquarters, eating up the scene through a chink in the office curtains, when the RSM did a smart about turn, shook his fist at the building and roared: 'I'll 'ave you for this, Jameson!'

He was a good sport and didn't labour the point later when I played the innocent. 'What, me, Sir! Would I do a thing like that?' The RSM actually paid the compliment of advising me to sign on as a regular soldier when the time came for us to part.

This lazy, easygoing world was suddenly turned upside down in June, 1950. Playing chocolate box soldiers came to an abrupt end at 4 o'clock on a chilly morning. Alarm bells rang, whistles blew and we were ordered to the square in full battle order, carrying everything but personal possessions. We thought World War III had arrived. Quite a prospect, living in the shadow of the Iron Curtain.

We stood there for four hours. Nobody seemed to know what the flap was all about. BFN Radio solved the mystery in its early morning news bulletin. On the other side of the world the Korean war had broken out. We were most grateful, knowing there was no way in which British Troops in Austria, or their French and American allies in the adjoining zones, could withstand the might of Russia. The Austrians assumed we would make a fight of it. We knew in our hearts it would be a case of hit the road for Trieste and get on a boat one jump ahead of Soviet tanks.

I remember a loony attempt to teach us to ski at the famous resort of Kitzbühel. A line of us were attempting to climb a gently slope, slipping, sliding and falling about like a bunch of clowns, when a group of skiers descended out of the blue and weaved in and out of our ranks at breakneck speed. 'Just watch those lads,' said the instructor. 'You'll be fighting that lot one day!' It was the Red Army ski team.

Overnight, Korea added six months to our period of service. Groans all round at the news, the loudest rising from those with demob charts inside their locker doors indicating they had only days or weeks to serve. Not that anyone complained too much. You could feel the global tension in the air. Britain was now involved in a war in the Far East and the Cold War winds blew as fiercely as ever in Europe. Spy fever gripped Austria, at the junction of the great East-West divide. It was to have dramatic consequences for some of us in uniform.

Sitting in the training office one day, I got a telephone call from an NCO at

Headquarters, British Troops in Austria, who had recently been on one of my courses. Something was tickling him. 'What a laugh,' he said, 'you'll never believe this. We've got a pink slip from the War Office on you.'

I wasn't laughing. A pink slip means Top Secret document. It was obvious what was coming. 'What's it say,' I asked nonchalantly, as if it didn't matter a damn.

'Listen to this. It says you're a Communist and must not be employed in any position of trust or placed where you can influence others.'

It had taken twenty months for the witch hunt to catch up with me. By now my beliefs had changed totally. Nevertheless it seemed odd that my Communist past had not hindered me in any way in the Army, especially as I was in great demand in Aldershot and Austria as a current affairs lecturer. I put it down to bureaucratic inefficiency. Now, everyone had the jitters. Someone obviously had been checking on subversives, real or imagined.

The major who was *O i/c Trg* (officer in charge of training) was most kind when he summoned me to his office a few days later. He hummed and hawed, red with embarrassment, clearly conscious an injustice was being done. Everyone knew I was a first-class speaker with a record second to none in getting people through their advanced trade tests.

Not realising, of course, that I knew about the pink slip, he put his message across something like this: 'Look here, Corporal Jameson, you're a bloody good chap. The other chaps like you and I like you. Sometimes things happen that have got nothing whatsoever to do with us. That's the Army, eh? What soldiering is all about.

'Seems these chappies back at the War Office feel its time for a change, bit of a rest, try something different, job for a Regular, that sort of thing. I mean, you'll be the first to appreciate, you are a National Serviceman. Ought to have Regular chaps training the troops. Know what I mean? Damned unfair, I know. That's the Army, eh? Do as you're told. Get on with the job. I know you're a good chap and will understand that, eh?'

Poor soul. He never did quite manage to get it out that I was to be posted elsewhere. I already knew that, too. The corporal in the outer office, another of my graduates, had told me at breakfast that I was being sent to Q (Movements) at HQ Klagenfurt as acting chief clerk.

More lunacy awaited me at my new barracks, Klagenfurt Garrison, near the centre of the provincial capital of Carinthia. The Garrison Sergeant-major was as mad as they come. One of his bright ideas was that everyone should have their hair shaved to a quarter-inch like himself, a thought that did not endear him to civilian soldiers. We decided that what grew under our berets was our own business.

It was Sinzenheimer who finally broke his spirit. The feud between Lance-corporal Sinzenheimer and GSM Smith deserves a place in British military archives. It began the day this conscripted son of a German refugee arrived to take up duties as the Colonel's interpreter. Some sticky fingered merchant pinched all his kit in the corridor as he checked in. Sinzenheimer was put on a charge for failing to exercise due care and attention in protecting War Department property. That was a mistake.

The GSM personally marched Sinzenheimer into the adjutant to answer for this heinous crime. Asked if he had anything to say, Sinzenheimer said: 'Yes, if you insist on employing a gang of thieves here, don't try to pin the blame on me.' Then he marched himself out again. The GSM almost had apoplexy as the adjutant recorded 'Case not proven.'

Smithy hit back by persuading the orderly sergeant to pull the fuses in Sinzenheimer's barrack block at *reveille*. He had been tipped that his adversary sat in bed every morning shaving, his electric razor plugged into a light socket, while the rest fought for a place in the washroom outside. *Now he had him!* As the 7.00 parade was called to attention, GSM Smith had but one object in mind. He marched straight to his man.

'Ah, good morning, *Mister* Sinzenheimer! I see we haven't had a shave this morning, have we, *Mister* Sinzenheimer?'

'No, we haven't,' says Sinzenheimer. 'And I shall be only too pleased to tell the Colonel why if you care to persist in the matter. He should be most interested in this morning's power failure.'

Another time Smithy was asking for complaints in the dining hall while on duty as orderly officer. He made the mistake of stopping before Sinzenheimer, hoping for a little fun. No chance. Before he could get a word out, Sinzenheimer proffered his big spoon with some glutinous substance attached to it.

'Would you try this blancmange? Sir,' he requested. 'I think you'll agree that if it were taken to the British Military Hospital for analysis it would be passed as unfit for human consumption.'

Taken aback, the GSM pulled away. 'No, no,' he protested, 'I never eat blancmange.'

'I'm not asking you to EAT it,' Sinzenheimer told him acidly. 'I'm asking you to TASTE it. That's your job, isn't it?'

The sergeant cook paid for that one. GSM Smith hit out in all directions, but never got the better of Sinzenheimer. Our hero, small, studious and a total stranger to all things military, eventually got his demob and went off to Cambridge, never to be heard of again.

Smithy once descended on me. A severe reprimand in that, while on active service, I did allow Room 53, J Block, HQ Klagenfurt Garrison, under my charge, to be in a filthy state. He found a bit of fluff under a bed. At 11.30 one Saturday night in May, 1951, the Sergeant-major staggered out of the Mess and put six radios, eleven bicycles and a doorkey under close arrest. Causing an obstruction and creating noise after lights out!

Poor old Smithy. They finally led him away after he set fire to his office. Unfortunately for him, one of the sentries had spotted him in the middle of the night emptying his files onto the flames. We reckoned it was all Sinzenheimer's fault.

Klagenfurt Garrison created a wonderful camaraderie among us reluctant warriors. There we were, all kinds and classes from every corner of the country, trying to keep our marbles in a military madhouse. A Geordie milkman with a brogue so thick nobody could understand a word he said was *muckers* with a bank manager's son from Orpington. A big country boy, a Regular, would take us to his married quarters where his petite wife fed us stew and dumplings and apple crumble. We even had a cultural corner making regular excursions to the Klagenfurt Opera.

There was one little chap who desperately wanted to succeed as an actor. He would lie on his bed – our favourite posture offduty – and declaim Shakespeare while the others jeered and hooted. 'Aw, put a sock in it, will you?' someone would yell, lobbing a boot over to reinforce his point.

Our budding thespian asked me solemnly on one occasion: 'Do you think I'll ever make it?' I could only speak the truth as it seemed to me. 'Sorry, mate, you've no chance. They'd never see you over the footlights.'

Thankfully, the barrack room raspberries never blunted his ambitions. That was Ian Holm, who put on an inch or two and became one of Britain's greatest actors. A mutual Army friend was Donald Churchill, who also became a top actor and playwright.

Working at Headquarters, British Troops in Austria, wasn't a bad old job. Q (Movements) is the Army's travel agency, arranging the transfer of military personnel by road, rail and sea. The chief clerk there was much relieved to see me. My arrival meant he could go off on leave prior to a posting elsewhere. He gave me a rundown on the office, handed me the keys and was off. Having never been trusted with keys before, I had a good nose round while the officers were at their lunch. Starting with the Top Secret safe, naturally. As well as returns listing Army strength in Austria, there was also an Order of Battle specifying in detail what would happen in the event of war.

Most interesting. I smiled to myself. Imagine what a real spy would have given to get his hands on that lot!

Now that I was on Headquarters staff, I soon got the chance to prove to any-one who might be watching where my loyalties lay. I caught a spy. Well, almost. It happened this way. At 2.00 in the morning, I was sitting reading a book in the guardroom in the main Headquarters building. It was my first spell of duty as all-night duty guard commander. I sensed someone behind me, looking over my shoulder.

It was a greasy looking individual, a civilian, wearing a black leather coat. I had seen him before, chatting up soldiers and their girl friends in *gasthöfe* around the town. If anyone was a spy, it had to be him.

'Gi'es a light, Corp,' he said, proffering a ciggy.

'Piss off!' I told him. 'Now. This minute.'

'Aw, come on, Corp. All the guys know me.'

'Yes, so do I. That's why I'm telling you to move. Fast. Otherwise I shall take that bayonet there' – pointing to a rifle and bayonet against the wall – 'and shove it right up your rear end.'

As you can see, I was feeling a bit sensitive about spies.

He shuffled off. His presence worried me. How had he managed to get into the Guardroom inside the main building? That meant he had passed through Austrian police on the outer perimeter, dodged British troops patrolling the grounds and got through two sentries at the entrance. None of them admitted seeing him. I noted it all down in the duty log, mentioning that I had seen him behaving suspiciously in town.

No sooner had I got my head down for a couple of hours in my room than the SIB are at the door. Two of them, in double-breasted suits and big jazzy ties. They obviously had been seeing too many Raymond Chandler films. The SIB, or Special Investigation Branch, is the Army equivalent of the CID. Detectives in plain clothes looking for thieves, black marketeers, conmen, deserters – and now spies. I told my story again and the man in charge, a Sgt Williams, thought that he, too, knew our quarry.

'Little short geezer,' he said, 'looks like a rat.'

'That's him, that's the one.'

'Right, let's go get him.'

We spent the next forty eight hours roaring about in a Jeep, turning Klagenfurt upside down. Every *gasthof*, bar, club, cinema, NAAFI. Places I never knew existed. We knew who we were looking for, and he must have known it, too. He had scarpered. I went back to my office.

Six weeks later I bumped into Sgt Williams in town. He beckoned me over. 'Brother, did you get me into trouble,' he said.

'Why, what happened.'

'Well, I was up on the Yugo border. Personal, not business, visiting my girl friend' – he said it too earnestly for me to believe him – 'when who should walk in but our chummy. Soon as I clapped eyes on him I knew it was him. Nasty looking bugger.

'I slip outside, call for some assistance. Could be dodgy, see, just me and him.

'When he comes out, we grab him. Get him out of there in no time flat. Trouble is, he got roughed up a bit on the journey and there was hell to pay.'

'Why was that?' I asked innocently.

'Turned out he was a Yank. American CIA agent.'

'The miserable bastards,' I said. 'Fancy spying on their mates.'

'Yeah, that's what we thought,' said Sgt Williams. 'He did tell us, but we didn't believe him. I mean, bleedin' Yanks on the Yugo border. Out of order, that, no mistake.'

Spies, spies, spies. They seemed to grow on trees. At one point in Austria we had no less than eight Royal Signals NCOs under arrest accused of selling official secrets to Communist agents. Even the RASC, which had few secrets to sell, had two Staff Sergeants in adjoining cells awaiting trial for giving comfort to the enemy.

Staff Sergeant Harry Drummond was the black market king of the British zone. He was said to keep a beautiful Hungarian countess in a castle on the proceeds of tyres, petrol, rations and other Army goods that had found their way into grateful Austrian hands since the end of the war. Arrested for extortion, he claimed to have VD and was sent to the military hospital for a check. While there he escaped by clambering down a drainpipe and fled to the Russian zone in Vienna. The Russkies pumped him dry, realised he was a racketeer, not a defector, and sent a message to the British Military Police to come into their zone and pick him up.

Staff Sergeant Harry Longmuir was a more pathetic case. He manned a lone petrol pump on the road from the border village of Villach to Trieste and had been ordering Army manuals in bulk and passing them to Communist agents. He actually got hold of 144 copies of something called *Staff Duties in the Field*, which purports to give the disposition of senior officers in wartime. What the Printing and Stationery Section, Royal Army Ordnance Corps, thought a petrol pump attendant wanted with several gross of restricted documents was never explained. Harry's defence was that the Communists were putting pressure on the family of his Czech-born wife and he had no alternative but to do their bidding.

We had to guard this prize pair before they were convicted. Drummond was calm and phlegmatic about it all. Because of his escape, he was held in a freezing stone cell with only his underclothes, straw palliasse and single blanket. He cadged fags, but never complained. Nor would he tell us how much loot he had salted away.

Harry Longmuir was different again. Small and skinny, where Drummond was tough and stocky, he spent hours pacing up and down in his cell, wringing his hands and telling anyone prepared to listen: ' 'Twasn't me, 'twasn't my fault.'

I was there on guard at 2.00 one morning when Drummond kept calling Longmuir's name through his bars until his compatriot opened his rheumy eyes and demanded to know what he wanted.

'They're going to hang you, Harry, hang you by the neck!' he hissed venomously. He rolled over on his blanket and went to sleep, leaving poor old Harry weeping in his cell.

In the event, Drummond got 10 years for betraying his country, instead of four for fraud. Longmuir, still crying, went down for seven years. Two Harrys from Scotland. They didn't bear the remotest resemblance to that third villainous Harry, the one named Lime.

That was Austria. The armies of four countries playing hopscotch on a crazy pavement of pretty girls, real spies and Nazis who were really democrats. Or was it the other way round? I wasn't sorry to leave when my demobilisation orders came through in July, 1951.

Major S. G. Scrutton, Royal Engineers, gave me a farewell testimonial: 'I have always found him to be most reliable and attentive to his duties, trustworthy and pleasant in manner. He is a clean, sober type and amenable to discipline.'

It was time to go home, repair my marriage and get on with my career.

The angels were waiting for me.

CHAPTER FOURTEEN

Poor man's American

G etting back to Reuters proved a great deal more difficult than arranging to be called up into the Army. By now Tony Cole had moved upstairs, presiding over the news empire from a palatial suite on the seventh floor. Top dog in the editorial was Geoffrey Imeson, a decent enough chap in his owlish spectacles. When he took them off for a polish, a sure sign he was feeling twitchy, he looked like a little boy lost.

The specs were treated to a bonus the morning I sat in front of Geoffrey's desk, fit and bronzed after my time in Austria, to inquire blandly how he planned to employ me now that I had served King and Country.

We left unspoken the chain of events that preceded my visit. I had written to say I was ready to return to duty, only to receive a terse letter from the Company secretary informing me with regret there was no room at the Reuters inn. Never say die, I shot round to the Hackney labour exchange, where the obliging manager immediately called the secretary to threaten action in the courts to secure my lawful reinstatement. Conscripts had a statutory right to be re-employed for a period of six months. A letter arrived days later with the appointment to see Mr J.G. Imeson, Assistant Editor.

'We've thought carefully about your case,' said Geoffrey, holding his spectacles up to the light of the window, 'and we accept that we are not being altruistic about it.' I wondered what altruistic meant.

'However, taking everything into consideration, the work you did in the past, that sort of thing, we have arrived at what we think is a solution that will satisfy both you and us.'

Geoffrey gave me an insipid smile. He was not enjoying this. Whatever the solution, I wasn't going to like it. We both knew that before he delivered his *coup de grâce*.

'We are going to retrain you as a teleprinter operator!' To his credit, he made it sound like six months in the Bahamas. I entered into the spirit of things, putting on an expression grateful and yet perplexed.

'That is most kind of you,' I said, 'and I'm sorry to have put you to all this trouble. However, much as I appreciate what you are doing for me, it is totally out of the question for one very good reason.'

'What's that?' Geoffrey inquired with a querulous frown.

'The National Union of Journalists' – I spelled it out – 'does not approve of its members becoming teleprinter operators.'

Geoffrey was prepared for such tardiness. 'Right,' he said briskly. 'You've got six months. No longer. You'd be well advised to start looking around for another job now. Meanwhile, we'll put you on the NOR desk.'

NOR stood for North America. The most exciting corner of the agency because it ran a world news service to newspapers and radio stations in Canada and the United States, home territory of our mighty rivals, Associated Press and United Press. Clients included such prestigious papers as the *New York Times, Chicago Tribune, Los Angeles Times, Christian Science Monitor* and *Cleveland Plain Dealer*. The desk also monitored the Soviet and East European world for the Voice of America, the CIA's radio station beaming propaganda behind the Iron Curtain.

A strange place to land an Englishman suspected of Communist sympathies who was still a trainee and had just spent two years out of the business. All but one or two of the desk personnel were American or Canadian. The North American editor was Stu Underhill, a Canadian of immense ability whom many thought would one day run the entire agency. He was a tall, austere man who laughed seldom and was not given to small talk.

I guess they lumbered Underhill with the dubious Jameson for two reasons. If I was to prove unworthy of a job after six months, this highly specialised American enclave was the place to fail. They didn't even speak the same language as us, though to be sure it was a close approximation. And if I were going to get up to any mischief on behalf of the Kremlin, this would be the place to do it – and be spotted in minutes. Brother, was I in trouble.

Stu Underhill said nothing of this at our first meeting, though a murmured aside showed that he knew all about it. 'You've got your work cut out in the next six months,' he warned me gently.

151

Work is my favourite occupation, especially writing. I threw myself into that job as if my life depended on it. In a way it did. I wrote powerful features that found a ready home in papers all over North America. I did my stints round the clock as a sub-editor – or rewrite man, as our cousins call it – and within months was often running the desk. I looked and sounded more American than Billy the Kid, acquiring a crew cut and smoking Chesterfields. What really saved my bacon was that early education in American literature. I knew as much about the American way of life as the natives. One guy, Emerson Chapin, worked next to me for three months without realising I was British. By the time the six months was up there was no mention of leaving Reuters.

My mentor Tony Cole, the editor I had failed so miserably, began sending the odd message of congratulation on some success or other. Herograms, we call them. I was delighted. One of my great regrets is that he died in January 1963 at the early age of fifty, before I became a newspaper editor. He would have liked to have seen his Cockney protégé justify whatever it was he had seen in me at the beginning.

A couple of years later I was promoted to the Central Desk, hub of the agency, and went through the ranks there like a dose of salts. By the age of twenty five, notwithstanding the earlier hiccups in my career, I was senior desk editor and often editor-in-charge, responsible for the entire world news service.

Best of all I liked the all-night shift. The permanent night owls were all a bit barmy. It must have been the odd hours. The editorial was like a tip at the end of several news cycles, waiting for the cleaners to arrive with the dawn. Discarded cups, saucers and plates everywhere, many of them serving as makeshift ashtrays. The floor a sea of paper; hacks regard the deck as a filing cabinet and rarely use wastepaper baskets. Most of the overhead lights were switched off and three or four bodies could be discerned in the gloom, stretched out on desks. Night workers snatching a couple of hours' kip so they could get through their day jobs.

This was the scene as Tony Cole made his routine check call sometime after midnight: 'Cole here. Anything doing?'

Digger Blore, night editor and wartime naval commander, never faltered in his response: 'Everything correct, Sir, and all departments bearing an equal strain!' Digger was a short, pugnacious Aussie who invariably had a long black cigarette holder clenched in his teeth. We always tried to get him to tell us tales of derring-do from the war years. One story was that he parachuted into Bucharest, capital of Nazi-held Rumania, in the full dress uniform of an officer in the Royal Australian Navy. 'So many bloody uniforms about the Jerries weren't going to spot another, were they?' he barked.

'Yes, yes, Digger,' I would twit, 'but did you wear your dress sword?'

Alongside Digger a showbiz type with black wavy hair and gold wristband, beavering away on two typewriters. A quick burst on one and then over to the second. This was Larry Forrester, handling news dispatches on one machine and writing film treatments on the other. He became one of Hollywood's major scriptwriters.

The main object of the night shift was to 'turn over' the previous day's file for evening papers, injecting any new material into the stories and somehow making them look fresh and newsy. In the case of a plane crash, for instance, you would write the blindingly obvious: *An investigation opens today into the crash* ... The important thing was to get the word 'today' into the text.

Again and again, the European Editor explained this to a flamboyant, bearded film extra working the night shift on his desk. This character kept missing the point. One morning the editor let out a great scream of pain as he sat reading the overnight file. His night sub had written: *Bonn, West Germany – Twenty two West German coal miners were still dead today 24 hours after a disaster* ... And so the journalistic career of the great James Robertson Justice came to an abrupt end.

Another night owl was the brewery heir Jonathan Guinness, son of Lord Moyne. His mother, Diana, one of the Mitford sisters, had later married Sir Oswald Mosley. Jonathan made no secret that he was firmly on the right – he later became chairman of the Tory Monday Club – and the leftwingers at Reuters gave him a wide berth. I always found him friendly enough. The lads knew he liked to swig a bottle of milk on the doorstep when he reached his Kensington home off the night shift. With the Dairy Marketing Board very much in mind, I tried to kid him into posing for a picture. Nothing doing.

Nigel Ryan, the first editor of ITN, was also a contemporary. I bawled him out once for getting the name of one of the EEC founder nations wrong. Sandy Gall, another famous ITN name, was also there. We would work alongside each other when he was between assignments as a wide-ranging foreign correspondent. Sandy told me once he infinitely preferred covering wars to sitting at a desk handling other peoples' copy. Author Freddie Forsyth of *The Day of the Jackal* was also at Reuters, as was David Chipp, who became the conscience of Fleet Street as editor of the Press Association agency.

Baron Reuter began his famous agency in the mid-19th century to carry commercial news to the great financial institutions. He opened his first office in London at Old Jewry, in the City. By the 1920s it was very much a news service. In my day, financial news was left to the poor relation of the outfit, something called Comtelburo for Commercial Telegraph Bureau. The numerologists who appeared to run it were forever trying to get their dispatches on to the news wires. They always got shoved to the back of the queue. 'Sorry, cock,' we would say, 'they've just formed their 29th postwar government in Italy. No room for your crap.' With the advance of technology, some visionary at Reuters realised people playing the markets in world capitals could make a fortune if they received news of exchange dealings and currency fluctuations ahead of the game. More importantly, they would pay handsomely for such a gift from the computerised gods. Reuters already had the communications network and the expertise. The rest was easy. Nowadays it moves financial information across the globe in seconds. The news service takes secondary place.

The microchip was Cinderella's metamorphosis. Reuters' financial services raised the value of the agency until it was worth more than most of Fleet Street put together. The proprietors who were supposed to run it as a non-profit making trust woke up one day to a unique opportunity. They floated it as a public company, financing much of their own transition to new technology from the proceeds.

Those of us who grew up in the place laughed cynically at the excitement created by Reuters' millions. Had we stayed, we would have been preferential shareholders with a fortune in our pockets. While we were there all we cared about was getting out. Not out of any disrespect. Simply to make a better living. Reuters always had to struggle to get more money from its newspaper owners. That meant we worked for minimum wages. I earned more as an *Express* sub-editor than I did as a senior editor at the agency.

My exit visa was the birth of the *London American*, a weekly newspaper designed for 110,000 Americans living in Britain and anyone else who might be interested, not least the dollar tourists coming over in increasing numbers year by year. It was very much an Anglo-American venture. The editor was an American advertising man, William J. Caldwell, and the chief shareholder Robert 'Mac' Boult, a Leeds clothing manufacturer.

It was Lawrence Thaw, one of my North American desk pals, who put me up for a job on the new paper. News editor, second only to the editor himself. It seemed an unlikely proposition. I was not American and had no experience of newspaper production, though desperate to learn it. There was also that little business of my Communist past.

Bill Caldwell brushed aside my objections when I went to see him in swish offices at Princes Arcade, off Piccadilly. He turned out to be a fierce Republican, but clearly was impressed by my honesty in raising the political bogey. Nothing to worry about, obviously, otherwise I would not have mentioned it. As for the rest, well I had run the North American service at Reuters and, hell, anyone could pick up newspaper production. I learned later they had looked for an American. The cheapest they could find came at £100 a week. They paid me £38.50 – a fiver more than Reuters.

So, in March, 1960, start of a new decade, I began another great adventure with the most oddly assorted bunch of newspapermen and women this side of *The Front Page*. I was thrown in at the deep end from day one. Caldwell was a thinker. All very well, but a newspaper runs on people who do things, not think about them. I had to take over the day-to-day running of the paper. The poor man's American, I called myself.

Caldwell's main role was to produce the esoteric diary of an American in Britain and write lengthy editorials reflecting on the state of East-West relations and the Eisenhower policy of brinkmanship, which he supported totally. I wondered whether he was a CIA agent because of a strange habit he had of making mysterious phone calls every time I raised ideas with him.

What about the death penalty, I would say. It's a big issue here, and the Americans seem to be at sixes and sevens about it. Some states do, some don't. The electric chair fascinates the British. Think we should run a piece.

'Well, now, let me see,' he would say, rubbing his chin. 'If you'll just give me a second, Derek, I'd like to ponder on that.' He would be reaching for the phone before I was out of the door. Most peculiar. I never did find out who he was calling.

Bill was an avuncular figure, short, grizzled, steel grey hair. He looked like a judge in a Hollywood movie and never quite fitted into the circus in the outer office where we worked. He disappeared without a word one day at the end of our first year when the paper began running out of money. I carried on as before, in control of the paper, only now there was no titular editor to consult.

It was lively enough for a weekly. Three or four pages of news stories relevant to Americans, some of British origin, others lifted from the American papers. Several syndicated columns like Sheilah Graham in Hollywood, Earl Wilson on show business, Irv Kupcinet from Chicago and Sylvia Porter on finance. Our own writers produced two or three pages of fashion and beauty, a two-page arts spread, some general features and one or two sports pages. Twenty pages for one shilling (5p).

The best coup we had was when CIA pilot Gary Powers, flying a U2 spy plane, came down over Russia on the eve of the 1960 East-West Summit. I managed to get hold of an American briefing document revealing that he had not been shot down, as everyone thought, but glided to earth with engine failure. There had been a second plane behind him 1,250 miles inside Russia. Our publication of this Top Secret report caused a five-minute sensation.

We did make a noble effort to improve understanding between our two nations, affectionately sending up their special relationship and looking at life from our own Anglo-American vantage point. We liked features that examined some of the more loony attitudes prevalent at the time. For instance, we summed up the British view of Americans in those days with a series of typical questions: *Is every American a millionaire? Women run America, don't they? Your crime wave is shocking, isn't it? Why is the divorce rate so high in America? Are many of your schools Blackboard Jungles? Why are you so beastly to the Russians?*

Despite our best efforts, the paper made little progress. The rich harvest of advertising revenue that was supposd to come our way failed to materialise. Canny advertising men quickly spotted that tourists were not likely to read an obscure weekly when they could get the *New York Herald Tribune* at every newstand. Before long there was not enough money coming in to pay our wages and printing costs. Promotion of the paper came to a standstill. There was no more capital forthcoming from owner Richard Boult. He was having troubles of his own in his clothing empire.

Every phone call seemed to be a creditor. Some of them even planted themselves on the chairs by the reception desk. Ron Beard, a former policeman and neighbour of mine, was sitting there one day. He had been sent by John Lewis stores to discuss the bill for an electric kettle. I started using the fire escape to get in and out after that. We moved office three times in a year, descending from the jet set world of Piccadilly to a decrepit warehouse by Blackfriars station, near Fleet Street. Disaster stared us in the face. We kept going stoically for 15 months. At the end we were down to four journalists. I was filling half the paper on my own.

Needs must . . . What better way to learn the newspaper business! In this crazy world I had the great good fortune to sit at the feet of the most famous journalist of our times. Arthur Christiansen, the shipwright's son who took the *Daily Express* to a wartime sale of 4,000,000 copies daily. Lord Beaverbrook, his proprietor, had declined to re-employ Chris after he suffered a mild heart attack. So he was putting his fund of knowledge to work as an editorial consultant and media odd job man. He even played himself in the film *The Day the Earth Caught Fire*. That's where I got the idea of pursuing a career in show business 25 years later.

The *London American* paid Chris £4,000 a year as editorial adviser, twice my salary as editor. I would take the page proofs to him every week and we would mull over them together. I would devour every word he uttered, totally enchanted. 'Think that headline's a bit strong,' he would say in his rich, dry bark of a voice. 'It's a nothing story, some chap objecting to quarantine regulations. He's obviously never seen rabies.'

Normally we met in his office at ATV, Associated Television, near Marble Arch. He was editorial adviser there, too. The company was connected in some way with Muzak and the piped wallpaper music emerged from every crevice. Even in the lifts and bogs. Not in Chris' office, though. 'Look at this, old chap' he said one day, beckoning me over. He had ripped the wires out of the wall. 'Can't stand all that guff,' he laughed.

Now and again he invited me to join him for a drink, an opportunity to pick his brains about Fleet Street and the characters he had worked alongside. I once asked him the question puzzling everyone in newspapers. 'Since you made such a good recovery, and are now as fit as ever, why did Beaverbrook refuse to take you back as editor of the *Express*?'

Chris snorted derisively. 'Don't think I didn't try. I put it to him fair and square "I want my job back." Know what he told me? "Forget all about it, Mr Christiansen. I don't wish to be shunned at your funeral".'

We were standing in the BBC pub, The Phoenix, behind Oxford Street, one day when an anxious-looking bloke began hovering around in the way they do in the presence of the mighty.

'Can I b-b-buy you a drink,' he finally stammered.

'Certainly, old chap,' said Chris without hesitating. 'I'll have a G&T and one for my friend, too.'

A drink means a chat, of course. It was soon clear that our benefactor had something on his chest. 'You don't know who I am, do you?' he asked Chris importantly. 'No' 'fraid I don't, who are you?'

'Well' – at last the moment of truth – 'you might be interested to know that you fired me from the *Express* in 1943 and do you know what I do now?' His voice rose triumphantly.

'No, what do you do?' Chris asked politely.

'I am the SENIOR HOME AFFAIRS EDITOR OF THE BBC.' Each word slowly and separately for maximum effect.

'Well, I was obviously quite right,' Chris responded briskly. 'Now what are you having to drink, old chap?'

Sadly, Chris played a lesser role as time went by. The paper now had another champion seen as the answer to all that troubled us. Cartoonist one day, managing director the next. The most extraordinary character of them all, Robert Guccione.

Bob was submitting cartoons to the paper from the beginning. He had a strong line, as we say in the business, but his subjects tended to be bizarre. The first, I recall, was an organ grinder and his monkey. A gorilla, in fact, carrying a young lady wearing not a lot under his arm from her room to his master playing below.

Not that anyone was going to argue with Bob about his drawings. He was passionately committed to his art, had worked on the celebrated *Village Voice* in New York and didn't give a toss whether people liked them or not. He was also a powerfully built Sicilian American, olive skinned with piercing eyes. Not a man to put down easily. Anyway, we paid him only £7 a cartoon. You don't get editorial control at those prices.

Bob had a job elsewhere, though he spent hours at a time with the paper, totally absorbed in everything going on. It was obvious to me that he was picking up every last scrap of knowledge about the publishing game. We talked a lot and his remarkable story emerged piece by piece.

He had been bumming around making a reasonable living with his pen and guitar in the south of France when the *gendarmerie* intervened. No work permit. Bob was given 24 hours to quit the country. Britain was the obvious place. He arrived with little money and no work.

'I asked a guy in a café where's the best place to find a job and he said "Try the *Daily Telegraph*," ' Bob told me. 'Cost me money I couldn't afford, but I got the paper and read it right there on the quayside.' Under Situations Vacant, he found an old-established dry cleaners in the City of London looking for a manager. They had an old fashioned name to match. Babcock and Tiller, or some such. An idea began to form in Guccione's brain. He was a go-getting American. He had driven a laundry truck as a teenager in San Francisco. He would call on Babcock and Tiller.

Ushered before one of the directors, Bob made his pitch. He knew all about dry cleaning in America, though was not on top of the way it was done here in Britain. He could learn easily enough.

'What compound do you use in America?' asked the director.

'V8,' said Bob.

'Never heard of that.'

'Well it's a kind of blend of all the cleaning fluids,' Bob assured him.

V8 is American canned vegetable juice. 'I said the first thing that came into my head,' Bob told me. 'Anyway, it was good enough for this guy. He gave me the job.'

Bob went into the dry cleaning business with a will. He renamed the firm Prompt Cleaners, and plastered the name in big red letters on the side of its vans, freshly painted white. He organised home collections and deliveries. American-style dry cleaners in London, he boasted. Business trebled in months. Bob was made not just manager, but general manager.

Nevertheless, relations between him and the oldest dry cleaners of them all were not of the best. The directors could not understand some of his funny American ways. Like giving the workers champagne when they topped production records. He was drawn more and more towards his great love, art. That meant the *London American*.

The day came when he quit Prompt Cleaners for good. We took him on the paper for £25 a week. That included all cartoons and other illustrations, plus a weekly satirical piece he was writing called The Solemn Column. Pathetic wages, but all we could afford.

We got along fine while he was one of my staff. He has said since that he learned much from me, though he hated me being his boss at the time. That did not stop him subsequently putting into practice much of what he had picked up under my tutelage at the *London American* in his own *Penthouse* empire. 'Now they all hate me,' he says wryly.

Now that he had a new role, managing director, Bob and I were soon involved in a ferocious battle over the contents of the paper. He already had the idea for *Penthouse*, the magazine that was to make him a millionaire several times over, firmly fixed in his mind. The inspiration was Hugh Hefner's *Playboy*. Bob had thoughts of his own on how that formula could be adapted to the British market and ultimately challenge Hefner in America. He was quite right. A man of his time. This was the threshold of the Permissive Sixties.

There was just one problem. I wasn't having any of it. And I ran the paper.

'Look, Derr,' he would say to me patiently for the tenth time. 'I'm not asking you to do anything you don't want to do as a professional. Half the stuff you're running comes from other papers. All I'm saying is that if we scalp the American sheets for good sex stories, you know, crime, divorce, rape, court cases, that kind of thing, we'll start selling some goddam' papers.'

'You mean turn us into a kind of American *News of the World*?' I would ask innocently.

His eyes would light up. 'That's it! You got it, Derr. Won't cost us a bean. What the hell's wrong with that?'

'Just one thing. I'm a newspaperman, not a pornographer. And I'm responsible for what goes into the paper. So you can piss off!'

There were times when I thought he would hit me. His eyes would bulge, veins standing out on his neck. Then he would turn on his feet and storm off muttering 'I don't know how anyone could be that goddam' stoopid!'

I would never budge. No wonder Bob got annoyed. And what about poor 'Mac' Boult, the owner? Just imagine, if he had got rid of me and taken up Guccione's ideas, that would have been the birth of the *Penthouse* empire and he could have shared all those millions instead of going broke in Leeds. Of course, the staff sided with me. What was left of it. They didn't fancy tit-and-bum, American style, any more than I did.

Barbara Taylor, the woman's editor, was caught in the middle. She had been Richard Boult's girl friend for several years. They met in Leeds when she was working for the *Yorkshire Evening News* and their romance continued after she came to Fleet Street to write fashion for the *Evening News*.

Now Barbara had thrown her lot in with the *London American* and naturally wanted it to succeed if only for the sake of Mac. She herself had grave doubts about the venture, though she loyally kept quiet about them. I felt sure she had backed Guccione's overnight promotion. Would she go for his survival kit?

Never. Not our lovely Barbara. She was too much of a professional. A tall, striking redhead with china blue eyes, Barbara had tackled the paper's problems with great gusto from the start, winning over all kinds of people, cultivating the advertisers and filling page after page every issue.

'I've always worked hard, you know, very hard,' she would say in those rounded Armley tones, her eyes opening wide. A girl from the back streets of Leeds going places.

With an eye on those 80,000 American servicemen in Britain, Barbara even managed to become first woman to break the sound barrier in a USAF F-100 Super Sabre jet fighter, roaring over the English countryside at 800mph. In the passenger seat, of course. That little epic did us a power of good with Major-General Mickey Moore, commander of the U.S. Third Air Force in Britain.

Like Guccione, Barbara made it, too. Have you recognised her? Barbara Taylor Bradford. After the paper folded, she went to Hollywood with dreams of writing the great novel. There she met and married producer Bob Bradford and eventually produced her blockbuster, *A Woman of Substance*. This other story of Yorkshire grit, not unlike her own, sold 12 million copies and became a major television series around the globe. Now they are into highly successful sequels.

'Ooh, Derek, fancy all this happening to us,' she says to me nowadays from her palatial New York apartment, 47 floors up. She still has her Yorkshire accent. 'Who would have believed it when we sat in that cold warehouse wondering how we were going to fill the paper.'

Alongside Barbara was the delicious Joanna Norton-Griffiths, cousin of the former Liberal leader Jeremy Thorpe, a girl with all the outrageous neck of the English upper classes. 'I say,' she would shriek, striding into the editorial, hands on hips. 'There's a most fearful stink in here! Why can't one of you blighters open a window.' Jolly hockey sticks in a world of cynical Americans. Jo used to keep me in fits. Today she is the wife of top peoples' vet Keith Butt. Then there was Maggi Nolan, our celebrity columnist whose entire life seemed to revolve around some Mayfair haunt called Siggy's. Her column went down a treat, though I could never understand the appeal of news items reading: *Mr Bing Crosby has just returned from New York, where he did a TV show for Mr Perry Como, who'll be coming to London to do a show next month.*

Associate editor Lawrence Thaw, the man who made it all happen for me in the first place, was my strongest ally in the fight to keep the *London American* going as a newspaper. He wrote powerful pieces on visiting Americans like James Thurber, Van Johnson, Sophie Tucker and Democratic party boss James A. Farley and even landed a rare interview with Caroline Benn, American wife of the Labour leftwinger Tony Benn, MP.

'Jeez, Derr,' he used to say, 'don't take any crap. You know what I mean, kiddo? You hear what I'm saying to you.'

Everyone else could hear, too, because Larry has a roar loud enough to shake the timbers, especially when anything desperate happens to disturb him. Like a typewriter ribbon getting snarled up. What fascinated me was his ability to get through a dozen cups of thick black coffee in one sitting, helped down with one French fag after another.

We met as sub-editors at Reuters. He has been in Britain for nearly 40 years now, has a lovely English rose of a wife named Sue, and is totally hooked on the place. Nevertheless, our strange little ways still manage to infuriate him. Once I took him to Battle, outside Hastings. 'There you are, Larry,' I said expansively, 'birthplace of the modern world.'

He snorted, thinking about it as we walked through the village. Then he spotted a fly inside a butcher's window.

'Jeez, look at that,' he hooted. 'One thousand years of civilisation and they can't even keep the goddam' flies off the meat.'

Lawrence Copley Thaw – he has dropped the 'Larry' these days – is pure pedigree stock. American aristocracy. His father and namesake was a Wall Street broker who also achieved fame as an explorer. His mother's second husband was of the Singer sewing machine empire. The name Thaw has a far greater significance for Americans than any of that. It looms large in one of the most celebrated murders in American history, as famous as Lizzie Borden and her chopper. In 1906, Lawrence's great uncle, Harry K. Thaw, stormed into Madison Square Garden and shot dead Stanford White, the greatest architect of his day. He discovered White had been dallying with his bride, showgirl Evelyn Nesbit, when she was barely out of school. Evelyn was the famous Girl on the Red Velvet Swing, an interesting divertissement White had installed in their love nest. Great Uncle Harry finished up in an asylum. He was released ten years later, only to be reincarcerated for beating up a young boy.

Larry's role on the *London American* at £27.50p a week embraced show business, music, ballet and striptease, as he likes to put it. He once got three of us to review the gyrations of a visiting American strip queen. Covering these shows, if that is the word, attracted advertising support. Larry roped in some powerful support in other directions. Charles Taylor, whose father, E.P. Taylor, ran Canada's biggest brewing dynasty, wrote a theatre column for £7 a week. R.B. Kitaj, now one of the world's foremost modern painters, reviewed the galleries for two guineas (£2.10p).

We even had an Irish Cherokee on the paper, the delectable Molly Brodney from Yankton County, South Dakota. Molly was the only staff feature writer. She came to us from the pages of American *Vogue* and was in London thanks to a transatlantic romance with a young Scottish laird, Mark Murray-Threipland. They married while she was working on the paper and today tend their fields and castles in the wilds of Caithness. Mark raises extraordinary pedigree cattle. Cream cows from Sicily, seven foot tall? I guess it makes sense to dairy farmers. Back in Greenwich Village, Molly's first husband became the first American publisher of the permissive age to print the works of Henry Miller, J.P. Donleavy and other writers once strictly taboo. They tell me he is now a millionaire.

Another high flyer on the paper was the sports editor, Jack Geiger, who had worked on a similar venture to ours, the Rome *Daily American*. I always thought Jack was a reformed gangster. He certainly had friends in the underworld.

Once I spent a weekend at his country retreat, the kind of place where they drink gin and tonic with breakfast, and a bloke in gumboots with a shotgun under his arm came across the fields to greet us. He may have looked like local squire to some folk. I recognised him instantly as one of the nation's top villains. There was also talk of Jack making a hasty departure from Britain in earlier years. Something to do with vending machines. The metal parts tended to disintegrate about a fortnight after some poor soul had invested his life savings in them.

'It's all hooey, Derek,' he would say. 'Take my word, there's bums out there would do down their own grandmother.'

He would laugh outrageously, his sadly twisted body shaking at the thought. Jack suffered dreadful spinal and other injuries in a crash after the war when he was flying with the U.S. Air Force as a jet fighter pilot. For two years he lay in a hospital bed, encased in plaster, fighting back after being told he would never walk again. The accident happened on the ground, strangely enough. Jack was on the tarmac in his fighter and a bomber coming in to land finished on top of him.

A lot of people were curious to know what had happened to this six-foot-two-inch giant, a former athlete, who now moved in a shambling, twisted gait, almost crablike. Jack wasn't shy about it and laughed off his misfortunes.

'Ask me why I never got a 100 per cent disability pension,' he would challenge people.

''Cos I landed my plane on the wrong goddam' airfield, is all.'

Jack's credentials were impeccable, despite my doubts. He married an English girl from the top drawer. Her father was something big in Robertson's jam. He himself left us to become a press officer with the USAF in Britain and in no time at all became Chief of Press with the Air Force in Washington. Sadly, he died not long afterwards.

I remember covering a murder trial at Colchester of a USAF man. Staff Sgt

Willis Boshears was accused of strangling a local good time girl, during a drunken debauch while his Scottish wife was visiting the folks back home. He hid the girl's body in his deep freezer for three days before dumping it in a ditch.

Boshears' extraordinary defence was that he had killed the girl in his sleep and didn't remember a thing. I recall the gist of the judge's words, summing up: *Never in the entire history of British jurisprudence has an accused person successfully claimed that he or she committed a felony whilst in his sleep.*

Jack, by now working for the USAF, strolled over to me as the jury filed out and whispered: 'He's going to get off.'

'Rubbish,' I said hotly. 'How can he? You heard what the judge said. And one of the jury's wearing a ban-the-bomb badge!'

Jack put a finger to the side of his nose, raised his eyes heavenward and said 'Don't forget I told you, buddy.'

He was quite right. Not guilty. I still can't make it out. What a merry chase we had through the streets of Colchester trying to catch up with Boshears before the USAF got him on a plane out to the country. Eddie Laxton and Stanley Meagher of the *Daily Express* almost ran me down as I stood in front of their fast sports car to stop them abducting Boshears. *The Express* bought the wife's story and had passed advance proofs around the Press bench with a lurid headline saying: I MARRIED A STRANGLER. I looked eagerly next morning to see how they had got out of that one. I KNEW MY MAN WAS INNOCENT, said the substitute headlines.

The fun and games could not last. An injection of cash might have saved the hard-pressed *London American*. None was forthcoming and the paper died in June, 1961. It was too sad an occasion for a wake.

Guch, as we called Bob Guccione, was kind enough to ask whether I would like to join him in a new venture. Dirty pictures. Hot Shots, Mademoiselle Fifi, Oriental Beauties. That kind of thing. Two guineas (£2.10p) for six.

'We'll make enough money in six months to launch our own magazine,' he said. I declined with thanks. Another fortune chucked away. Bob was right as usual. The money rolled in. He and his wife, a former ATS officer named Muriel, were next seen counting bundles of banknotes on the floor of their luxurious new apartment in Chelsea's Cheyne Walk. Their neighbour was Cecil King, then boss of the Mirror Group.

Four years later Bob flooded the nation's letter boxes with tens of thousands of leaflets in which the high and the mighty hailed the birth of Britain's new sexual revolution, available for all to share in the columns of the new glossy magazine *Penthouse*. The Post Office obliged by prosecuting Bob for sending offensive matter through the mails. He was fined two hundred quid and went from the court to a BBC TV studio to tell *Panorama* viewers and anyone watching in Fleet Street that the new age of sexual liberation was upon us.

The free publicity was worth a million. First copies of *Penthouse* were in the newsagents within days. More than 100,000 copies were snapped up at 5/- (25p) a time. The most *London American* sold was 43,000 after its expensive launch. By the close it was down to 17,000 copies.

I had no regrets. Within minutes of the *London American* folding, Arthur Christiansen appeared with soothing words and got on the phone to the man sitting in his old chair, Bob Edwards, editor of the *Daily Express*. I crossed the road to the Black Lubyianka, where Bob treated me to his famous smile and took me on his staff as a features sub-editor.

At £35 a week I had to take a pay cut. It didn't matter. At last I was working for real newspapers.

CHAPTER FIFTEEN

All you need is love

L ife on the *London American* changed me totally. Reuters had been a
cloistered, almost monastic existence. Round-the-clock shifts. Off to
Fleet Street by bus, nose stuck in a book, clutching my brown paper
bag of cheese and chutney and liver sausage sandwiches. Overnight, I became
a man about town, leaping into taxis, dining at the best restaurants. All
expenses paid, naturally.

The new lifestyle of a rising young executive wrecked what was left of my
marriage. For years we had struggled along, trying to make a go of it, though
Jackie never really trusted me after the Elle episode. She had always been
what is euphemistically called highly strung. By the mid-50s her mental state
had deteriorated to the point where she was spending up to three months a
year in psychiatric wards. Manic depressive, was the official diagnosis.

We moved out of our Hackney slum in 1955 as my career progressed and
took a new apartment at Denmark Hill, in the southeast suburbs. The
Greater London Council built the show estate for higher income tenants lest
anyone accuse the ruling Labour party of working class bias. Hoping to
consolidate the marriage in this first home of our own, we had a second child.
Peter, bright red hair and clever with it, was born on May 21, 1956, ten years
after his sister Barbara. Both of them have never been anything but
marvellous kids. Peter went on to win a State scholarship to Dulwich College,
the last to be granted before the loony left killed off the scheme whereby
children of ordinary families could secure a place in public schools. Peter
followed his old man into newspapers, though eventually he chose the saner
world of advertising.

Journalists formed the bulk of the population in Ruskin Park House, our
new abode. It is only minutes from Blackfriars on the Catford Loop line.

167

Since dad was in Fleet Street, too, Barbara and Peter had no problem growing up as members of the middle classes, even though it was something new in the Jameson experience. King of the kids thereabouts was one Kelvin MacKenzie, whose father edited a South London weekly.

'Will you stop that bloody noise,' I used to yell over the balcony of our third floor flat while Jackie was having the vapours inside. Like so many people with mental troubles, she couldn't stand any intrusion by the external world.

Kelvin would shuffle off, brothers Craig and Drew alongside. Their mates Kit, Jonty and Pip Miller wouldn't be far away. Kelvin, a right little terror, grew up to become editor of *The Sun* and Craig worked for me as assistant editor at the *News of the World*. Drew went to the *New York Post*. Kit is a journalist, too, though another claim to fame is that he was once the boyfriend of topless model Samantha Fox. His father, Gary Miller, was a famous pop singer in the Fifties. Brothers Jonty and Pip are actors.

Jackie's life increasingly became a living hell. Any attempt to relate to the real world usually ended in disaster. She would set out on a shopping expedition, brimming with confidence and happy to be going out. Half an hour later she would be curled up in a ball on the floor of a supermarket, crying piteously 'I can't, I can't ...'.

It was always a nightmare trying to get her into hospital. The psychiatrists knew that was exactly what she wanted. Once inside, she would cling to the staff and other patients, placidly accepting massive doses of tranquillisers and begging them to put her to sleep for up to two weeks at a time. Narcosis, they call it.

She didn't even flinch from the dreadful weekly ECT sessions. They pumped tens of thousands of volts into her over the years in electro-convulsive therapy, condemned by many nowadays as barbaric. This ghastly ritual always made me think of the electric chair on death row in American jails. They would shave Jackie's temples for the electrodes, wrap her in a white robe and strap her to a padded couch, rubber gag in mouth. Then they would knock her out with a pentathol before switching on the current.

'Must she go through all that again?' I would ask, not that they ever take any notice of relatives. 'It never seems to make the slightest difference.'

'Calm her down, Mr Jameson. Calm her down. If she doesn't calm down, she'll never be able to go home,' the sisters would say.

Jackie took it all with abject resignation. Her raven hair turned grey at these sessions. Her only complaint was that she was losing her memory. After two or three months of this farce in the name of Freud, they would send her home. Wan, broken, staring blankly at the world like a trapped animal. She would lie on her bed for hours, biting a tightly clenched fist, body heaving uncontrollably. About the only thing you could say for it was that she was not screaming and raving. That would follow later.

For ten years, I did my best to be a caring, decent husband. Not that I was always the Good Samaritan. There were times when I would go crazy myself. More than once we finished wrestling on the floor. Jackie crying and screaming while I spat out my hatred at what she was doing to our marriage, the kids, our lives. Nothing ever got through. It was like trying to communicate with a zombie.

I did all the housework, went out shopping, washed clothes in the basement launderette and looked after the kids, managing to work my anti-social hours at Reuters with the help of kindly neighbours aware of my predicament.

The headshrinkers even had me going to psycho-analysis myself. Across London to Frognal in Hampstead five times a week for fifty-minute sessions with an analyst to discover myself and so help my poor, stricken wife. It brought me a great deal of enlightenment, lying there on the couch talking a great deal of rubbish. I don't think it helped Jackie much.

Although the interminable talk cleared my own mind, I never did quite get the hang of what it was all about. The analyst was a cool lady from Eastern Europe. I never found out exactly where. That would have been telling. Every statement becomes a question. The analyst asks, you answer. Never the other way round. That is against the rules. I sent her a Christmas card, one of 50 or so dispatched that year.

'Why did you send me a Christmas card?'

'Why, didn't you want a Christmas card?'

'That is not what I asked.'

'Well, I sent lots of Christmas cards. Dozens of Christmas cards. I ALWAYS send Christmas cards. So I sent you a Christmas card.'

'Why does it make you angry?'

'Because it's a bloody stupid question. Why shouldn't I send a Christmas card? Everyone sends Christmas cards.'

'It gives you pleasure to send me a Christmas card?'

This went on for the whole fifty-minute hour. I still don't know what was wrong with that Christmas card. Sometimes, in exasperation, I used to challenge her to come and lie down with me.

'You'll learn more about me in five minutes on the couch, than in five weeks sitting there,' I would throw at her.

'What is it you think I wish to learn about you?'

Long hours at the *London American* meant I was no longer able to play mother and father at home as I did in the past. Jackie had not been able to cope with my new life – any change in normal routine would bring on a crisis – and was back in hospital again. That left me in a difficult spot. Caught up in the frantic business of running a paper, I could hardly drop everything and rush home to give Barbara and Peter their tea.

My secretary at the *London American* came to my aid. She could see my problem and volunteered to do kitchen duty for me. Not once or twice, but several times. Shopping, cooking, baby sitting. She took over all my chores. I was overwhelmed. There had never been anyone before I could count on so totally. I fell in love. The real thing. Exciting, ecstatic, extraordinary.

Maggi was her name, one of the new liberated creatures of the 60s. Dark and potent in white Courreges boots and Mary Quant minis. Snub nose, wisp of hair over left eye, husky voice. She came to me by way of boarding school and Edinburgh University, where she had walked the streets barefoot and drunk too much wine. Some had a new word for her: beatnik. To me she was a goddess. She had a classy accent, and cared about my kids.

I never did understand what she saw in me. Then that is true of all the women in my life. They cast me as romantic, emotional, slightly crazy, despite my efforts to appear conventional, hard-working and ordinary. A bread-and-cheese man never more happy than when he is working at his trade, crafting words. Still, I do like a cuddle and did grow up in a world of women. I guess that gives me a headstart on most men.

It was hardly a match made in heaven. Maggi, rebel daughter of an RAF officer killed in the war. Jameson, hellbent on career, troubled marriage, slum kid made good. For all that, the chemistry was there. Having a woman to rely on after all those arid years lit a spark that blew my mind. Maggi felt the same about me. We were desperate about each other.

170

'I'm going to take you home, get you in bed and keep hold of you for the rest of your life, Maggi,' I told her the first night we managed to get out together.

'Yes, I know,' she said. 'Sounds wonderful.'

And so it was. Love is not about how a man and a woman appear to the rest of the world. It is what they bring to each other behind closed doors in that wonderland where all the passions run wild. The more you have suffered, the greater the emotion. It feels like stealing apples from God. That's how it was for us. Maggi and I loved long and hard and often through that summer of '60, wrapped around each other in an Earls Court bedsitter while the Everly Brothers sang *Walk Right Back* and Elvis sighed *Are You Lonesome Tonight?* Maggi was also gone on a new British singer named Adam Faith.

Guilt destroyed our affair, as it has many another. Jackie was out of hospital, which had enabled me to flee in search of happiness. The greater my love for Maggi, the more worried I became about Jackie's mental state and what it might be doing to Barbara and Peter. I went back home. For no apparent reason, without any discussion, I packed my suitcase on Easter Sunday morning in 1961 and took a bus to Ruskin Park House. She gave me hell.

There was a lot of see-sawing after that. The way men do. Back with Maggi one day, off home the next. A toss up between guilt and desire. One wins and immediately surrenders to the other. It is the story of a million shattered lives. In the end Maggi did the only sensible thing. She called it quits, said there was no point in going on.

That's when I really went crazy. Wrote long, ardent, stupid letters that sometimes got posted. Staked out her flat. Phoned at all the wrong times. Talked her into occasional meetings. I was working at the *Express* by this time and she was secretary at the *Sunday Times*. I bowled in there one day and hovered about in the corridor, then finally burst into her office.

'Get out of here,' she said through gritted teeth. 'You'll get me fired.'

In comes the stiff, military figure of Sir Denis Hamilton, wartime comrade-in-arms of Field Marshal Lord Montgomery and now editor of the *Sunday Times*. 'What's the trouble?' he asks. 'Can I help?'

'Ah, yes, Sir,' says I. 'My name's Derek Jameson. I look after Photonews on the *Daily Express* and it occurred to me you might be able to use something of that kind on the *Sunday Times*. All those acres of space. Have you got any openings for a Saturday casual sub?'

Maggi sat there seething while he wrote out a note to the Chief Sub-editor. *This chap works on the* Express. *Anything we can do for him?* I got the job, too. It didn't last long. One Saturday they handed me what looked like the manuscript of a paperback to sub. A story of Britain's prospects in the Common Market. 'How much of this d'you want?' I asked the Chief-sub. 'What it's worth, old boy, give it what it's worth.' When he came to paste the galley proofs to a dummy page he discovered I had sent only four paragraphs to the printer. 'What bloody fool subbed this?' he roared. 'How am I supposed to fill half a page with four paras?' They didn't ask me back again. Pity, really. They could still do with a Photonews.

Faced with such lunacy, Maggi fled abroad. We had a final meeting. I remonstrated with her, desperately pleading that she should believe in my love. Even threatened to lay down on the runway to stop her plane taking off. When none of that worked, I gave her a shove and sent her sprawling halfway down the stairs at Chancery Lane Underground station. Fortunately she was not hurt.

She went to Paris and married an American Greek, by whom she had two sons and a daughter. I went to my bedsitter in Paddington and played the Everly Brothers for several weeks, crying in the night. Love hurts; rejection hurts more.

My despair over losing Maggi had driven me from home once again. Paddington was a good place to forget, though it took time. I was one of only three men in a block of service apartments occupied almost exclusively by club hostesses and other ladies of the night. I never got involved, as they say, but they cooked me huge Sunday dinners, dished out lots of sympathy and listened to my lectures on the virtues of saving money. Most of theirs went on Italian waiters.

I was something of a hero among the girls. Returning from the late shift early one morning, the lady in the next flat started hollering blue murder just as I put my key in the lock. I went and hammered on her door. It was flung open by a huge black man wielding a carving knife. She was on the floor.

Petrified, I did the first thing that came to mind. 'Police, police!' I yelled at the top of my voice. He jumped back, startled, then bolted up the corridor.

Obviously he thought I *was* the police, not requesting their assistance. The girl was none the worse for wear. Apparently he seemed to think she should be sharing her earnings with him. God knows what her father would have made of it. She told me he was a vicar in Surrey.

Another love affair that went wrong sent me scuttling back to Ruskin Park House yet again. This time it was a wonderful lady who took me to her heart because she felt so sorry for me, stuck in that tiny bedsitter on my own. Unfortunately she was engaged to one of my closest friends, who threatened dire deeds against my person when he discovered what was going on. She reviewed the situation and, quite sensibly, opted for her one true love. They married shortly afterwards. I went home in disgust, promising to stick to the straight and narrow. I still got hell. Jackie hit me with just about every pot and pan in the kitchen. Not the best way to settle down to a quiet life.

Career still came first. I put in eighteen months at the *Express*. It made a splendid post graduate course after the *London American*. Although already in decline, the *Express* in those days still boasted that it was the world's greatest newspaper and its professional standards were remarkably high. A sub-editor could be fired on the spot for getting a proper name wrong. Subs and re-porters would give up secure jobs in the provinces, come to the *Express* only to be told after a fortnight: 'Sorry, old boy, you aren't quite up to our standards. You'll find an extra week's pay when you collect your cards at the Cashier's.' This climate of fear, which existed in varying degrees on all news-papers, was to rebound on managements later in the Sixties. The workers got wise, backed the militants and came under the protective umbrella of Chapel power. The unions were to dictate terms for the next two decades until the computers of the new technological age changed all the rules.

All this was a long way off as I plunged into the hectic features department of a top daily newspaper, handling everything from cutting three lines out of the horoscope to producing the famous William Hickey column. The hours were long – 3pm to 3am many days – and the work gruelling. Nothing concentrates the mind so much as the knowledge that one slip might spell the end of a promising career. There were still laughs a'plenty.

One of my jobs was producing the readers' letters page, *Dear Sir*, and naturally I helped it along a little by writing many of them myself. Once I invented a doctor's wife in Streatham complaining that her husband had been called out on an emergency at 4am. When he got there, he discovered the crisis was a sick poodle belonging to a neurotic spinster. What happened? It turned out there was a doctor with the unlikely name I had chosen living in the same Valley Road in Streatham. Apologies all round.

Another letter was from a proud mother who said her three children, aged seven, nine, and twelve were all born on the same day, September 15. Was this a record? I added a sentence of my own: *Mind you, my husband and I only screw on Christmas Day.* It was meant to be deleted in the composing room after everyone had had a laugh. We never reached that stage. The head printer suddenly descended on the features department, waving a galley proof of readers' letters. 'What imbecile sent down this rubbish about a mother of three?' he demanded. I had to own up. 'How dare you,' he thundered, 'you're corrupting my staff!'

Head printers put the frighteners on sub-editors in all newspapers. It is the only hope they have of getting their paper out on time. This one was particularly awesome. A devout Methodist, he was known as 'Bananas' because of his huge hands. He could grab hold of type and make up a page with those long fingers quicker than any compositor I ever met. As we scurried about his composing room like worker bees, chopping and changing page layouts, adding and deleting copy, re-writing 'busted' headlines that didn't fit, Bananas would suddenly roar: 'We're running fifteen minutes late, gentlemen. All sub-editors kindly leave the floor immediately!'

It was panic stations all round because the executives upstairs would be anything but amused if we locked up pages with holes in them, especially the editor at that time, a whizzkid down from Oxford named Roger Wood. He had replaced smiling Bob Edwards, forced out in a coup engineered while his lord and master was ill in the south of France. Lord Beaverbrook recovered and Bob was reinstated. There have been many editors of the *Express*. Bob is the only man to have got the job twice.

Right now, Roger was in the chair and breathing down my neck. Chubby and auburn, with a deceptively languid air, he was even more terrifying than the head printer. Our parting words came over a cookery column I was handling. The copy claimed good old-fashioned home cooking was making a comeback as the British were fed up with French, Italian and other foreign grub. I had to think fast. A three-deck headline, not more than seven characters to a line. *Ta-ta to/sauce/tartare,* I wrote.

Roger, who was later to become editor of the *New York Post* and one of Rupert Murdoch's chief lieutenants, strolled over to the bench where I was working half-buried in page proofs.

'Did you write this headline, dear boy?' he asked, pointing to my little beauty.

'I did,' I said grandly, 'in all of ten seconds.'

'He shook his head solemnly. 'I think that's the worst headline I've ever seen in my life. Are you not happy on the *Express?* Perhaps you should talk to someone about it.'

'Perhaps you should go and fuck yourself,' I said. 'I had ten minutes to get that page away and it was a shambles.'

Roger laughed. 'It's all right, Derek,' he drawled. 'We all know you're thinking of leaving.'

Of course, he was right, on both counts. It was a lousy headline and I was being courted by other papers. Poaching is one sure sign of success in our business. At the Mirror Group, the great tabloid veteran Hugh (now Lord) Cudlipp was reshaping his papers to meet the new affluent age. The school leaving age had risen, every boy and girl aspired to pass the 11-Plus, and he clearly thought the time had come to take his titles upmarket. An old-established and much loved picture paper, the *Sunday Pictorial,* was renamed *Sunday Mirror* and the hunt was on for fresh hands to match its new image.

I was not all that interested when the call came from Reginald Thomas Payne, editor of the *Sunday Mirror* to go and see him. I regarded Sunday papers as semi-retirement and was doing quite nicely on the *Express,* thank you very much. So I didn't bother with the proverbial interview suit when I made my way to the red and blue *Mirror* skyscraper at Holborn Circus, up the road from Fleet Street. I wore an old brown suede jacket.

Reg Payne was a darling. One of the funniest men I ever met, from the grand old school of rough, tough, shrewd editors. He said I had been recommended and asked what salary I would want to join him. Feature sub to start and then, all being well, picture editor in view of my *Express* work on the famous Photonews feature.

I asked for £50 a week, which was ridiculous. I was getting £40 at the *Express.* He said he would let me know and I assumed that was the last of that.

Then something happened that endeared me to Reg forever. There was a knock at the door and he yelled 'Come!' A none too prepossessing bloke put his head round the door.

'What d'you want, you evil looking bastard?' Reg shot at him. His caller made a hasty excuse and left, the way they do on Sunday papers.

'Who was that?' I wanted to know.

'THAT was the FOC,' said Reg.

Any editor who dared address the NUJ's top man on a paper, the FOC (Father of the Chapel), in those terms had my vote, not because I was against my own union, but just for the sheer audacity of it. You have to admire courage, however misplaced. As I was going out of the door, Reg said to me: 'Well, I hope to see you, cock! That's a funny name you've got, isn't it?'

'Funny?' I said. 'What's funny about it?'

'Jameson Derek! Sounds phoney to me. Or a poof,' says Reg.

'My bloody name's not Jameson Derek,' I says to him. 'It's Derek Jameson.'

'Oops, sorry, cock. I asked Jack Gourlay (columnist Logan Gourlay) if he knew any useful subs at the *Express*, and he said, 'Yes, there's only one worth bothering with. His name is Jameson. Derek, that is.'

'Sorry, Jameson, er, Derek!' What madness. I had to work for this bloke. It took Reg a month to clear that £50 upstairs before he called to say the job was mine. Eric Raybould, managing editor at the *Express*, a blunt Northerner who wore red braces and carpet slippers, shook his head at the news. 'You're a bloody fool, Derek. Keep your nose clean and you could make features editor here.'

'They're paying me fifty quid,' I told him in astonished tones.

'You what!' he said. 'Take it lad, take it.'

So began a fifteen-year love affair with Mirror Group Newspapers. I had learned to read on those *Mirror* cartoon strips and now I was about to become one of their executives. Who knows, maybe one day I'll make editor of the *Daily Mirror*, I thought. *The angels are watching.*

Picture editor of a successful tabloid paper in the Swinging Sixties was one of the best jobs in the business. I was courted by all branches of show business, eager for picture stories in the respectable *Sunday Mirror*. We had the resources to buy material from top agencies and photographers, and there were about a dozen staff photographers eager to click their shutters on the ideas buzzing around the editorial.

I had a splendid assistant, Brian Clifford, who comes from my part of the world and shares my sense of humour. We never stopped laughing. He went on to become picture editor of the *Daily Mail* and other papers and today is a big wheel in BBC publicity and promotion.

This was the birth of the Beatles era and we were among the chosen few to be granted a photo-session on an early visit to London in 1963. They had already shot to fame and I decided to accompany Frank Charman, our chief photographer, on this important assignment.

The best we had come up with at short notice for the venue was the rather sparse Embankment Gardens, at the side of the Thames. Frank was not despondent. He had been in the business forty-odd years and was a famed animal photographer. Compared with chimps, pop groups were no problem. Unfortunately he had not taken into account the redoubtable John Lennon, who soon made clear he did·not like London, public gardens, photographers, newspapers in general and the *Sunday Mirror* in particular.

Just to add to the shining hour, Frank Charman in true Fleet Street style could not remember Lennon's name. He insisted on calling him 'Mr Bannion.'

'Hey, lads, what's this bloody rag?' John wanted to know. 'This picture'll never make. What a right doomp to bring us. It's all roobish.'

'Now, now, Mr Bannion,' says Frank, totally unperturbed. 'This won't take long. If you would kindly go over to that tree and swing on the branch with both hands.'

'Swing on tree! I'm not a fookin' ape, wack. I'm off. Ta ra.'

And off he was. We were left with three Beatles, which isn't the same thing at all. Luckily, Frank had got them as a foursome on their arrival. Back at the office, the editor wanted to know whether we had got good Beatles pictures for the centre spread. 'Marvellous!' I said. He didn't hear me mutter under my breath 'Well, three of 'em, anyway.'

Poor old Frank was better off taking animal pictures. We told everyone that when he went on his frequent trips to London Zoo, the chimps would spot him and jump up and down gibbering 'We're going to be in the *Sunday*

Mirror, we're going to be in the *Sunday Mirror!*'

Once he spent a great deal of money on a chimp of his own and kept it in the garden shed. The idea was to teach it to say 'Brook Bond tea,' assuring his fortune for all time. Sadly, he turned his back on the brute at feeding time and it took a lump out of his thigh. Frank had to have eighteen stitches.

Reg Payne had built a team around him equal to his constant quest for a strong, vigorous paper. We kept him happy most of the time, though he would be the last to admit it. My constant moan: 'If I gave him a world exclusive on the Lord Jesus returning to earth, he would toss it aside and say "What's this bloody rubbish!" '

His deputy was a tough, all-knowing *Mirror* veteran named Joe Grizzard, who missed becoming a great editor himself. Wrong religion. At work, Joe was a human whirlwind, striding through the editorial like something out of a speeded-up film, poking his nose into everything, making angry demands. Off duty, he was a quiet, contemplative orthodox Jew, an elder of the synagogue.

There was the occasion when Joe was running the paper from the back bench, the bridge of a newspaper which controls production and sends final news pages to the printer. It had been a hectic day and Joe suddenly keeled over. We stretched him out on some chairs and summoned the duty nurse.

I went to Reg Payne's office with the bad news. 'Joe's collapsed, Reg.' I said. 'We've got the nurse to him.'

'Christ, that's terrible,' he said. 'Is the first edition away?'

It turned out to be a mild case of hypertension. Joe was back the following week, raving and roaring, driving us to ever greater heights of endeavour. Underneath the flintstone, hearts of pure marzipan. Like the day another of my photographers let me down. He went out on Friday lunchtime to shoot a certain winner for the centre spread, those middle pages always hungry for pictures. Normally we would have the pictures and design the pages on Friday evening. Five o'clock, six, seven, no sign of him.

The moment I dreaded arrived. Joe came storming out, arms waving like windmills, jaw thrust out. 'Where's this spread?' he demanded in an ugly tone. 'Sorry, Joe, something's gone wrong. We'll have to lay it down in the morning. The photographer's disappeared. Hasn't even checked in.'

'Not checked in! He should be flogged with syphilitic spiders, the useless bastard!'

Next morning, there was still no photographer. I was summond to Reg's office, craftily taking an alternative spread with me. Reg and Joe looked suitably outraged, breathed fire all over the place and raised no objections when I assured them the erring snapper would be sacked the first moment I clapped eyes on him. That he was. The following Tuesday when we resumed work. 'You're fired,' I told him. He tried to say something. 'I don't want to know,' I spat. 'Tell the editor. He'll probably shoot you!'

An hour or two later the internal hotline went on my desk. 'Come in here. Now!' Reg and Joe looked at me balefully. 'What did you say to that photographer?' Reg asked. 'Didn't say anything,' I answered chirpily. 'Just told him he was fired.' I thought they would be pleased.

'You evil bastard,' Reg shot at me. 'I've a good mind to fire you!'

'But he went out and didn't get any pictures,' I protested. 'You know very well what happened. Christ, you gave me enough stick!'

'Pictures,' said Reg. 'Pictures! How the fuck could you expect him to take pictures when his young daughter had just run off with a gipsy fairground worker. What have you got for a heart – stone? Well, I've unsacked him and next time it could be you for the chop. Out!'

That was the *Mirror*, Big-hearted, loony, always at fever pitch.

In 1963 Reg landed the story of the decade, Christine Keeler's confessions of her affair with John Profumo, Minister of War in the Macmillan Government. She shared her favours with him and the Soviet naval attaché, Ivanov. Reg got a call saying there were two girls in the front hall, Christine and her friend Mandy Rice Davis, and they would speak only to the editor. He saw them and out tumbled the story of their antics with various members of the Establishment, notably the Minister of War.

'Yes, all very interesting,' says Reg, 'but where's the proof?'

At that, Christine tips the contents of her handbag on to his desk. Purse, make up, keys, the lot. And a letter from John Profumo.

Reg checked out her story and published the letter when the Minister denied there was anything improper in his relationship with the call girl. The first word was enough to ruin him. *Darling . . .*

By strange irony, people in high places ultimately destroyed Reg Payne's career. He was brought down by the Establishment rallying to the side of Tory statesman Lord Boothby, friend and wartime aide of the great Winston Churchill. Boothby's postwar television appearances had make him a great favourite with the public. He came across as a man of good humour and common sense.

There was little sense about a curious friendship he formed with the Kray brothers, the most notorious gangsters in the land who ultimately received life sentences for murder. Boothby had mixed with them socially, involved himself in their business affairs and even made a fuss over them being denied an export permit. Reg went into print in 1964 with the story of this strange alliance. He considered it most certainly not in the public interest. He carefully omitted Boothby's name. That fooled nobody. Boothby immediately wrote to *The Times*, complaining that he had been gravely maligned. What looked like the libel action of the century was shaping up. The *Sunday Mirror* was well prepared with a dossier of evidence and pictures.

Enter Cecil King, patrician Chairman of the *Mirror*'s owners, the International Publishing Corporation. This lesser member of the Northcliffe dynasty caved in without a fight. He said he did not want the *Mirror* papers to appear to be waging a vendetta against homosexuals. Boothby got £40,000 damages and a handsome apology.

Reg was fired, though innocent on all counts. Boothby's relationship was improper and Reg had consulted King before publishing the story. Hugh (now Lord) Cudlipp, King's deputy and the man who later drove him from office, had been on holiday at the time the story broke. Cudlipp awarded his close friend Reg a strange consolation prize: Editor of the lowbrow weekly *Titbits*. Reg did get back to Fleet Street eventually as deputy editor of *The People*, another *Mirror* paper, though he never occupied an editor's chair again. He retired early with health problems.

I never really hit it off with the new editor, Michael Christiansen. My theory was he knew his father had a high regard for me, and therefore feared I might sit in judgement on him. The old class nonsense also got in the way. He seemed to think working class people were all very well in the office, though you wouldn't actually invite them to dinner.

Once Ben Jones, one of Fleet Street's top glamour photographers, came to me with the story that comedian Bruce Forsyth had run off with Anthea

Redfern, the girl he later married. Model Anthea had been involved with one of Brucie's close friends, club owner Louis Brown. The picture story made the front and middle pages.

'How much shall I pay Ben?' I asked the editor. 'Oh, seventy-five quid should do it,' said Mike. 'He's only a photographer.'

'So is Tony Armstrong-Jones,' I shot back, knowing that Mike really meant he was only working class. What made me livid was that Mike had just paid a top-drawer writer named Philippa Pigache thousands for some so-so baby feature. I paid Ben £400 and told him to bung in heavy expenses.

Mike loved all sports, especially cricket, He once interviewed an aspiring sports reporter from Manchester, said nothing about his career, but was delighted to know he had played cricket at school. The job was his provided he went back north, got his cricket gear together and returned the following Sunday to turn out on some village green. The lad was happy to oblige – and was out for a duck.

I was at the match myself, strictly as a supporter. Mike's second wife Chris, who had been a *Mirror* secretary, wanted to know why I wasn't playing. I told her I didn't. 'You won't get far on this paper if you don't play cricket,' she told me. A strange lady. She even had the gall to ask me once how I managed to become editor of the *Daily Express*, a job her husband coveted in view of his father, with my 'drinking problem.' I hardly drink. It doesn't agree with me. Three lagers and I'm anybody's.

In view of our rather difficult relationship, I was somewhat confused when Mike told me with his usual exuberance that I was to be promoted. It sounded fair enough. Assistant editor in Manchester, in charge of the *Sunday Mirror* stake in one of the most exciting new developments in national newspapers: Four-colour printing in Irish editions out of a brand new plant on the outskirts of Belfast. I took the job. Only fools oppose an editor's wishes in Fleet Street. But I had this niggling doubt in my mind. The whisper in the office was that Mike wanted to get rid of me.

In the event, it was lucky I did not play cricket because those Irish editions of the *Sunday Mirror* made my reputation.

CHAPTER SIXTEEN

Fame in the North

I arrived in Manchester in 1965, my first time in the city I came to regard as my second home. Those blunt Northerners, with their total disdain of anything facile or phoney, suit me perfectly. I guess that's what makes me a *Coronation Street* addict. No sooner had I arrived than the *Mirror* lads insisted on teaching me some of the local dialect. I had run into trouble trying to buy a tea mug in Woolworth's on my way to the office. 'Where can I find a mug?' I asked a girl at the nearest counter. She looked at me blankly. 'Mug,' I said. 'You know, MUG. China mug, tea mug, toothbrush mug.' Realisation dawned on her. 'Ow, you mean moog,' she said, 'over int'corner.' She came chasing up behind me. 'Asta gorrit?'

It's always easy to get on with people you like. It didn't take me long to learn that you must never get hoity-toity, putting on Southern airs. *Thawants-ta wash thi eeroil aht*, the Lancashire printers would kid me when I made out their lingo was beyond me.

I threw myself into the job with manic enthusiasm, delighted to be doing something new in newspapers. News in colour. I had preached it for years. There were weeks when I changed fifteen of the *Sunday Mirror*'s forty pages for Irish readers, with three or four sports pages on top of that. We had to change pages between Eire and Ulster because the Catholic Republic frowned on any mention of birth control, was not too keen on sex and regarded football pools as the work of the Devil. They took money that might have gone to the Irish Hospitals Sweep.

Within a year I had turned the Irish circulation of 55,000 copies weekly into 210,000, largely due to my colour projection of Irish favourites like the Pope, the Kennedy clan and British soccer teams of Catholic inclination. My favourite frontpage of this period had a big splash headline saying THE

PILL *and* THE POPE. Alongside that a girl in a white sharkskin bikini in a blue lagoon and across the bottom of the page: MANCHESTER UNITED IN COLOUR.

Traditional circulation gimmicks of this kind became irrelevant when Ulster erupted in violence in 1969. There was now a harder, tougher edge to the competition. The newspaper that succeeded best was going to be that which understood most what was happening in that stricken province. I had seen the trouble coming and moved quickly. Sales in one city alone, Derry (Londonderry), quadrupled in a single day when I signed up Bernadette Devlin to write a column.

Snatching her under the noses of rival papers did my reputation no harm. She was acclaimed worldwide like the latest pop idol when she was returned by Mid-Ulster as Britain's youngest ever woman MP at a by-election in 1969. Bernadette is a bonny fighter and we got along fine together. She loved to imitate my dark brown accent. 'Jameson here!' she would mimic as she phoned from various points along the frontline of the great civil rights movement she symbolised before the Provisional IRA with its more lethal message took over the Republican campaign.

I was not so keen on the company she kept. We signed her at 40 guineas (£42) an article, peanuts by today's standards. I was shaken by the response of Loudon Seth, her close friend and agent, as we sealed the contract in my office.

'Now we'll see who's got the fastest sports car in Ireland,' he said as he added his name to hers in red ink.

Stone me! We had made her a second Joan of Arc, the humble carpenter's daughter fighting for her oppressed people, and here was this toffee-nosed academic by her side talking about bloody sports cars. Mind you, Bernadette didn't let down the side. Her columns were all about suffering, unemployment and deprivation among the poor of Ulster, a mixture of romantic nationalism and Marxist logic. There was no mention of sports cars. She herself had grown up in poverty in County Tyrone, the third of six children reared on State benefits. Her father had been forced to emigrate to England to find work. Her mother and father died, both aged 46, before she found world fame.

Since we both grew up the hard way and became teenage revolutionaries,

Bernadette and I had much to talk about. We never got anywhere. She studied at Queen's University, as did one of her sisters, and all the family received a good education. The State looked after them all their lives. Ma Wren never received a halfpenny in benefit and most of us had to leave school at 14. Compared with my generation, Bernadette and her contemporaries were in the sports car league. At least we had jobs and the hope of a better future. Most of the poor in Ulster have neither.

People and stories are the lifeblood of a newspaper. Although based in the Manchester production centre, I never missed an opportunity to visit my staff in Ireland. Apart from anything else, it allowed me to witness Ulster's agony at first hand. It also brought my first ever television appearance, on Gay Byrne's *Late, Late Show* in Dublin. In the audience were several Provo supporters and one gentleman told me hotly that I was a tool of British military intelligence.

'That'll be the day,' I told him. 'Listen, I was in the Army. Two years' conscription.'

MAN IN AUDIENCE: *'Do you consider it cool, objective reporting to glorify a murderous British occupation army in the northeast of this country?'*

JAMESON: *'Well, that's an interesting question because it is phrased in terminology that to me is about 50 years out of date. You talk about a murderous British army in the north. I don't think anyone really can defend an army, they've just got a job to do. We don't like the idea of some kid of 18 from Northampton, unemployed – can't get a job in the local boot factory – going into the army and someone on a roof with a high powered rifle blows the head off his shoulders. Now, should we refer to the man with the rifle as some kind of folk hero?*

'I read in the magazine Hibernia *today about the old British game of conquer and rule. We are not interested in conquer and rule. We're no longer a world power, an imperial power. We're just a country trying to make a living in the world and all this is crapology about the murderous British Army and occupation of the North. Occupation? You don't think the British people want to be in the north of Ireland. We'd like to see a situation where they could get out tomorrow.'*

AUDIENCE: 'What about the hysteria over the four shot soldiers?'
JAMESON: 'The ones lured into a flat by the women? What do you
want us to do, stand up and cheer because they were lured there and shot dead
at seven minute intervals with a bear gun?'

So it went on, back and forth, a verbal onslaught by the Provos as I attempted to give the Irish some understanding of what ordinary men and women in Britain thought about the troubles in Ulster. Pat Heneghan, the *Mirror*'s circulation manager in Dublin, wrote afterwards: 'You were top of the topical talk all weekend. No longer will we be called the gutter press in the Irish Republic.'

Appearing elsewhere on the same chat show was James Saville, OBE. 'You're the guv'nor,' Jimmy said to me afterwards. 'The way you handled that audience. You're wasted as a newspaper editor. You should be in my business.' Perhaps that's where the idea came from. The Irish love Jimmy, who has raised so much money for their charities with his marathon runs. We both agree that the Irish are wonderful people and, like the rest of us, the vast majority want nothing to do with those who seek to impose their will with the bomb and the bullet.

A great friend in Dublin is Ulick O'Connor, barrister, journalist, poet, author, playwright and, in earlier years, a champion pole vaulter and boxer. He himself doesn't drink, but was with me at one 2 am session in the bar of the former Intercontinental Hotel. 'I'm not sure how long we can continue with Bernadette Devlin,' I told my colleague Gordon Clack, 'London reckons her column is pure Marxist propaganda.'

Suddenly, a bloke appears at my elbow, no bigger than a pint pot, and says to me: 'Don't you be mentioning the name of Bernadette Devlin.'

'You what?' I say.

'There's not an Englishman born fit to mention the name of Bernadette.'

'If you washed your lugholes out before earwigging, you'd know I was a friend of Bernadette Devlin,' I told him.

Ulick, at the other end of the bar, realises an altercation is going on and comes down to find out what's happening. I tell him. He picks up trouble by the lapels, shakes him and says: 'I'll break every bone in your body if you upset my friend!'

The night manager appears, orders Ulick out. 'You'd be setting two stones to fighting,' he tells one of Ireland's most distinguished sons. 'Get the President of Pan American Airways on the phone,' Ulick says to me. What's he got to do with it? 'He is a personal friend of mine and they're major shareholders in this hotel.' What's his name? 'Never mind his so-and-so name, get him on the phone.'

While all this palaver is going on, a bloke comes round writing down orders on the back of an envelope. 'What is it you're having?' he says to me. It's the same little fellow who started all the trouble in the first place. *That's magical Ireland*.

Manchester produced more upheavals in my personal life. Before leaving London, my marriage all but over, I got heavily involved with a gorgeous young French girl named Eve, one of the pioneers of the Page 3 school of art, though she also worked as a fashion model.

Eve was married to a rally driver, a thought that scared the pants off me on occasion when she invited me into a friend's adjoining flat and I could hear him through the wall, watching sport on the telly. He phoned her once or twice while I was there. 'It's all right darling', she cooed, 'I'm just doing my crochet with Joyce.'

She left him to flee with me to Manchester, packing a bag and walking out on the marriage with no more than a scribbled note. Eve reckoned it would not have come as any surprise because her husband was in love with an old girl friend, someone I knew well. She was a top fashion writer in Fleet Street.

Eve and I were fine so long as we were together. It was an extraordinary affair. There I was with this wonderful French mistress, five feet seven inches tall, green eyes, ash blonde – 35-25-35, every man's fantasy – and she wanted nothing more than to read and watch telly. Newspaper pubs bored her, she didn't like the pictures and when we went out to dinner all she would eat was two hard-boiled eggs and a cold tomato. Only a diet-conscious model girl would have the nerve to go into a top restaurant and order a hard boiled egg.

Fed up with hours alone in a service flat while I was away at work, she returned to London after three months. I used to zip up and down the motorway like a lovesick schoolboy, often driving for seven or eight hours to spend a little time with her. Sadly, absence doesn't make the heart grow fonder. It kills love at the roots. Without human contact, it withers and dies. Eve and I began to grow apart. The last letters were lovely, though.

Derek to Eve: *Many ways do I love you. Most of all when you are in my arms and it is you and me alone. My hands run down your beautiful face, trace the outline of your long body and open you up like a flower. Your eyes are bright stars burning into me, your lips reach deep into my soul, your hands bring me peace, your body embraces mine. I am at peace.*

Eve to Derek: *I pray to God that I'll never have to go through this separation again. I can't stand it. I'd do anything not ever to be cut off again. I see through you, feel through you, think through you. I have lost independent judgement, which no one else achieved in me before you. Even going to the laundry with you had something ceremonial and symbolic about it.*

That was the warning bell, all right. Model girls who feel that desolate, are likely to seek comfort elsewhere. Adrian was his name. Male model and parachute jumper. My spies told me he liked to lie in the bath for hours while she waited on him hand and foot. Eve would have liked that. Not that it lasted. I heard subsequently she was living in Germany with a motorbike rider.

This time, I grieved to Sonny and Cher's *I've Got You, Babe.* There were to be no flowers in the spring for me, but the song seemed to sum up what I felt about Eve. Come to think of it, Sonny and Cher's romance did not last, either.

At least my transfer to Manchester broke the usual ritual. There there was no scuttling back to Ruskin Park House. I had told Jackie about Eve and we were now officially separated. With the passing of the years, Jackie was now more mature and better able to stand on her own feet. Barbara and Peter were both at boarding school.

Barbara played mother hen to the girls of St Mary's, Bexhill-on-Sea. She got religion at one point and was baptised and confirmed on the same day, which is more than can be said for her father. She grew out of it. Peter was boarding at Dulwich College. A natural rebel, like his father, he made awful sounds in the Punky Lazar Hot Five and organised football in the sacred quadrangle. The sports fields recognised only rugger and cricket.

Ultimately, Jackie divorced me for cruelty. It was the quickest way in those days short of the ludicrous farce of hiring a private inquiry agent to collect evidence of adultery. I wasn't having any of that. Instead, I agreed to simplify matters by not contesting the action. Jackie threw the book at me. Since I said nothing to the contrary, the judge awarded her care, custody and control of the children. Strange justice. For much of her life, she had been incapable of looking after them. In the event, Barbara came to live with me above an insurance office in Wilmslow Road, Manchester. Peter also came north after school. He served his apprenticeship as a reporter on the *Rochdale Observer*.

I threw myself into work with manic enthusiasm, delighted to be in the thick of things in the huge printing centre at Withy Grove in Manchester. It was a Victorian mausoleum of a building. Marbled halls and pillars at the front, a decaying wreck at the back. It was owned by the Thomson organisation, successors to the old Kemsley empire, and the *Mirror* papers leased the plant alongside the *Daily Telegraph* and *News of the World*. In its day ten national newspapers were produced under that one roof. There was nothing quite like it anywhere in the printing world.

My job was pioneering stuff in national newspapers. Withy Grove compositors made up pages in lead as part of the now obsolete hot metal process. Art proofs would be taken of each page and wired by facsimile transmission to the *Mirror*'s big new Irish plant on the outskirts of Belfast. Within minutes the negatives would be turned into printing plates. The papers were printed on a web offset press able to handle colour pictures produced in the plant's own colour laboratory. These techniques, still foreign to Fleet Street, marked the birth of the new age of technology in national newspapers.

In the end, Withy Grove fell victim to the system it was pioneering. Facsimile transmission destroyed Manchester as a major production centre. London can now wire pages north, making it no longer necessary for newspapers to maintain a big staff in Manchester to duplicate pages for editions going to Scotland, Ireland and the north of England and Wales.

Perhaps sensing the axe hanging over our heads, we all worked like stink to make our papers successful, to show those effete jokers in Fleet Street how it was done. I thought nothing of working twelve or thirteen hours on Fridays, then repeating it again the following day. Saturday is press day on a Sunday paper.

There was great affection for us Londoners in Manchester. We were anything but toffee-nosed. Three of us on the *Sunday Mirror* kept the printers happy. The others were Robert Wilson, my assistant, and Tony Smith, the sports editor, both now senior executives on the paper in London. We were a rowdy lot. Laughing, kidding and cajoling, between us we spurred the Thomson compositors into superhuman efforts. We would lock up fifteen pages for Ireland, change the lot for Scotland and then throw out half of those pages for the Northeast edition. Three editions in three countries in the space of 40 minutes.

People are always asking me how I became a Fleet Street editor. It was not sipping aperitifs in the Savoy Grill or even El Vino's wine bar. It was right there in Withy Grove on that hot, noisy, greasy 'stone,' as we journalists call the composing room. The name itself goes back to medieval times when the monks produced their illuminated manuscripts on a flat stone slab. There are no stones in computers.

That composing room was so large we reckoned the operator at the far end of the serried ranks of linotype machines was only ever seen when the compositors shared out their Christmas club money. The *News of the World* was on the opposite side and I would produce a huge pair of binoculars and read their page proofs as they were pinned to the wall on a spike about half-mile away. It worked, too. We once got a *NoW* exclusive into our first mainland edition because of what I had jokingly read on that wall.

Our boss in those days was Jack Stoneley, a quiet, kindly feature writer who caught the eye of Hugh Cudlipp by launching the *Mirror* pets club. He sometimes raised his eyebrows at our antics, but let us get on with it. I was to replace him as Northern editor a few years later, not that he held that against me. Today he is a highly successful author.

The only time I ever saw Jack really mad was when I showed him with delight a spread of colour pictures for the Irish editions.

'Look at that, Jack,' I chortled. 'See that girl. Fur bikini, fur hat, fur leggings. Not only did she make them herself, but she raised the mink that produced the fur. Not bad, eh?'

He went white and bright red in turn. 'So long as I am editor, never, ever, again show me anything like that,' he thundered. I had forgotten the pets club bit.

Jack's deputy was Harry Richardson, a lumbering giant who thought nothing of sinking six or seven pints in the lunch break, then sending the boy out for a double portion of fish and chips. He would put these in a drawer at the base of his desk and devour them by the fistful as he schemed pages or read copy.

Harry was responsible for pictures, a legacy of his wartime days in aerial reconaissance in the RAF. As a photographer put them on his desk, fearing the worst, Harry would scan them balefully and snort: 'You've got a right load of bloody rubbish here. What did you do, shoot them in t'cellar through nylon sock?'

He fancied himself as a singer and, egged on by us, would swamp many a cabaret singer in those days by suddenly launching into 'Old Man River, that Old Man River...' He died of cancer a few years ago and thankfully did not see the demise of Withy Grove, where he had spent most of his life. Too much booze, too many late nights. He shook me once, as we were looking for a taxi at some ungodly hour, by sighing 'Ah, well, Derek, another day off the end of our lives.'

Manchester's nightlife in the Sixties had to be seen to be believed. There were more than 300 clubs in the city centre. Working late at nights, we were known in about half of them. We also knew all the best places to get a midnight meal. Then it would be one for the road in the Press club and home to bed by 3 am. Back on the desk at 10 o'clock, raring to go.

Social life on newspapers revolves around the office pub, in our case *The Swan with Two Necks*. Every paper has its favourite boozer, though people from other titles are welcome even if they are there only to find out what their rivals are up to. They're a thirsty lot, newspapermen and women. Not so much for beer, but rather endless chat about this or that story, gossip, scandal, football, politics. You name it, they'll discuss it. Talk is in their blood. What better way to wind down after the heat of the day than to sort out the world with your soulmates in the saloon bar. Life beyond those pub walls can be excruciatingly boring. Some will spend more hours here than they do at home.

The pub is also a haven for the lovelorn. The perfect place to impress the ladies. All those heroics, all that bonhomie. Safe, too, as angry wives with dinner on the table call yet again to find out what's happened to him. 'Just having a drink with the boys,' he will say. 'Be there within the hour.' What the more lecherous don't say is 'Just having a drink with that gorgeous new blonde in the sports department.'

I have spent too many hours in newspaper pubs, not for the beer and chat so much as the opposite sex. I adore women. One in particular at this stage of my life. I was knocked out the moment she walked into the *Mirror* office to be interviewed for a secretary's job. We exchanged glances and that was it. Bang! Once again I was smitten. You can't get much dafter than that.

What is it about love? How can a sane, reasonably sensible person fall for a total stranger before a word has been exchanged? It gets worse. To be honest, it was not the unknown girl that attracted me so much as her hairstyle. Rich and luxuriant, honey in colour, pinned up high above the collar, Grecian style. God help me, I was mesmerised by a head of hair.

Naomi was her name. Small and pert, a friendly smile, nicely brought up in one of the better suburbs of Manchester. I formed a magnificent obsession for her that almost destroyed me. Not yet 21 when she landed the job, it was her first experience of love with an older man. She responded happily enough. The doubts came later.

It was great while it lasted. A real hearts-and-flowers romance just like the story books. Whispered exchanges in the office, messages left on the desk, telephone calls halfway through important meetings. She would meet me at the station on my return from trips to London. I would drive her to her door every night. That was the problem. It was getting to be too heavy, too intense. Naomi was not ready for lifelong commitments, least of all with a much older father of two.

She tried to let me down gently. I was having none of it. She began leading her own life, refusing to go out with me, making dates with others. I would raise hell between clenched teeth. The poor girl was in a spot. She loved her new job, but what do you do when one of the bosses has a severe case of obsessive jealousy?

I caused a dreadful commotion at one office party, grabbing hold of Naomi when I came upon her sitting on the stairs, chatting to a photographer. 'Why are you doing this to me? How dare you! We're getting out of here. Now.' The usual mindless rubbish. Unrequited love makes fools of us all.

Overwhelmed by the gale force of my emotions, Naomi blew hot and cold. The relationship continued on a now-and-again basis. Everything ducky for a few days, then she would feel trapped and go her own way. I would rant and rave, then ignore her. Within days we would manage to find ourselves alone in the office, usually when the others had gone to lunch. I would saunter over with some outrageous line of chat.

'You can go to hell and back, marry the Pope and never speak to me again, but you will never find anyone, anywhere, anyhow who will love you the way I do!'

'I know, Derek. You've been dreadful these last few days. I don't want to hurt you, I want us to be friends.'

'Of course. I'm a lunatic. Will you have a drink with me tonight?'

'All right, but I must be home early.'

And so it would be on again, more or less. My heart would soar, the smile back on my face, and there would be knowing looks in the office. Derek and Naomi were together again in The Swan last night. *Will he never learn? It just isn't going to work.*

In love there are givers and takers. I never realised the obvious truth staring me in the face. We were both takers. But then it took me half a lifetime to grow up. Some people never reach maturity. For years I suffered with this *maladie d'amour*. I had to be sure that my lover belonged to me totally. The honeymoon period had to last forever. I was obsessed by Naomi because I was never sure of her love. She moved away from me because she was certain of mine.

Every time we split and went our own ways, the old emotional see-saw would start up again and draw us back to each other. Buffeted about in these stormy waters, the day had to come when we made for a complete break. We both got seriously involved elsewhere. Naomi was going steady with someone outside newspapers and talked of getting married.

I found a real live angel. My second wife, Pauline, a girl from a poor family in Manchester who was so beautiful with her lustrous black hair, wide brown eyes and ivory skin that she was known to everyone at the *Mirror* as the Madonna. Pauline was only seventeen years old when we met on a blind date. A friend insisted on taking me along to cheer me up. She fell for me completely. Total, unswerving devotion. Within weeks she moved into the flat in Manchester and looked after me as nobody had ever done before. Pauline even put the toothpaste on my brush before I cleaned my teeth. She was much too good for me. Still is. We remain good friends.

In those days, we had lots of fun, went to parties, took trips out into the marvellous countryside surrounding Manchester. Barbara and Peter loved her sweet nature, as everyone does. She is especially blessed where children are concerned. They take to her like cubs round a mother bear.

It wasn't going to work, though. I knew it from the start and caused her the most awful suffering. I still had this dreadful obsession for Naomi and tried to make a break. Pauline wasn't going to give up without a fight. She kept coming back, loving me all the more.

Once I raced out after midnight to rescue Naomi when she got stranded in town. Pauline insisted on coming, too, threatening to lie down in front of the car if I wouldn't take her along. I finished up in the middle of Manchester's Piccadilly, doors open, headlights on, the pair of them spitting and snarling at each other. People standing in a taxi queue nearby had a field day.

Another time, it shames me to confess, I was all set to marry. We had been together nearly three years. Like any bride-to-be, Pauline was deliriously happy. The banns were up, wedding invitations ready to go ... *Pauline Tomlin and Derek Jameson are happy to invite you to THEIR WEDDING at The All Saints' Registry Office on Monday, August 19th, 1968, at 2.30 followed by a Wedding Breakfast and Reception at the Gourmet Restaurant, Bloom Street.*

Still uncertain, I suddenly cancelled the lot. Pauline should have given me the elbow there and them. She still persevered, her devotion so overwhelming that she could not see the danger signals. I wanted it to work, too, despite my doubts. You can't turn your back on a love like that.

Suddenly, my career took off all over again. Just two weeks after this fiasco, I was recalled to London to take over all production at *Sunday Mirror* headquarters in Holborn Circus, just off Fleet Street. I was going home again. My Manchester colleagues presented me with a gold watch and a dummy front page sending up my Irish web offset press: WEB MAN IN ABDUC-TION DRAMA HORROR.

I took Pauline with me. It had not worked too well in Manchester. Perhaps everything would be different in London.

CHAPTER SEVENTEEN

The road to the top

I took an elegant mansion flat at Parliament Hill Fields, on the southern slopes of Hampstead Heath. It was a splendid place to pause, draw breath and think about where I was going. Manchester had been the perfect launching pad. The difficult bit, I figured, was to make the right impression in Fleet Street itself in the face of fierce competition.

The bug of ambition flourishes in the crash! bang! wallop! world of popular newspapers. It is no place for the faint hearted. One good story or picture can make a lifelong reputation, deserved or not. Many made it by lucky chance and possess neither talent nor ability. There are the creeps and jesters who spend their lives getting up the editor's arse, as we say in newspapers. Usually via the drinks cabinet.

Since they are too busy polishing egos to bother much with the actual business of producing words, pictures and pages in newspapers, these hangers on frequently succeed better than the people who do the actual work. They learned early in the day that you get ahead not by telling those at the top what they ought to know, rather what they want to hear.

I've met them all in my time and could name a few but for the aforementioned law of libel. Editors who made it thanks to their cosy little dinner parties where the proprietor's wife had such a lovely time talking to her favourite telly person. Senior executives too coy to mention halcyon days at boarding school with you-know-who. Those who reached the heights for no other reason than they happened to know someone supposedly famous who put in a good word with the owner.

With my background and accent, there was only one way I was going to succeed. That was by working my balls off. As always. Like many another, I am one of those people who have had to graft from the cradle. Time and again in my career I lost out to the old boy network. The only answer was to snort scornfully and get on with it.

London was a doddle compared with the hurly burly of Withy Grove. I supervised the flow of early pages at the beginning of the week, a task that did not tax me overmuch since the features department could look after itself. My chance to shine was in my dual role of night editor on Fridays and Saturdays when we began moving news pages and wrapping up various editions of the *Sunday Mirror*. This meant I was left in charge of the paper for lengthy periods late in the week, an experience that was to prove useful in later years. The editor, Mike Christiansen, would take his cronies off to lunch or dinner secure in the knowledge that Jameson knew what he was doing. Too true. I couldn't wait for them to get out of the building and leave me to it.

'There they go – the quality street gang!' So I would tell my subs as Mike and his top executives made for the cars waiting to take them to the best restaurants where they would eat, gossip and play daft games for hours at a time.

Mike was sports mad, especially if a gamble was involved. He became fascinated with a Chinese dice game called *yatse* at this time and played every time an opportunity arose. He also carried a plywood box around under his arm. This was *close the box*, another little diversion that got them all highly excited.

Mike was the only cloud on my horizon as I embarked on this new phase of my career. Though he brought me down to London in the light of my successes in Ireland, I was under no illusions that he had much time for me. My rise in pay was negligible, despite the higher cost of living, and he had tricked me out of my title. At the interview leading to the appointment, I told him I assumed my position as assistant editor would remain since this was a promotion.

He had a great dome-shaped bald head, which he would clasp like a football and stare into the distance when lost for words. He did it now. I should have known something was amiss. 'I see no reason why not, dear boy,' he said.

I went on holiday, my first real break for a year, and got a call from a friend on my return. 'Congratulations,' he said. What was all that about? 'It says in the *Press Gazette* that you've been appointed production editor of the *Sunday Mirror*. From that moment on I advised everyone not to believe anything until they see it in writing. Titles are important in Fleet Street. Those who know can tell at a glance whether a person is going up, or coming down. Assistant editor was a stepping stone to the top. Since he had taken mine away, I would have to get back up there all over again.

Mike did it so not to offend his cronies. When I protested, he said: 'Don't worry about it. You are assistant editor to all intents and purposes. You've got a bit of green carpet and two telephones like all the rest'.

I wasn't too bothered. My hunch was that he would not be editor for long. Mike had started brilliantly on taking over from Reg Payne in 1964 after the Boothby affair. Clever serialisations of books like Desmond Morris' *The Naked Ape* had taken the paper's circulation to 5,364,000. He seemed to have run out of puff by the time we entered the seventies and was becoming rather eccentric, to put it mildly. One of his strange decisions was to publish the biography of an artist who liked to sniff lavatory seats.

In the event, he survived until 1972, three years after my return to London. He was invited to go with the usual golden handshake. Mike turned it down. With two young children by his second marriage to raise, he preferred a high salary elsewhere in the *Mirror Group*. He was made deputy editor of the sister *Daily Mirror* and surprised everyone by becoming editor for a brief spell two years later. Like his famous father before him, he was forced to quit after a heart attack. He died in 1984, aged 57.

For all our differences, I felt terribly sad at the loss. He was a better editor then most, with inspirational flashes of genius, and yet laboured all his life under the handicap of being his father's son. In his case it was not true to say that he only got there because of Arthur Christiansen. Mike started on the ground floor as a wartime junior reporter on the *Daily Mail* and worked his way through the ranks to the top. How sad that he should end his days selling second-hand books on a stall in Colchester market.

Mike's career at the *Mirror* ended mysteriously. Although he certainly had heart trouble, there are those who believe his departure was not entirely related to his state of health. Could the stairs have been greased for him? He himself told me that he had made a good recovery and was perfectly fit.

In August, 1975, he vacated the editor's chair for three months to join a development committee set up to plan the introduction of computerised production at the *Mirror*. The new technology was a watershed in the life of

Fleet Street, but there is no way in a million years that the editor of the nation's biggest selling newspaper, as the *Mirror* was at that time, was going to leave his office to sit on a development committee. He had only been editor for nine months.

At the time of his departure, the *Daily Mirror* had published what it called a no-nonsense guide to sexual knowledge. 'Allow your children to read it at your discretion,' said a Page 1 announcement. There was complaint of pornography to the Press Council. It was not upheld. Whether the material was out of place in a national newspaper was a matter of editorial judgement, said its adjudication. Mike Christiansen said the idea for the five-page spread came from the Family Planning Association.

Mirror hands knew there was an extraordinary story behind these events. Five years earlier, in July, 1970, the now defunct *Mirror Magazine*, a colour weekly given away free with the paper, had come out with a similar guide to sexual knowledge. 'Allow your children to read it at your discretion,' said a Page 1 announcement. It never reached the streets. Lord Ryder, chairman of the *Mirror's* owners, the International Publishing Corporation, killed it on the spot, supposedly for economic reasons. Most of us at the *Mirror* preferred to think the condom dangling from an erect penis on Page 11 was responsible.

Editor of the magazine when the axe fell was the urbane Michael Molloy. Acting editor of the paper five years later in the absence of Mike Christiansen was the same Michael Molloy. Christiansen never returned to his editor's chair. Defending that guide to sexual knowledge was one of his last editorial acts. Molloy was confirmed in the job in December, 1975.

Little did I know the time was not far off when I, too, would be caught up in *Daily Mirror* politics. Right now I was fully occupied on the Sunday paper and introducing Pauline to the delights of my home town. She could not have been more happy free of the temptations that had made me so difficult in Manchester. Having taken her away from her large family, I felt more loving and protective towards her than ever before.

Everyone at the *Mirror* adored her. Pauline became fast friends with one of our neighbours, Jill Evans, then a *Daily Mirror* feature writer. Jill is a close friend of mine and had helped me find the flat on Hampstead Heath. Today she runs a news bureau in Hollywood. In those days she lived in the next block with a loony character named Gordon Winter.

On the face of it he was a Yorkshireman who had emigrated to South Africa and was now working in London as a freelance journalist, selling pictures and stories to Johannesburg newspapers. He turned out to be a spy for BOSS, South Africa's notorious bureau for state security. Gordy later defected and exposed his paymasters in a book called *Inside BOSS*. At one time both sides were after him. His spying activities in London brought death or long spells in prison for many black activists.

I had my doubts about him because of his habit of taking pictures everywhere he went. I swear you could not go to the supermarket without his camera coming out and he would start snapping away. He had thousands of negatives stored in boxes. Nobody was allowed near them. 'Will you put that bloody camera away, Gordon,' I would remonstrate with him. 'You'll have us all arrested.' He would laugh like crazy, his blond head thrown back. 'Don't worry, Dekky,' he would say. 'It's only my little hobby.' The rogue snapped me with a bloke he reckoned was the London commandant of the IRA. He turned out to be a publican from Kilburn.

Once Gordon called me on the telephone and said in an urgent whisper: 'Look out of your window and you'll see me go to a car. If the guys inside grab me, dial 999 and report I've been abducted.' They came alright, though he must have sweet talked them out of trouble. He would never tell me what that was all about.

For years, Gordon touted around an explosive story in which a male model named Norman Scott alleged he had been involved in a homosexual affair with Jeremy Thorpe MP, the twice married and highly regarded leader of the Liberal party. No newspaper would touch it because nothing had appeared in court. It became obvious later that Gordon's motive was to discredit Thorpe, then a leading light in the anti-Apartheid movement. Thorpe and three associates subsequently did appear in court. They were acquitted of charges that they conspired to murder Scott, but the Old Bailey trial in 1979 destroyed the Liberal politician's glittering career. What seemed to upset public opinion most was that Scott's Great Dane, Rinka, had been shot dead by a hit man on Exmoor in October, 1975.

With her great love for children, what pleased Pauline most about London was being able to play mother to my son Peter, on visits from Dulwich

College, and Jill's two sons, Paul and Simeon, by her former marriage to Fleet Street production executive David Francis. In this family atmosphere it wasn't long before Pauline decided on a child of her own. The marriage plans so abruptly shattered in Manchester had deprived her of the one thing she wanted to make her life complete. Well, marriage might be out, she decided, but she could still have a baby.

Being a totally single-minded person, she announced one day that she was off the Pill, planning a baby, but not to let it bother me. It was her decision and hers alone. She would not marry me now at any price. Her wish soon came true. She was pregnant. 'Never mind all that rubbish in the past,' I told her, 'we're getting married.'

'No way,' she would say. 'You wouldn't marry me when you had the chance, and you're not going to now. I'm having a baby because I want one. So mind your own business!'

Of one thing you may be certain: No bastard is going to inflict the suffering he or she went through on an unborn child of theirs. The more adamant Pauline became, the more eager I was to get married.

I even enlisted the aid of the highly formidable ladies at the *Mirror.* By now most of the top people in London had met Pauline and were enchanted by her. I even managed to get her alongside Marje Proops for some sound advice. 'Of course you must marry him, my dear,' she said. 'He's a pain, of course, but you know what men are.'

She finally relented and we married at the Hampstead register office on 27th September, 1971. The reception was at the City Golf Club, one of Fleet Street's more trendy meeting places. There were 150 guests and 200 gate-crashers. Several punch ups and two guests breathalysed and banned. A real old-fashioned wedding.

'Never heard language like it in my life,' said the bride's mother. 'I thought journalists were supposed to be educated people.'

Ben was born the following May. He has grown up a big, happy-go-lucky lad with a taste for rock and heavy metal bands, like his half-brother Peter. Daniel, my youngest, born five years later, is quieter and more studious. Of course all that could change as he gets older.

I had known my career at the *Sunday Mirror* was not going to advance much under Mike Christiansen. The new editor should make all the difference. He was Bob Edwards, who had taken me on at the *Express* fifteen years earlier. He didn't remember me – names are not Bob's strong suit – but his greeting was warm when his deputy, the same Joe Grizzard of earlier days, explained the role I played in getting out the paper.

Bob, like me, has Fleet Street in his veins. As editor of the leftwing weekly *Tribune*, he had caught Beaverbrook's eye with the help of his friends, the Labour leaders Michael Foot and Nye Bevan. He was editor of the *Express* twice, fell foul of Beaverbrook's heirs and finished up as editor of the other *Mirror* Sunday paper, the *People*. Now he had crossed the bridge of sighs that linked the offices across Fetter Lane to run what had been his main rival. Bob appears very top drawer with his closely cropped grey hair and permanent tan – he spends much time at sea on his yacht. But I was impressed by the fact his father had been a milkman. Years later, reading Bob's autobiography, I learned he had owned a dairy. Bob also wrote that I am a better radio and TV presenter than I was a newspaper editor. There's only one answer to that. *Well, he would say that, wouldn't he?*

New editors like to shake up things a bit if only to let the troops know they are there. Bob was no exception. Within weeks of his arrival he decided the Manchester office was looking distinctly moribund. His solution was to appoint a new Northern editor, someone who knew the place well: Derek Jameson.

Taking up office brought about one of those gaffes that can give you the creeps for years afterwards. Bob and I had taken the train to Manchester on Monday evening, normally a day off on Sunday newspapers, and booked into the Midland Hotel. He was not going to shirk the awful business of getting rid of the incumbent face to face, and had arranged to meet my old boss Jack Stoneley for breakfast the following morning. He would break the bad news over the eggs and bacon. I was to join Bob later and we would descend on the office together, installing me before anyone had time to draw breath.

All neat and tidy – we don't hang about in newspapers – until I decided that, while awaiting Bob, I might as well go down to the dining room for an early breakfast, getting out of the way before his meeting with Jack. I ate my eggs and bacon, then lingered too long over the newspapers. When I finally made a move, who should I bump into but Jack. He had arrived early and was about to have a coffee before his appointment.

'Derek,' said Jack warmly, greeting an old friend. 'What are you doing here?'

'Oh, this and that,' I said lamely. 'I've got a bit of business up here.' He must have feared the worst. There was no way a senior executive from London would be on his patch without him knowing about it. I felt like a rat.

The transfer of power could have been worse. I kept well out of the way as they mourned Jack's departure in the pub. There was still some flak. The Northern news editor, Bill Boustead, Jack's best friend, made some philosophical remarks about people who put a needle in a gramophone to make sure it plays a certain tune. I got the gist.

'Get stuffed,' I said, 'I've never once thought of returning to Manchester since the day I left three years ago. Are you implying that I plotted Jack's downfall?'

'Something like that,' said Bill. 'Anyway, you can have my job, I've no wish to continue working for this lot.'

Sleep on it, I advised him. Dramatic gestures are all very well. However, they don't pay the rent. He didn't pursue the matter. Robert Wilson, my old running mate on the stone, shed a few tears for Jack. That shocked me. He was a close friend and I had been best man at his wedding. Still, newspapermen are a sentimental lot. I forgave him.

I steered clear of Naomi, though could not resist a whispered 'You know what they say about bad pennies!' Being married and an editor, I had decided to behave. A brave resolution. Pity I didn't keep it. Before long the old chemistry got to work and we had the odd tête-à-tête. Nothing heavy, though. My feelings for her were genuine and I wanted to know what she was doing with her life. She was the same free, independent spirit. Nowadays I hear she has settled down.

There was another fling with a sensational lady who caught my eye wearing a Russian fur hat. We would drink tea and munch cheese rolls in the lunch break and discuss the meaning of life. A lovely girl named Tina. It all came to an end when she sensibly decided to stay with her husband.

At the office it wasn't long before Bill Boustead took early retirement and quit, a chance for me to make one of my mates news editor. Ken Bennett is a Scouse who could bring tears of laughter to the eyes of a stuffed parrot.

'You're mad, you, Jameson,' he used to say as I danced a jig in his office over some loony story he had managed to land. 'We don't even know if it's bloody true yet.'

I would say something like: 'Course it's true! Where else but Chester zoo would they give polar bears hot water bottles to sleep with at night?'

It was Bennett and his mate Mike Taylor, then deputy editor of the *Daily Mirror*, who created havoc at my wedding. Ken was the best man and they swam through the day on a sea of lager and Bacardi rum. Mike is a fanatical Manchester United supporter and obviously thought he was at a match. Propped against a pillar at the ceremony, he woke up with a start as the registrar intoned 'This young couple, united in love . . .'

'UN-I-TED, UN-I-TED,' roared Taylor, waving an imaginary scarf and making rattling noises.

The pair of them finished up at Bloomsbury police station. Taylor had been arrested driving my future mother-in-law back to the Hampstead flat. Bennett was there in a forlorn attempt to persuade the officers that, without the services of their guest, Michael Taylor, millions of readers might well be deprived of their favourite *Mirror* the next day. 'Very interesting, Sir,' said the desk sergeant. 'You'll have to have a word with Marje Proops about it.' Mike was banned for a year. It was a brand new office Triumph, too.

Running the *Sunday Mirror* in Manchester seemed tame compared with the frantic pace of my earlier spell in the north. At least I could keep an eye on my beloved Irish editions, though the magic of the Belfast plant was missing. The IRA casts a baleful eye on any British commercial venture in the province. The Provos blew up the plant in 1972 leaving more than one hundred of their fellow countrymen out of work.

Funnily enough, I heard about it in an Irish bar on holiday in Majorca. There was to be a great deal of banter between the Irish in there and myself over the troubles in Ireland. One day my chief adversary told me: 'Well, now, the lads have been and gone and done it. They've put a bomb under your plant in Belfast. It's been on the wireless.' I didn't believe a word of it. 'That'll be the day,' I said. 'They'd have more chance getting into Fort Knox.' The next day's *Mirror* arrived the following morning. IRA WRECK MIRROR PLANT said the splash headline.

My lovely plant, scene of so many early triumphs. I had even made newspaper history there in 1966 by publishing the first on-the-day colour picture of earth taken 850 miles up in outer space. We had been the first Fleet Street paper to sell copies in the Irish Republic printed in Ireland. Our successes had taken national sales to over 5,000,000. Strangely enough, the bombing of the Belfast plant made no difference to sales. Editions flown in from Manchester without colour and with less Irish news actually sold more copies. We put it down to the reputation we had made for ourselves in that shortlived Irish operation.

I managed to cause a stir when an aspiring Conservative party leader named Margaret Thatcher visited Manchester and gave a background briefing for editors at the local Tory club. More of the schoolmarm then than she is now, she admonished me for leaning back in my chair.

'Sit up straight, you'll go through the window like that,' said the future Prime Minister.

'That'll make more of a story than this lot,' I told her.

Getting ahead in life often owes more to good luck than sound judgement. The important thing is to be in the right place at the right time. My big chance came by accident with the retirement of the great Sir (later Lord) Hugh Cudlipp as Chairman of the International Publishing Corporation, as the Mirror group and its associated interests was then called. Hugh Cudlipp had been the driving force behind tabloid journalism for four decades and now those who had flourished in his shadow were paying tribute in traditional style. One long round of farewell parties in every corner of the empire.

We wanted the Manchester thrash to be especially memorable. This was his cradle. Well, almost. The fiery Welshman had spent some of his early years as a young reporter working in Blackpool, Manchester and neighbouring Salford. 'In Manchester, I really learned what journalism was about,' he was to write in his inside story, *Walking on the Water*. 'I met most of the first class operators who were later to fill the editors' chairs on the newspapers in London.' It could not have been a long love affair because he was editor of the *Sunday Pictorial* in London by the age of 24. We drew a veil over the fact he had walked among us but briefly and hailed him as one of Manchester's own.

Hugh Cudlipp was the youngest of a remarkable trio of brothers who simultaneously became Fleet Street editors, the sons of an enterprising commercial traveller best remembered for selling goods on tick to poor shopkeepers caught up in the depression. Hugh rose to become head of the mighty *Mirror* empire, nudging the aristocratic Cecil King off his pedestal along the way, but to us lesser mortals he was your actual copper-bottomed, total newspaperman. Pugnacious, cigar clenched in teeth, forever questioning and challenging, it was Cudlipp my generation admired most. He told a rattling good story, too, and was witty with it. His sayings have become newspaper folklore. Some examples:

Here's one secret you don't know – you're fired.

Will you please put a small panel on Page One explaining that I had nothing to do with the production of tomorrow morning's paper?

The spike is the least complicated of newspaper accessories.

Not only does dog eat dog in Fleet Street, but when the snack has been digested both dogs join the Tail Waggers' Club.

The first time I met him was when he was taking a call in his office. Hugh beckoned me inside, shoved the phone in my hand and barked: 'See who this is. He talks so bloody posh I can't understand a word he's saying.' It was some promotions man wittering on about nothing important.

To the master, a fond farewell. A great rollicking, nostalgic, boozy lunch was laid on in Hugh's honour at Manchester's Midland Hotel on November 29, 1973. It happened to be my 44th birthday. I took a back seat when it came to the formal speeches, leaving those to my opposite numbers, Led Woodliff on the *Daily Mirror* and Alan Hobday of the *People*. They could do the waffling. For myself, I took the humble position of chairman (in theory, a non-speaking part).

What a shambles! Some 300 hacks making whoopee at the firm's expense. They raised the roof. I had to keep these well-oiled revellers occupied if only to prevent them wrecking the joint. For two hours I stood there, telling jokes and anecdotes, ad libbing, reading the riot act. Soothing words of praise one minute, a stream of invective the next. It was one of my greatest performances.

Cudlipp must have been impressed. Few doubted his hand was behind my sudden promotion early in 1974 to key job of Northern editor of the *Daily*

Mirror. It must have been one of his last acts before retiring. With one mighty bound, as they say in *Boy's Own*, I was within grasp of my life's ambition to be editor of the world's greatest tabloid paper.

The problem was that it was fast losing that title to the self-proclaimed soaraway *Sun*. No man is perfect. Cudlipp had made perhaps his greatest mistake in handing the *Sun* on a plate to the Australian entrepreneur Rupert Murdoch. The price was a joke: £50,000 down and a further £600,000 over six years out of profits – if any. Cudlipp obviously thought Murdoch could never make a success of it. After all, the Mirror Group had tried hard enough, spending millions translating the old *Daily Herald* into the only paper born of the age we live in, *The Sun*, as the advertising agents put it.

Murdoch shrewdly spotted Cudlipp's mistake. The old Welsh wizard's magic had gone wrong. He had taken his papers upmarket, believing the more affluent and better educated workers wanted a product to match the new age of prosperity. They didn't. They wanted the same formula as before. Get-rich-quick prizes, plenty of birds and football, the news served piping hot. *The Sun* leapt in to fill the gap. By the time I arrived, it had already mopped up a million of the *Mirror*'s readers in the south and was now looking for similar dividends in the north. My brief was to stop the onward march of Rupert's men, many of them former *Mirror* employees.

There's nothing quite like a newspaper war. I pulled every stunt in the book. *The Sun* had a fatal flaw and I exploited it with ruthless energy. The paper had no plant in the north. Rupert was not going to get involved in that costly business. It meant *The Sun*'s first edition, destined for our very own patch, had to be locked up and running on the presses by 7.30 pm at Rupert's ancient *News of the World* plant in London's Bouverie Street.

My first editions in Manchester were not off stone until 10.00 pm, and those for the heavily populated Merseyside and Manchester areas after midnight. The London news desk could spot any tasty stories in *The Sun* and give us a matcher or spoiler – duplicate or destroy its exclusivity – while *The Sun* was still in a train at Watford junction.

That wasn't the half of it. *The Sun*'s early deadlines meant they had trouble getting in late football results. What a shame! We not only boasted a full results service, we also ran big pictures and match reports. Three pages of them in the case of glamour teams like Liverpool and Manchester United.

We hit every late-breaking story with great zest, particularly those in the north, knowing there would not be a word in *The Sun*. All the skills and tricks I had learned up there on the stone, locking away page after page of the *Sunday Mirror*, served me well now I was running the *Daily*.

One campaign I recall fondly was to find the oldest budgie in Britain. We published a picture of the chief contender, the most evil-looking brute this side of the Timor Sea. Bald, plucked and indignant, it stood there on its perch and aroused the sporting instincts of the north's budgie lovers. The letters poured in by the thousand. London thought our Page 3 bird the ultimate in low taste. Within a week they were running the story themselves.

There was one area where we were not supposed to compete. Page 3 birds. *The Sun*'s very own trade mark. The *Mirror*'s bosses in London frowned on unadorned pulchritude. 'It's alright in that comic,' they pontificated as sales went down the pan, 'but it's not the *Mirror*, old boy.'

To hell with that. My job was to stop *The Sun*. I have already told the story in relation to the libel action of how I craftily paid half-price for *The Sun*'s Page 3 overs and published them a few days later. London screamed in pain. What was I doing putting nudes into the *Daily Mirror*? demanded Anthony J. Miles, Cudlipp's successor as editorial supremo.

'Okay, Tony,' I told the big boss in London. 'If you don't mind *The Sun* overtaking the *Mirror* in the north, then we'll stop printing nudes.'

'Well, I'm not saying that, am I, cock?' said Tony, the most irascible man I ever met in newspapers, bless his socks.

Miles had made his name as editor of an esoteric diary in the *Mirror* called the Inside Page. It won the inevitable awards and had taken him to the top. First features chief of the *Mirror*, then editor and ultimately editorial director. Obviously losing a million copies to your main rival doesn't make an editor all bad.

Perhaps he didn't know that the *Mirror* had many times published topless girls in the course of its history. Most famous was the wartime strip *Jane*, recently enjoying a revival, and the paper actually pioneered nudes in 1938 with a study called 'Apple Orchard.' True, you could not tell whether it was a boy or a girl, but topless it certainly was.

I carried on doing my own thing in Manchester regardless. The fight to stop *The Sun* was a thundering success. By 1975, we were putting on over

60,000 new readers a month and *The Sun* was going backwards. In March that year I had this announcement posted on all notice boards:

NOW FOR THE GOOD NEWS! The Daily Mirror's *Northern circulation in February showed another increase of 61,000 copies to 1,357,972, the highest February sale in history. And we did it purely on the strength of the paper, without any promotion or advertising – a magnificent achievement by everyone in Manchester (London helped too!).*

'Everyone in Manchester' added up to one of the best teams of journalists to be found in any editorial. You can combine the talents of 100 journalists and produce zilch. In Manchester we made magic together. Bob Sands ran production. He was a dry, phlegmatic Mancunian who had to be restrained from 'going back' (changing) to a page every time a proof was put in front of him. In charge of reporters was Leo White, another large helping of Yorkshire grit and easily the best news editor in the north.

For light relief there was my night news editor, Maurice Wigglesworth, a legendary figure in newspapers who seemed to live on bangers and bitter. Round and rasping – he really was Mr Five-by-Five – Wiggy could frighten the toughest reporter out of his skin. It was always done with utmost courtesy. Everyone, from chairman to messenger, was addressed as 'Sir.'

I first heard Maurice in action sitting in the editor's cubicle – horse-box, we called it – in the main editorial. He was on the phone to a reporter in Belfast who had failed to cover a major newsbreak.

'You don't know why we missed t'story? I'll tell tha why, Sir. 'Cos tha's a fookin' idiot, that's why, Sir!'

His verbal sparring partner was George Harrop, the natty, punctilious night picture editor, who was reputed to have once been a cinema organist. The two were a better double act than Little and Large. I used to earwig on the pair of them behind my frosted glass partition.

Wiggy: *Stop picking tha nose, George.*
Harrop: *How dare you, Maurice, I was brushing away some fluff.*
Wiggy to himself, after long pause: *If there's one thing I hate worse than a nose picker, it's a fookin' liar.*

George was a dab hand at one-liners himself. Ada came trundling her tea trolley through the office one afternoon, a darling old girl of 80 who wore a heavy black snood over her thinning hair. 'There she goes,' George turned to me, 'the Angel of Mons.' We had a general manager thereabouts named Paul Rochez, who liked a drink or three. He came staggering into the newsroom with a crony on one occasion, bouncing off the walls. 'There you are, Maurice,' said George, 'Rochez and Rico-chet.'

Cudlipp said if ever Wiggy left Withy Grove, the place would fall down. He wasn't far wrong. Maurice retired after 21 years in 1976, the beginning of the end of that great crucible of newspaper craft. George Harrop was not far behind him.

It was people like these who rallied to the fight. Together we beat *The Sun* at its own game, a success that produced few bouquets from London. It was not lost on *The Sun*. Sir Larry Lamb, the former *Mirror* man who then edited the paper, taking it from 750,000 copies to well over 4,000,000, put on record: 'In his role as Northern Editor of the *Daily Mirror*, Derek Jameson successfully inhibited the growth of my own newspaper, *The Sun*, in his area at a time it was strikingly successful everywhere else. I regarded him as a formidable opponent.'

My reward was a six-week trip in the summer of 1975 to the United States. It was anything but a rest cure. I visited 14 newspapers from New York to Los Angeles studying new technology 'to see how it all works before we computerise production at Holborn Circus,' as I said in a letter to Anthony Delano, then head of the New York bureau. Having spent a great chunk of my life tearing out my hair in composing rooms, I was an instant convert to a system in which one computer can do the work of 500 linotype machines.

No sooner had I got back from the States than I was asked to go to London to act as editor for a month. Michael Christiansen had suffered his mild heart attack and the acting editor, Mike Molloy, was on holiday. It was clear that Christiansen was coming to the end of his editorship.

My arrival in sleepy August caused a flurry of speculation that I was to be the next editor in view of those hard fought battles in Manchester. I stirred up a storm of activity in that all too complacent London editorial, producing some lively newspapers in the middle of an IRA bombing campaign.

Had there been a free vote on who should fill the editor's chair, I would have won by a landslide. One cheeky sub-editor, Des Lyons, actually put it to Tony Miles that the job should be mine. 'What? With that accent!' he said. That says it all. Not the sort of chap you would propose for the Reform Club. Apparently I don't speak properly, as the ten million people who listen to me every day can testify.

I advised people to put their money on Mike Molloy, a *Mirror* man since he was out of school, who had achieved fame as an art editor of great distinction. He put down his pencils to become a features executive and never looked back. Mike is a smooth character, unfailingly courteous and unruffled in any crisis. He was also the executive closest to Tony Miles. I was right. He was made editor in December, 1975, and held the job for more than 10 years, something of a Fleet Street record. Miles disappeared with the arrival of the new owner, Robert Maxwell. Molloy remained in the editor's chair for another year, then was created editor-in-chief and shifted to run the *Sunday Mirror* for a spell. He also writes fine detective thrillers in his spare time.

There were rumours that the non-editorial members of the board pressed for my appointment, pointing to the circulation successes in Manchester, but Tony Miles threatened to quit if such an outrage were inflicted upon him. If nothing else, Miles is brutally honest and has never disguised his distaste for me. I once produced the *Daily Mirror* virtually single-handed for four days in Manchester during an NUJ stoppage, an achievement that only the most proficient among us would seek to emulate. On my next visit to London, I awaited the odd word of praise that must surely fall from Tony Miles' lips, however reluctantly.

At first I thought he wasn't going to say anything. He huffed and puffed, wrinkled up his face, scratched his nose. There was something he had to say, but he obviously was avoiding it. At last it came out.

'Those papers of yours, cock!'

'Yes, Tony,' I said brightly.

'I'm ashamed to think they will be put into museums as a permanent record of the *Daily Mirror* during those days!'

That's Tony Miles. He gave me more laughs than any man I ever served. These days he runs a lurid tabloid in the United States and Canada. You know the sort of thing. AMERICA LEFT MAN ON MOON. I wonder if he still calls *The Sun* a comic?

Miles may not have cared for my accent, but he appreciated my expertise as a production man. Now that Molloy was in the editor's chair, he appointed me development editor of all the *Mirror* papers while still retaining the job of editor in Manchester. My brief was to launch the training programme necessary for journalists to switch from hot metal to photo-composition. The response was less then enthusiastic. Apart from a few hi tech visionaries, most senior executives viewed new technology with deep suspicion.

They could see major problems ahead and took the view it was a management plot not to improve production, but to cut staff and save money. The print unions shared their gloom. The *Mirror* finally switched to computers and video screens, the first major group to make the change. It took five years of negotiation to get there. Within a year, prior to Robert Maxwell's arrival, it was clear that the production of all papers had been seriously impaired and the number of employees had risen.

That was all to come later. Right now I was up the creek. Editor in Manchester one day, commuting to London the next to organise the massive switch to new technology by five national titles - the *Daily* and *Sunday Mirror*, *The People*, *Sporting Life* and *Reveille*. I think that Miles was expecting me to fall flat on my face. Not likely. My day would come.

I can read Fleet Street like a book and knew before long some rival organisation would be knocking at my door. Mike Molloy hastened the process in November, 1976, by inviting me to London as his managing editor, number two on the paper. To the surprise of many, I accepted with gratitude. It helps to be in the right spot. In any case, Mike and I had always been good friends. We had a similar background in that Mike began work at the old *Sunday Pictorial* as a 15-year-old messenger, tearing the teleprinter tapes. A job I knew well. He later went to Ealing Art College and, apart from a two-year stretch at the defunct *Daily Sketch*, has always worked for *Mirror* papers.

My first summons on high came from Rupert Murdoch the following summer. He took me to the Savoy for lunch on a Saturday. The idea was that nobody would see us. When we arrived, Ted Blackmore, the *Mirror*'s production director, was sitting at the next table with his wife. Sod's law. Rupert and I didn't discuss newpapers. He already knew all about me. We were more interested in a top drawer wedding party at a round table nearby. Was it a shotgun marriage, we wondered. Why was one half of the table not speaking to the other? That's the joy of Murdoch. He is real people. Cockney accents don't frighten him.

He obviously wanted me to join him, declaring when we parted that it was too early to make a move. I should sit tight until hearing from him. All was revealed the following day in a Sunday paper headline: MURDOCH BID FOR EXPRESS GROUP.

Rupert called me at breakfast at home a few days later. It astonished me to think of him dialling the call himself. Most tycoons of his magnitude have trouble opening a car door.

'Things haven't worked out,' he said, 'but thanks for your interest. I'm sure we'll work together one day. 'bye now.'

Murdoch's £10 million bid for an interest in Express Newspapers had just failed. He had it all wrapped up, but was robbed of the prize at the last minute. The shipping and construction consortium, Trafalgar House, owners of the QEII, Ritz Hotel and much else besides, intervened and won over Sir Max Aitken, ailing son of Lord Beaverbrook. Rupert had sought only a stake and management control. Aitken preferred to sell out completely to Trafalgar for £14,592,560 – the fixed assets were worth over £50 million – rather than allow the Australian into the Black Lubyianka.

Word swiftly buzzed round Fleet Street that Rupert was after me. I was not surprised in early August to get a call from Charles Wintour, an *Express* director and famous former editor of the London *Standard*. How about a spot of lunch? He had played a key role in thwarting Murdoch's plans.

Charles, known to some as The Headmaster because of his solemn air, soon got to the point. Victor Matthews, Trafalgar's new Chairman of Express Newspapers, wanted to meet me. Would I care to lunch with him at the Hotel Bristol, off Piccadilly? That I would. Lord Matthews, as he is now, was a man who made good sense to me. A poor boy from Islington, next door to Hackney, he started life as a clerk in a building company and had become one of the top industrialists and financiers in the country. Short, dark and decisive, he weighed me up with his nutbrown eyes as we sat down to lunch in his newest hotel.

'You don't have to worry about being here like this,' he said. 'I have come through an underground passage from Trafalgar House next door. Nobody knows we are meeting.'

'Oh, I'm not worried about that,' I said breezily. 'I met an old friend, Bernard Shrimsley, editor of the *News of the World*, on my way here and he said to me: 'When are you taking over the *Daily Express* then?' My mouth again.

'How in God's name did he know about that?' asked Matthews, deeply shocked at his first experience of Fleet Street's omniscient grapevine. It would not be the last. The answer was simple, though I didn't let on at the time. I had been seen getting into Charlie's car the previous day.

We discussed the proposition, though Matthews made it sound like a hypothesis rather than an imminent appointment. I wasn't fooled. I knew the *Express* needed a tabloid expert urgently. It had changed shape to the smaller size, but it hadn't worked. The paper was a mess.

'I'm flattered and delighted,' I said. 'There's just one problem. Like most top *Mirror* executives, I'm a supporter of the Labour party. I don't think you want a Socialist running the *Express*.'

'Oh, I don't think that matters,' he said airily. 'You wouldn't be stupid enough to try to turn it into a Labour rag. There are plenty of precedents. Beaverbrook always employed Socialists.' He was thinking of Michael Foot and Bob Edwards, of course.

'Well, if it doesn't worry you, it certainly doesn't worry me,' I said. 'I'm not all that strong in the faith these days, anyway.'

The call came that afternoon, creating a dilemma for Mike Molloy. He was just off on a three-week holiday. 'Don't worry about it, Mike. I'll tell the *Express* I can't be there until September and carry on running the *Mirror* until you get back.' He went off happily enough, leaving me in the unique position of being in charge of two rival daily newspapers simultaneously. Little did I know there would be a repeat performance in years to come involving the *Daily Star*.

As it was, Tony Miles was having none of my dual role at the *Mirror* and *Express*. He descended on me with all guns firing, accused me of treachery and told me to get out of the office by lunchtime. It was then 11 am.

'Christ, Tony,' I said, 'have a heart! I've been at the *Mirror* for fifteen years. You can't expect me to evacuate in two hours.'

'Just get your things out of there at the first minute. I want you OUT!' he stormed. Tony then harangued me on the internal hotline, calling five or six times, demanding to know why I was still in the building. I finally made my exit in the middle of the lunch break, trailing cardboard boxes and plastic carrier bags loaded with my stuff.

The editorial director then gave orders that I was not to be allowed back into the *Mirror* skyscraper. For the next couple of weeks I had to meet a secretary on the pavement outside, who would hand over my personal correspondence, including an armful of letters congratulating me on my appointment to the *Express*.

Good old Tony, game to the end. He genuinely believed I was guilty of gross betrayal by accepting a bigger and better job. I should worry. All it meant was that I planted myself two weeks earlier than expected in the chair where the great Arthur Christiansen had sat. Editor of the *Daily Express*. In many ways the most coveted job of all in the world of newspapers.

Outside the window that August day in 1977, beyond the net curtains swaying in the breeze, I could see Reuters and the back alley where it had all begun more than 30 years earlier.

Oh well, I thought, *the angels have brought me this far. Now I guess it's really going to get tough.*

Index